'Want to make the world a better place? Learn how to be an entrepreneur! In *See, Solve, Scale*, Danny is masterful at breaking that intimidating word into simple, clear steps that anyone can follow'

Evan Sharp, co-founder of Pinterest

'Danny Warshay is an entrepreneurial hero unlocking the power of entrepreneurship for the rest of us. Read it, roll up your sleeves and change the world'

Andrew Yang, former 2020 Presidential Candidate, entrepreneur and non-profit founder

'In my work, I've studied how organisations can create optimal environments to foster creativity and innovation. In this book, Danny Warshay describes the process you need to succeed in those environments. If you are an entrepreneur or ever dreamed of creating something that matters, this book is a low-risk, high-reward resource for making it happen'

Teresa Amabile, Baker Foundation Professor and Edsel Bryant Ford Professor of Business Administration, Emerita, Harvard Business School

'Brown University doesn't need a business school - it has Danny Warshay. For liberal arts grads with a passion to improve the world and be their own boss, *See, Solve, Scale* helps you escape Plato's cave and see the entrepreneurial light. Entrepreneurship is full of minefields. You'll be glad to have Danny lead the way'

Barry Nalebuff, Milton Steinbach Professor at Yale School of Management and co-founder of Honest Tea

'*See, Solve, Scale* makes what has been exclusive Ivy League training accessible to everyone. It is now my go-to recommended reading for all entrepreneurs we engage within the diverse communities we serve and beyond'

Marcos Gonzalez, founder and Managing Partner of VamosVentures

'Danny Warshay's *See, Solve, Scale* makes a fundamental connection between a liberal arts education and entrepreneurship. We at liberal arts schools teach our students how to observe acutely and analyze deeply. It turns out, as Danny demonstrates, these skills translate perfectly to the role of entrepreneurs, which is to identify a problem and seek a solution. That he does so with stories and examples of a diverse set of founders of all ages and backgrounds makes this the perfect book for all aspiring entrepreneurs'

Mary Schmidt Campbell, Ph.D., President, Spelman College

DANNY WARSHAY is the founding Executive Director of the Nelson Center for Entrepreneurship and Professor of the Practice at Brown University. He began his entrepreneurial pursuits while an undergraduate at Brown as a member of the Clearview Software startup leadership team. Apple acquired Clearview, and since then, he has co-founded and sold companies in fields ranging from software and advanced materials to consumer products and media. Danny received an MBA from Harvard Business School. He lives in Providence.

See Solve Scale

How Anyone Can Turn an Unsolved Problem into a Breakthrough Success

PROFESSOR DANNY WARSHAY

PIATKUS

PIATKUS

First published in the US in 2022 by St. Martin's Press,
an imprint of St. Martin's Publishing Group
First published in Great Britain in 2022 by Piatkus

1 3 5 7 9 10 8 6 4 2

Copyright © Danny Warshay, 2022

The moral right of the author has been asserted.

A CIP catalogue record for this book
is available from the British Library.

ISBN: 978-0-34942-735-5

Printed and bound in Great Britain by
Clays Ltd, Elcograf S.p.A.

Papers used by Piatkus are from well-managed forests
and other responsible sources.

Piatkus
An imprint of
Little, Brown Book Group
Carmelite House
50 Victoria Embankment
London EC4Y 0DZ

An Hachette UK Company
www.hachette.co.uk

www.littlebrown.co.uk

For my family, especially the memory of my father

BD BARNES 16
@ MINDSTRING. COM
+1 919 399 2074
SEPT 2022

Vision without action is just a dream, action without vision just passes the time, and vision with action can change the world.

—NELSON MANDELA

CONTENTS

PART 3: PITCHING

INTRODUCTION

Food scarcity, illiteracy, inequitable access to education, climate change, violent conflict in the Middle East, poverty, pandemics: as a society, we face these problems and so many more that are in dire need of solutions. As individual consumers, we also confront problems daily, such as challenges to our sleep-related experiences and confusing dietary choices. In big companies and other established organizations, we face problems that result from doing things the same way for too long, fail to innovate, and risk obsolescence. And our research scientists, on whom we rely to discover solutions to many of these kinds of problems, are frustrated when their standard research methods no longer create the breakthroughs we count on. More than ever, we need to see and empower ourselves as entrepreneurial problem solvers, even if we have been held back by a lack of confidence and training, to develop large-scale solutions with impact.

The premise of this book is that anyone can become an entrepreneur and a solver of problems when armed with the right tools—not just those who conform to the entrepreneurial myth of swashbuckling heroes unbound by rules, on the hunt for unicorns. I have written this book to empower those of you who may not see yourselves as an entrepreneur because you don't fit this stereotype. This does not mean that the process is easy. It's challenging, and it can be frustrating and even intimidating. It also does not guarantee you success. But my experience teaching entrepreneurship to thousands of students has shown me that there is a vast, untapped entrepreneurial layer of society that has been neglected because of strong biases the conventional world of entrepreneurship sustains. At the same time, this book is designed to solve a problem all entrepreneurs face: too often, they are making things up as they go, relying on instinct and intuition in places where a structured process would make their lives easier and more efficient and their startups more successful.

Just as all new products need to offer something that differentiates them from their competitors, the *See, Solve, Scale* Entrepreneurial Process does this in three ways:

- It teaches entrepreneurship as a **structured process for solving problems**, using an anthropological approach to figure out what problem to solve. This prevents the expensive and often fatal mistake many entrepreneurs make of developing a solution in search of a problem.
- It teaches **entrepreneurship as a liberal arts skill**. Like other liberal arts, we can adapt its lessons across all types of contexts, from classic business startups to established corporate, nonprofit, and governmental organizations, and even more unexpected contexts like academic research labs. Studying history in college did not make me a historian, any more than learning the scientific method makes people scientists. And yet I have drawn on my history training, and science students draw on theirs, in all sorts of unexpected ways. The *See, Solve, Scale* Entrepreneurial Process has produced many traditional entrepreneurs, including some you will meet in these pages. It has also empowered many within established organizations and elsewhere who previously had not seen themselves as entrepreneurs.
- It is based on rigorous scientific research and is animated by entrepreneurship experiences—my own and many others'. This **practice-backed-by-research** draws from my combined roles as entrepreneur and teacher.

Once you see how *See, Solve, Scale* works, you will see why the standard notion of who can be an entrepreneur is so limiting. If you are what I call an "entrepreneurial underdog," you will become unleashed from self-doubt and armed with a system proven to help you tackle this process. If you are an investor, you will start to uncover a broader pool of potential entrepreneurs whom your competitors may never consider. Among the things you will learn:

- Entrepreneurs **do not need abundant resources**. In fact, early in this process, scarce resources can be a benefit and abundant resources are often a burden. After reading this book, you won't worry about not having enough money, expertise, education, or pedigree. And if you happen to have abundant resources, you will learn techniques to prevent those resources from getting in your way.

- **There is no "entrepreneurial psychological type."** For example, you do not need to be an extrovert. In fact, the creative strategies of introverts add disproportionate value to entrepreneurship teams. Research I will share proves that diversity is a critical characteristic of successful entrepreneurship teams. As an important part of this diversity, different personality types complement each other and lead to greater success. You will no longer feel blocked because your personality differs from the image of the stereotypical entrepreneur.

- Entrepreneurs **do not need to come from,** live in, or be trained by **the "right crowd,"** such as Silicon Valley, developed countries, or elite universities. They do not need to adhere to gender and racial stereotypes. I realize that when only 2.3 percent of venture funding goes to women,[1] 1.5 percent to Latinx founders,[2] and 1 percent to Black founders,[3] this may sound naive. These dismal percentages are explained in part by research from my Brown University colleague Banu Ozkazanc-Pan and her coauthor Susan Clark Muntean that concludes "an investor is highly likely to rely on stereotypes" when deciding who to fund.[4] This approach can and should change. While far too often sexism, racism, and unconscious bias perpetuate these numbers, the hopeful news is that you are more likely to succeed if you recruit diverse team members from beyond your own crowd and beyond your own strong network ties.

- **Successful entrepreneurs don't always invent something from scratch**. You can build on prior inventions and translate existing models to new contexts. This knowledge will empower you if you

feel stymied or intimidated by your current level of technical, design, or creative skills.

While entrepreneurs vary in their resources, personalities, and backgrounds, I want to warn you about common entrepreneurial tendencies
that can work against you. In their groundbreaking research that led to the
development of behavioral economics, Nobel Laureate Daniel Kahneman
and Amos Twersky demonstrated that our biased intuition can cause errors in judgment. In Kahneman's words, they "documented systematic errors
in the thinking of normal people, and traced these errors to the design
of the machinery of cognition rather than to the corruption of thought
by emotion."[5] In other words, as humans, our judgment is influenced by
things outside our awareness, even when we think we are being rational
and logical. At critical junctures throughout this process, therefore, I will
caution you that sometimes relying exclusively on your intuition will be
a mistake, as doing so will cause you to make these following common
errors in judgment:

- More than half of venture teams are formed with friends and
  family, though research shows that those teams are less likely to
  succeed.
- To find and recruit team members, you may be tempted to mine
  your network of close contacts, yet you are better off tapping your
  weak ties more than your strong ones.
- Even in diverse teams, many focus on what they share in common, rather than leveraging the full range of diverse expertise
  and insight available.
- Overfamiliarity can cause us to miss what in retrospect seems
  obvious.
- Our enthusiasm for solving problems can cause us to converge
  too early on a potential solution, rather than forming a portfolio
  of options.
- We rely too heavily on "Corporate Immune Systems," which reject not only actual threats but also valuable innovations that
  compete with existing ways of operating.
- Because we tend to think more is better, we cling, we covet, we

accumulate, despite the benefits of scarce resources that I reference above.

- We suffer from fixedness—a cognitive bias or a mental block against using something (e.g., an object, an idea, a service) in a new way—which often inhibits our ability to see solutions to a problem.
- In a creative process, we tend to add things, which often makes products more complicated, rather than subtract things, which often yields simpler and better solutions.[6]
- At the same time, many entrepreneurs have a hard time thinking big as they believe that the way to mitigate the inevitable risk of starting a venture is to keep it small, tidy, and easy to get your arms around. This tendency gets in the way of scaling over the long term.
- Our personal and organizational resistance to failure limits our ability to learn, iterate, and improve, and it reduces our ability to think big.

Because this theme of human error is so powerful, throughout each step of *See, Solve, Scale*, I have created "Caution" callouts that will help you identify and avoid these common stumbling blocks.

I began the journey to developing the *See, Solve, Scale* Entrepreneurial Process as a college undergraduate, when a group of fellow Brown students and I addressed a data-collection and data-management problem that office workers faced, built a software startup to solve that problem, and sold the company to Apple. Perhaps like you, I was a complete entrepreneurship novice, and I discovered I loved learning and doing all the steps in this process. After a period developing my skills at Harvard Business School and in brand management at Procter & Gamble, I spent several more years launching, growing, and harvesting startup ventures in fields ranging from software and advanced materials to consumer products and media.

Teaching anything forces you to zero in on its essence. And so I was able to hone this process during the last sixteen years of teaching the *See, Solve, Scale* Entrepreneurial Process to over three thousand mostly liberal

nts at Brown University; MBA students at Yale and Tel Aviv
_____; and corporate, nonprofit, and governmental professionals
throughout the world. To date, this process has spawned many successful
classic startups that have made their founders millions of dollars, as well as
many other successful ventures in the nonprofit world and in other unexpected contexts. These entrepreneurs are creating solutions to significant
problems that range from food waste and the deforestation of the Amazon
to illiteracy and the Middle East's transition away from an oil-dependent
economy. As my Brown colleague Stephen Porder, a professor of ecology,
says, "I spend all semester depressing my students about environmental
problems like the climate crisis, famine, drought, pollution. And then I
send them to you, Danny, to learn how *to solve them.*"

In writing *See, Solve, Scale,* I have embraced and benefited from this
same process. In years of both doing and teaching entrepreneurship, I
identified an important problem: a much wider group of aspiring entrepreneurs needed a process that would help them solve consequential problems (**Step 1: See: Find and Validate an Unmet Need**). The structured *See,
Solve, Scale* Entrepreneurial Process I had developed was doing that on
a small scale for roughly forty students in each new class (**Step 2: Solve:
Develop a Value Proposition**). And then many of my students nudged me
to write this book as the third critical step (**Step 3: Scale: Create a Sustainability Model**) to share this process with millions of aspiring problem
solvers who may not even know they are entrepreneurs.

Among a wide diversity of entrepreneurs whom this process has empowered, here are a few of the classic business entrepreneurs I describe in
more detail in later chapters:

- Ben Chesler was distraught when he learned about the billions of
  pounds of food we waste every year. How could we throw away so
  much perfectly good food when there are so many people starving? And so he channeled his frustration into building Imperfect
  Foods—a company that fights food waste by finding a home for
  "ugly" produce, sourcing it directly from farms and delivering it
  to customers' doors for about 30 percent less than grocery store
  prices. Ben and his team built Imperfect from a startup to a thriving venture-capital-backed company doing over $250 million in
  sales and saving over 150 million pounds of food waste.

- Gwen Mugodi shook her head in frustration when she realized so few children in her native Zimbabwe and neighboring African countries learned to read because of the lack of native language reading materials. She is now using her startup, Toreva, to publish reading materials in native languages and is teaching African children to read.

- Tyler Gage, Dan MacCombie, Laura Thompson, Charlie Harding, and Aden Van Noppen cringed at the low wages Ecuadorian farmers were paid and at the deforestation of the Ecuadorian Amazon that was devastating these farmers' land. They launched the RUNA beverage company as a vehicle for empowering Ecuadorian farming families with a fair trade wage and for reforesting the Amazon. They raised over $25 million from investors and ten years after its founding sold the company to Vita Coco.

- Scott Norton wondered why Americans obsessed about a wide variety of mustards, but cared about only one brand of ketchup. To fill that variety gap with condiments that are better for you and better tasting, Scott cofounded and built Sir Kensington's condiment company and later sold it to Unilever for $140 million.

- Luke Sherwin questioned every part of the mattress-purchasing process and cofounded Casper sleep company, which reinvented the mattress industry and is now generating over $400 million in annual revenue as a public company.

What isn't "classic" about these entrepreneurs is that they all were liberal arts students who learned the *See, Solve, Scale* Entrepreneurial Process in my Brown courses and at our Center for Entrepreneurship.

An even wider range of unexpected entrepreneurs learned this process in my workshops in corporate, nonprofit, academic, and governmental contexts throughout the United States, and in China, Egypt, Portugal, Bahrain, Slovenia, South Africa, Jordan, Palestine, Israel, the UK, and Jamaica. Here are a few of them:

- Micah Hendler, a member of the Seeds of Peace peacebuilding organization, figured if Israeli and Palestinian teens could sing together, they could live together, and so he started the Israeli/Palestinian Jerusalem Youth Chorus. It took learning the *See,*

Solve, Scale Entrepreneurial Process for him to envision how to think bigger and to scale his vision into Raise Your Voice Labs.

- May El Batran, an Egyptian Parliament Member, and Dan Stoian, a U.S. Department of State executive at the US Embassy in Bahrain, each saw a need to teach citizens of these Middle Eastern countries how to use entrepreneurship to solve their country's economic and social problems. Each invited me to conduct *See, Solve, Scale* Entrepreneurial Process workshops as a catalyst for economic development. When in 2008 May and I led some of Egypt's first entrepreneurship training sessions, there was barely an Arabic word for entrepreneurship, and the economy was so tightly controlled that the Ministry of Commerce had to approve these sessions. Those students have now become leaders in fields of social entrepreneurship and other movements having impact. And now I return yearly to lead workshops at RiseUp—the Middle East's largest entrepreneurship summit, teeming with thousands of entrepreneurs from the region.
- Patrick Moynihan, a Catholic deacon, founded the Louverture Cleary School in Haiti to educate young Haitians from very poor families. This was literally God's work into which Patrick poured his soul for thirty years. Patrick used this *See, Solve, Scale* Entrepreneurial Process to begin to scale his enterprise to a system of ten tuition-free boarding schools providing 3,600 students with a quality education and 1,200 alumni with university scholarships each year.
- Executives at established companies including CVS, Delta Dental, a large family-owned South African shampoo manufacturer, and a Slovenian hardware manufacturer all thirsted for a way to regain the energy and enthusiasm that had launched their companies years ago. They all have used this process to overcome forces that inhibited their corporate innovation to drive internal entrepreneurship.
- Neuroscientists, chemists, and psychologists who never imagined that entrepreneurship was relevant to their scientific research were shocked to learn that this process could help them reinvent their methods: to discover more meaningful problems to target and to achieve more sustainable outcomes in their solutions. As

Brown neuroscientist Chris Moore noted after my Bottom-Up Research workshop, "While I never would have imagined that an entrepreneurship workshop would have helped me see it, your training will now significantly change the way we do brain research."

Imagine being armed with the same tools that will empower you with a way to solve problems that *you* care about. Too often when we think about entrepreneurship, we think about only shiny new tech gadgets. There is nothing wrong with those things. But there is another layer. On a deeper level, when you see these and other entrepreneurship examples, you are seeing interesting people using this method to solve important problems. Some of them are making money, some are doing good. Many are doing both

See, Solve, Scale is a "Swiss Army Knife" that has utility in both expected and unexpected ways. It is everyone's entrepreneurship. Including yours.

———

This book is designed to mirror the experience of my students. Like they do in the classroom, you will explore entrepreneurship as a structured process (part 1); then you will delve into the three discrete steps—See, Solve, and Scale—detailing each step through case studies and examples (part 2); and finally, you will learn how to pitch your venture to investors, team recruits, and other stakeholders (part 3).

By the end of this book you will learn how to:

- Define what entrepreneurship is and see that it applies to a much wider range of contexts than you may have imagined
- Leverage key academic and practical insights to form a successful venture team
- Master the structured *See, Solve, Scale* Entrepreneurial Process
- Observe and listen like an anthropologist to identify important problems to solve
- Design solutions to those problems initially on a small scale
- Create models to amplify those solutions on a much larger scale
- Hone and enhance your analytical, writing and verbal skills to communicate your solutions

- Develop entrepreneurial confidence in some ways far outside your comfort zones
- Build your entrepreneurial network and stay in touch with me by joining the online network of other *See, Solve, Scale* readers worldwide

In order for this to work as it has with my students, I refer you to videos and other resources used in class to reinforce your understanding of the material. These are essential. The other part of the course that is essential is developing a network of peers with whom to share ideas and perhaps collaborate. In class, my students work in close-knit groups where they can share and reflect on what they have learned. For you I have arranged a private online group where you can meet and interact with a community of fellow readers and, if you like, to stay in touch with me. You can learn more about this online network and access additional relevant content and resources at dannywarshay.com.

Just like in the classroom, participation is 30 percent of the grade.

Let's get started.

PART 1

Entrepreneurship: A Process, Not a Spirit

I teach entrepreneurship around the world, and I often hear people describe something they call "entrepreneurial spirit." It seems to refer to something innate. You either have it or you don't. I don't buy this.

Imagine if we taught the engineers in charge of building our bridges to rely on a similar "bridge-building spirit." That would be insane. In bridge building, there are fundamental principles that follow a step-by-step process that can be taught and learned. While each bridge is different—functionally, operationally, and aesthetically—there is a beginning, a middle, and an end to building a bridge, a structured building process that you can master and apply.

Over the course of my own career, I have launched several successful entrepreneurial ventures. With each new company, I became more mindful of common principles and a series of steps that increased our likelihood of success. It turns out that while every entrepreneurial venture is different, just like in bridge building, there is a beginning, middle, and end to this *See, Solve, Scale* Entrepreneurial Process that you can master and apply, and this is not dependent on some inherent quality you happen to have.

CHAPTER 1

THE LIBERAL ARTS ROOTS OF THIS STRUCTURED ENTREPRENEURIAL PROCESS

I studied European intellectual history at Brown University in the 1980s. In those days, Brown was not the first place, or even the twentieth place, you would have thought of if you were interested in business. Then, as now, the university had no business school. It took pride in the purity of its dedication to the liberal arts, and its student body had a reputation for being quirky, progressive, and not pre-professional. It had its own names for things: a major was a "concentration," letter grades were optional, and even the pass/fail option was known as "SNC" (satisfactory/no credit).

Brown was not a hotbed of students looking to succeed in business. To be sure, some graduates ended up in business careers, and in those days that typically meant working as consultants or investment bankers. Although very few of my peers pursued the startup world, what attracted me to it in the very early days of the tech boom was an opportunity to team up with a few other Brown students on a software venture called Clearview. I was drawn to the romance of being our own boss, as well as to the lure of a life-style that stories of Silicon Valley had begun to popularize on campus. The "create your own rules" counterculture reminded me of the Brown ethos I was experiencing as a student. We eventually sold Clearview to Apple.

Although then I did not envision a structured process of entrepreneur-ship, in retrospect I see some of the early influences on the process that later became the basis of my teaching. I liked the idea of solving a problem that held people back. Based on my partner Matt Kursh's observations in his father's medical office, we set out to automate mundane but important office-management tasks. I am sure we did not call it Bottom-Up Research then as I would decades later, but in some ways we were anthropological, as we observed and listened to detect a strong need for automating the design and management of forms that were the front end of data collection in any office. We iterated (again, not knowing that years later that concept would be so central to this process), and we focused our Value Proposition on solving that strong and enduring unmet need. We provided a software system that empowered office workers to create their own beautiful forms on the newly launched Macintosh and then collect and manage data on electronic form equivalents.

I got a rush out of seeing our products in use in all sorts of offices and hearing customers rave about the efficiency impact they were driving. I had never known that something as mundane as office forms could be so exciting. At that point, in the mid-1980s, I didn't know that entrepreneurship offered an exciting kind of work experience and life. I only knew that I liked it.

Throughout the rest of my career, in several other startups across a wide range of industries, I built on that first entrepreneurship experience. I was never the domain expert in any of them: not the tech-savvy programmer, not the food scientist, not the journalist. Instead, I was focused on the business side of the company, and with each startup, I gained more experience in this structured Entrepreneurial Process. Later, when I circled back to teach at Brown, I was able to see how elements of my own experience could inform a process that I could teach.

Fast-forward sixteen years. In 2005, I got a phone call out of the blue from Barrett Hazeltine, a legendary Brown engineering professor whose courses were among the most popular in the entire university. The engineering department was looking to formalize the teaching of entrepreneurship, he told me, and it was looking for a successful entrepreneur with a range of business experience. He liked that I had entrepreneurship experience, had studied at Harvard Business School, and that I had also worked at an established company like Procter & Gamble. Would I be interested in returning to Brown to teach?

I had never taught anything. And what the heck did he mean by "teach entrepreneurship"? Was that even possible? To develop our products, my Clearview partners drew on their Brown computer science training and their obsession with Macintosh software, but to grow the business, we had relied on our best judgment and on raw liberal arts skills. Further, Brown still had no business school. In the university's liberal arts environment,

I would encounter students without even basic business trai explained that the university was responding to the fact th numbers of Brown students were being drawn to the growing popularity of internet startups. It was looking for someone who could meet the needs of Brown students in ways that would integrate the teaching of entrepreneurship into its liberal arts–based curriculum. I'm not sure everyone in Brown's leadership knew exactly what entrepreneurship was or how it would fit. Still, I liked the sound of what Barrett described. This was an opportunity to return to Brown and teach what I had experienced in my career in the same liberal arts environment I had so valued as a student.

I soon found that I had overestimated my Brown students' familiarity with business fundamentals. Partway through my first semester teaching, when I asked my students to evaluate the financial status of a company depicted in a case study, a student named Scott Norton sheepishly raised his hand to ask "what's an asset?" Of course there's no reason why a college student would know a given business term, and I realized that if Scott— one of my best students (and someone who would later build a wildly successful company)—did not know what an asset was, then neither he nor any of his fellow students had any clue about accounting basics or about how to "keep score" in business. It felt like teaching advanced music composition to students who couldn't read music.

It was then that something important dawned on me. The point of a liberal arts curriculum, as the former president of Harvard, Derek Bok, had put it, was, "to create a web of knowledge that will illumine problems and enlighten judgment on innumerable occasions in later life." It was about critical thinking and problem-solving skills *unrelated to a specific body of knowledge*. Studying European intellectual history had taught me how to formulate important questions, to think critically, to seek and evaluate evidence from primary texts, to use research to develop rational answers, and to communicate persuasive arguments on paper and in a presentation—all fundamental skills that had been essential throughout my career, particularly in my startup roles.

And so I began to worry less about whether my students knew the difference between a debit and a credit. I would arm them with a fundamental skill that all Brown students—regardless of their primary focus of study— could master and apply in all sorts of professional contexts, throughout their lives after Brown. In short, not having a business school restricting what entrepreneurship was or who should learn it was an advantage. It gave me freedom to teach a more expansive approach to entrepreneurship to many more students whom traditional approaches had ignored.

As I distilled the fundamental traits that entrepreneurial startups in my career had in common, they all had a similar objective: *to solve a problem*. As I mention above, that first startup that I was part of and that we sold to Apple, Clearview Software, identified a data-collection and data-management problem that frustrated many office workers. *Getaways*, a startup travel magazine and internet startup company that I cofounded, sought to address the challenge that hundreds of bed-and-breakfasts faced to attract travelers to their properties. The focus of this particular liberal art—entrepreneurship—that I could teach at Brown, therefore, was a *process for solving problems*.

To avoid retelling only my own startup experiences, which may not have been replicable or even relevant, I looked for rigorous research and case studies to inform this process. The freedom I had to define and teach a more expansive approach to entrepreneurship also empowered me to draw from a much broader range of academic disciplines than exclusively from the business and technology examples that dominated entrepreneurship. With great pleasure, to highlight this broader potential impact of entrepreneurship, I included a case about the Aravind Eye Hospitals chain in India on my first syllabus. In addition, I created a formal alumni network of my former students and workshop participants, who would provide a continuous feedback loop and enable me to hone, refresh, and improve the process based on their entrepreneurial experiences. For these alumni, this real-time discussion keeps things current and allows them to continue to learn from me and from each other.

Over the subsequent fifteen years, I continued to refine that process as I have taught it to thousands of students at Brown and elsewhere around the world. This structured process involves three fundamental principles that all aspiring entrepreneurs can master and apply.

1. <u>See: Find and Validate an Unmet Need</u>: what is the problem you are looking to solve? This is the most critical part of this structured process and demands an unexpected investment of time and effort.
2. <u>Solve: Develop a Value Proposition</u>: through an iterative process, develop a small-scale solution to that problem.

3. Scale: Create a Sustainability Model: expand your solution to have big, long-term impact.

This structured process applies to a wide range of problems and results in a wide range of Value Propositions and Sustainability Models—not only conventional businesses. In short, as a methodology not an ideology, *See, Solve, Scale* has empowered my students to solve problems in contexts far beyond business, including research labs, peace-seeking nonprofits, and economic development initiatives of US embassies. Yes, this method has made a lot of people a lot of money, but for many more people, it is about something bigger. Many of these entrepreneurial solutions are "doing well by doing good" and have made the world a better place.

While traditional notions of entrepreneurship focus on business applications of technical inventions, this process has turned out to be useful to would-be problem solvers in a range of contexts. Traditional notions of entrepreneurship focus on business outcomes. This process considers a business model as only one of many Sustainability Models that empower you to solve a problem at a large-scale over the long term.

Just as learning the scientific method does not lead many of my liberal arts undergraduates to become scientists, and learning how to write does not lead many to become professional writers, these fundamental skills prove essential throughout their professional lives. Mastering the *See, Solve, Scale* Entrepreneurial Process does not necessarily lead my students to become entrepreneurs in the narrow business tech sense. Instead, it proves essential in their wide range of professional endeavors. Entrepreneurship is not just for business anymore.

The *See, Solve, Scale* problem-solving approach reflects and leverages my own liberal arts background; it draws on influences of the humanities, arts, sciences and social sciences; and it treats entrepreneurship as a liberal art of its own. While this book includes references to familiar entrepreneur heroes like Steve Jobs, you will also encounter insights from Einstein, Pasteur, St. Augustine, Maya Angelou, mathematician Ruth Noller, and James Baldwin. And you will hear an even more diverse set of inspirational voices that the process of writing this book has introduced me to, including sociologist Bertice Berry, botanist Robin Wall Kimmerer, and scholar of Chicana cultural theory, feminist theory, and queer theory Gloria Anzaldúa.

CHAPTER 2

THE BENEFITS OF SCARCE RESOURCES

Don't engage with someone with nothing to lose. It's an unequal fight.
　　　　　—Baltasar Gracián, *The Art of Worldly Wisdom*

When you ain't got nothing, you got nothing to lose.
　　　　　—Bob Dylan, "Like a Rolling Stone"

With every new cohort of students I have to start by breaking down several preconceptions that limit aspiring entrepreneurs. Chief among them is that entrepreneurship rewards those with access to resources: financial resources, team size, time, pedigree, connections, knowledge, and experience. In fact, I tell my students, the opposite is true. Particularly in the early stages of the process, successful entrepreneurs benefit from having scarce resources. Scarce resources provide discipline to fail fast and fail cheap and iterate quickly to discover an innovative solution worth scaling. They motivate you to increase efficiency by collaborating with people who bring complementary skills and experience. In exchange, they often require you to share the risks and rewards of your venture.

On the other hand, paradoxically, abundant resources can hinder you. At times, they can force you to be too conservative. Because you are so focused on preserving them, they blind you to new opportunities and innovations, and you become too fixed on a particular outcome. At other times, they can make you overconfident. By removing the incentive to share risk, abundant resources can motivate you to make bets that you would not make if you had scarce resources. And without the incentive to share risk, you miss the opportunity to collaborate with others who may add value to your venture.

Many entrepreneurial ventures never get started because their potential founders are paralyzed by their perceived lack of resources. The three stories that follow will show you that this should not be the case.

R&R and the Nontrivial Benefits of Total Scarcity

R&R,[1] a classic Harvard Business School case study, tells the story of a startup founder, Bob Reiss, who identifies a lucrative opportunity to create a TV-themed trivia board game in the wake of the runaway success of Trivial Pursuit in the 1980s. Bob is a good example of someone who has a great idea but faces some significant hurdles in bringing it to market. He is also a good example of a geographic follower that I describe in more detail in the Solve: Develop a Value Proposition step. He had noticed the success of Trivial Pursuit in Canada and knew from prior experience that successful Canadian products tended to do ten times the sales when they entered the US market.

The hurdles? Bob lacks capital, he has only one part-time employee (an assistant), he has no one on his team who can design a game, manufacture it, or pick, pack, and ship it; he has no recognizable brand; he is not able to do credit checks or collect his customer payments; and what's more, he estimates that he has a limited window (eighteen months to two years) in which to get in and get out to capitalize on this trivia game's opportunity's short life cycle that is inherent in the faddish toy industry.

Bob has no doubt that his game idea focused on TV trivia is lucrative (an assessment that will later be proven correct). But given his basic lack of resources, Bob might well have given up before he got started. Instead, he responded with a discipline that allowed him to think as an entrepreneur to solve for those scarce resources.

After making that list of all of the things he'll need to get started, Bob determines that he'll need roughly $5 million in startup capital, a daunting amount to be sure. You probably don't have $5 million in cash lying around, and you may not think you could raise it. Bob's response is to shift what otherwise would be fixed startup costs (in hiring a game designer, manufacturing capacity, a sales team, a credit department, etc.), to variable costs that the venture incurs only if and when his product is sold. All of the functions that Bob lacks—design, manufacturing, distribution logistics, finance, sales, and marketing—he outsources to experts. Because he can't afford to pay them up front, he offers these experts a percentage of sales. This has several virtues. Among them is that it shifts some of Bob's risk to his partners in exchange for sharing the upside with them if they succeed. It also gives them the incentive to do everything in their power to make that happen. Rather than hiring the designer of the trivia game as an employee or even paying him a lump sum up front, for example, Bob pays the designer a percentage of the game's eventual sales. Bob will make less money than if he'd had the money to pay everyone up front. But he'll also incur significantly lower losses if things don't work out.

Bob eventually brought his game, *TV Guide*'s *TV Game*, to market. In the next two years, it would sell over 580,000 units and earn Bob over $2 million. All because he didn't let his lack of resources stop him from following through on a very good idea.[2,3]

Casper Mattress: No Experience, No Knowledge, No Problem

In the beginner's mind there are many possibilities, but in the expert's there are few.
—Shunryu Suzuki, *Zen Mind, Beginner's Mind*[4]

As a veteran of the gaming industry, Bob Reiss had in-depth knowledge of product life cycles, relationships with experts to whom he outsourced the business functions, even the initial insight about the potential popularity of a new trivia game. Unlike Bob, many first-time entrepreneurs often face a fundamental scarcity: a basic lack of experience and knowledge. But in the early stages of a startup, this, too, can work in your favor.

In 2014 two of my former students, looking for an entrepreneurial opportunity, zeroed in on a fundamental problem with a product we all buy many times throughout our lives: a mattress. In particular, they identified problems with the process of buying a mattress: you had to go to an uncomfortable showroom, and then follow that with a frustrating delivery service that required you to wait at home for large blocks of time. Further, because none of the big mattress brands appealed to people their age, there were too many undifferentiated choices. And it was unclear how to make a choice that would lead to satisfaction with a product they would live with for years. So Luke Sherwin and Neil Parikh set out to reinvent every step of the buying process. The only challenge? They knew nothing about mattresses other than that you slept on them.

This scarcity of knowledge and experience set them on a course of exploration unbounded by assumptions that guided the industry, which among other things, accepted the idea that a consumer needed to test and buy a mattress in person, and other inconveniences related to delivery and commitment that puzzled Luke and Neil.

Benefiting from their lack of knowledge about why things had to be done a certain way, they began to ask questions. What if instead of shopping for a mattress in an uncomfortable retail showroom, you could shop online from the comfort of your home? What if instead of having to manage a challenging and inconvenient delivery of the mattress, it could be delivered to your door via UPS? What if instead of having to make a high-pressured decision to purchase a product that will last eight to ten years, you could try out the mattress at home for up to 100 nights, and if you were not satisfied, you could ship it back for a full refund?

Because the incumbent mattress industry had built up its sales and distribution infrastructure years ago, these assumptions about how you had to sell a mattress had guided them for decades. It took a fresh look from mattress rookies to see the problems and use current technology to create solutions.

All of these new steps of the mattress-buying process are now possible because the Casper founders didn't know any better. Consumers loved the idea of not having to shop for a mattress in person, and they loved receiving their new mattress in shipments alongside all the other things they were now used to purchasing online. Compared to the long-term commitment mattress stores asked their shoppers to make on the spot, Casper's 100-night trial gave consumers the confidence they needed to try out this new approach. Casper quickly expanded to more than 1 million customers and generated over $400 million in annual revenue. It raised another $100 million in private funding, bringing its total to about $340 million, and in early 2020 completed an initial public offering[5] with its stock sold on the New York Stock Exchange.

Karim Lakhani, an innovation expert and professor at Harvard Business School, reinforces this ability of those like Luke and Neil lacking domain expertise to solve problems: "Big innovation most often happens when an outsider who may be far away from the surface of the problem reframes the problem in a way that unlocks the solution."[6]

Pussyhat Project: From Personal Constraints to Inspiration

Freedom is found in the context of limitation.

—monastic proverb

In limitations one can also find inspiration. Jayna Zweiman would have liked to go to Washington to join the hundreds of thousands of others at the Women's March in 2017. As she told a room full of Brown students, however, she was recovering from a serious head injury that made it difficult to travel or be in large crowds. Undaunted, she sought another way to make an impact. She and a partner conceived the idea of engaging people in knitting circles across the country to create a sea of pink hats at Women's Marches everywhere. They created a project with a central website where they published their manifesto, shared how to join, and offered a free base pattern for the hats. These came to be known as Pussyhats, both because they included cat ears and as an effort to reclaim a term that the new president had used in a misogynistic statement caught on tape. The hats would make a bold and powerful visual statement of solidarity and allow people who could not participate in person themselves—whether for medical, financial, or scheduling reasons—a visible way to demonstrate their support for women's rights.[7]

Jayna acknowledges that her own health experience inspired her to conceive and co-launch the Pussyhat Project. An architect, she likens this dynamic to what she had experienced in designing buildings with what at first appeared a limiting design constraint. As Jayna put it during our interview, "In architecture, from limitations come inspiration. When you look at so many buildings it is clear that someone had to come up with a good way to figure ways around constraints like zoning requirements or costs. And that's usually what makes the building sing. If you have all the resources you think you need . . . you usually don't come up with something as meaningful and fantastic."

Bricolage: Creating Something from Nothing

In *Stretch: Unlock the Power of Less—and Achieve More Than You Ever Imagined*, Scott Sonenshein of Rice University endorses this power of resourcefulness, of leveraging what you've got, of stretching your scarce resources rather than chasing to control more.[8] The popular word in the entrepreneurship literature for this approach is *bricolage*. And it was not a business expert, but an anthropologist, Claude Lévi-Strauss, who first introduced this term. In his landmark 1962 anthropology work, Lévi-Strauss defined a bricoleur as "someone who makes do with whatever is at hand."[9] This term would soon be extended to other fields including sociological ethnography, political science, women's studies, interpersonal relationships, complex information systems design, legal studies, education, evolutionary genetics, biology, and economics.[10]

Rutgers entrepreneurship researcher Ted Baker and his research collaborator Reed Nelson define bricolage as "making do by applying combinations of the resources at hand to new problems and opportunities."[11] Supporting the benefits of scarce resources, Baker and Nelson's research demonstrates how entrepreneurs use bricolage to "create something from nothing." Entrepreneurs do so "by refusing to treat (and therefore see) the resources at hand as nothing"[12] and "by exploiting physical, social, or institutional inputs that other firms rejected or ignored."[13]

Recycling and reusing what otherwise we would consider "single-use" products—think Henry Ford reusing his vendors' shipping crates in the bodies of his cars—are physical forms of bricolage. Engaging customers or suppliers in co-creation is a bricolage approach. Capitalizing on amateur and self-taught skills—like when Oregon track coach Bill Bowerman used a waffle iron to invent the first Nike running shoe—is a typical entrepreneurial form of bricolage. Bricolage can help fill a market "white space"— for example, repurposing magnifying lenses as inexpensive magnifier reading glasses—with products or services that would otherwise not be available. Ignoring, working around, or even not knowing accepted institutional rules are bricolage approaches that entrepreneurs often use when reinventing industry standards.[14] The Casper founders are a good example of this last bricolage approach.

One of the most inspirational examples of bricolage I know answered a question that baffled Simon Berry. An aid worker in Zambia, Simon asked why Coca-Cola's distribution system could deliver Coke bottles to within an arm's length of everyone on earth, but we had not figured out a way to deliver lifesaving diarrhea medicines to children in developing countries. Simon and his team collaborated with Coca-Cola to design a package of lifesaving oral hydration salts called a Kit Yamoyo that could fit in the available space in between the necks of bottles in Coca-Cola crates. This

Photo credit: Simon Berry, who figured out that ten Kit Yamoyos could fit into one crate of Coca-Cola by using the unused space between the necks of the bottles.

example of what Scott Burnham calls the difference between "this is" and "this could be" started to expand the distribution network for these life-saving medicines.[15]

Most relevant for *See, Solve, Scale*, Baker and Nelson modify and expand the meaning of "making do" in their application of bricolage to entrepreneurship. "We consistently observed a conscious and frequently willful tendency for firms in our sample," they explain, "to disregard the limitations of commonly accepted definitions of material inputs, practices, and definitions and standards, insisting instead on trying out solutions, observing, and dealing with the results."[16] By not focusing on "limitations" of one kind or another that might make our approach unworkable, and by trying something and adjusting based on the results, we end up with something more valuable.

I love sharing this counterintuitive insight about the benefits of scarce resources and the stories that prove it when students worry that entrepreneurship for them is impossible because they lack money, or experience, or high-level connections. My students at Brown and around the world worry about this. Everywhere from Providence to Zhengzhou, China, Ramallah, Palestine, and Kingston, Jamaica, seeing Bob Reiss in action has a perceptible effect on their body language—you can see the students straightening up, getting excited as they realize that their relative lack of resources might just work in their favor.

When I taught my Entrepreneurial Process course in China, after the session on the benefit of scarce resources, a student named David thought of the idea for a more-convenient, less-expensive workout facility. He had wanted to open a gym, but the lack of affordable space to open a typical workout facility had deterred him. Now, he reconsidered. As he puts it, "what we usually see is the 'Walmart size' gym, which is in a huge space, a wide range of expensive equipment, open for limited hours. Ours is a 24-hour '7–11 store' type of gym: only 300–400 square meters, good location, app-based, with smart controlled devices, providing super convenient services at a competitive price." David's customers can buy long-term or short-term memberships, and even purchase by the hour on their app. Their app controls registration for personal trainers and group exercise, and smart devices control the door and lighting systems, so they don't need employees on-site in the middle of the night. David calls their space-constrained approach "4 A.M. Fitness," and says it was inspired by NBA star Kobe Bryant, because, as David says, "he was known as the hardest trainer in the league."

Scarce resources spur creativity, impose discipline, and push us to think beyond what has been tried and true. I hope it's clear by now that you should not let concerns about your lack of resources deter you from following your entrepreneurial path.

Burdens of Abundant Resources

Freedom's just another word for nothin' left to lose.
—Kris Kristofferson, *Me & Bobby McGee*

It is impossible for a man to learn what he thinks he already knows.
—Greek Stoic philosopher Epictetus

The flip side of scarce resources being a benefit is that abundant resources can be a burden. They can make you conservative about protecting those resources and therefore reluctant to risk them when facing opportunities. Being flush with abundant resources can also make you overconfident and thus vulnerable to new competitive threats and complacent about the need to innovate. If you are like Luke and Neil, this creates an opportunity to compete against industry incumbents stuck in their ways because of this burden. If you are someone in that incumbent industry, this flip side may be an important warning that you need to address.

Before reading about R&R above, who do you think would be more likely to capitalize on a game opportunity, especially considering the time constrained by the faddish nature of the product with a limited life span—a one-employee startup lacking the in-house functional expertise needed to execute, or a world-class toy company with tens of thousands of employees and billions of dollars in assets? I would have bet on the big toy company, and if you are like most rational people, you would, too. Yet, often a long-standing world-class company, and its smart managers, as professionals, have too many resources to lose to risk pursuing this board game opportunity.

It turns out that entrepreneurs have different risk/reward profiles than non-entrepreneurs. Consider Bob Reiss—the entrepreneur in R&R—versus the VP of product development at a big toy company. What's the upside for that VP's career—not from the company's perspective—of pursuing the game opportunity? A pat on the back? At best perhaps a promotion? Maybe a small bonus? In such a large company, most employees do not have a meaningful stake (equity ownership or otherwise) in the success of the opportunity. What's the downside of failure? The VP could lose her job.

Now consider Bob. If the game opportunity that he and his outsourced team have created succeeds, he has unlimited potential upside. There's no guarantee that he will achieve that level, or any level, of success. But even as he has shared some of that upside with his outsourced partners, a percentage of infinity is . . . infinity. So, in contrast to the VP at a large game company, Bob has significant potential upside if his venture succeeds.

What's Bob's downside? He invested zero dollars of his own money. His house is not on the line. He did not max out his credit cards. The capital and resources for this new venture came from one outside investor and from all the various outsourced partners whose resources Bob has attracted. One meaningful resource that might lose value if this venture failed is his social capital—his reputation, his professional and personal relationships that he has developed over the years, which have enabled him to call upon, say a game design expert to create this new product, or the firm that will do credit checks and collect his receivables. Compared to a VP of Product Development's risk/reward profile, however, Bob's looks attractive: unlimited potential upside and no catastrophic downside.

BIG TOY CO. VP	BOB REISS
Modest Upside	**Unlimited Upside**
• Promotion • Pat on the back • Bonus	• A % of infinity is . . . infinity
Significant Downside	**Modest Downside**
• Lose her job	• No $ invested • No credit card debt • No house on the line • Hit to social capital

Given her unattractive risk/reward profile, what might the corporate VP do? What might her tendency be when she sees this new game opportunity cross her desk? She might start relying on the abundant resources they control to try to reduce their risk. Deploy teams to do more research perhaps in focus groups. Tell the legal teams to take an even closer look at the patent landscape to double-check they are not infringing on anyone's intellectual property. Triple-check that the manufacturing process in which they just invested their resources is producing perfect products. All rational decisions to protect the resources they and their companies currently control. All decisions that as the big toy company's shareholders, we might rationally support; and behavior that is based on their control of abundant resources. But this is all behavior that will make them miss these new opportunities.

But hold on. All hope is not lost for corporate managers facing these kinds of obstacles. Like Bob Reiss, even these established company managers can deploy *See, Solve, Scale*. If this is you, as you will see as we progress through the three steps, you can use an anthropological approach to see that there really are new problems that your existing products are not solving, problems that your overconfidence or even hubris may have caused you to miss. You can adopt mindset guidelines I share below that can help you overcome the burdens of your abundant resources and solve those problems. And eventually when it comes time to scale these new solutions, you can learn how to use your resources to your entrepreneurial advantage.

––––

I want to share one more example of a company that was a leader in its field. Its wealth of resources made it overconfident, vulnerable to a new competitive threat, and complacent about the need to seek new opportunities. When Tony Ridder was appointed CEO of the company that bears his family name, the media company Knight Ridder, which published newspapers, had sustained success in its field. Newspapers are an example of an industry that until the internet age had what we call "high barriers to entry," meaning that there were obstacles that new newspapers would have to overcome if they wanted to compete with established newspapers. Those barriers included high up-front costs to get started (e.g., printing presses) and loyal circulation bases. Those seemed to ensure the established company robust profit margins into the foreseeable future.

The foreseeable future arrived with the advent of the internet as those strong barriers to entry began to fall. None of these new online entrants needed to spend lots of money on printing presses and distribution to get started. And with more targeted content, they could compete against Knight Ridder's most profitable advertising channels and erode the value of its large circulation bases.

At the time, Knight Ridder seemed a good bet. After all, compared to a handful of unknown startups with limited funding and no experience, it had billions of dollars of assets; thousands of experienced salespeople, Pulitzer Prize–winning journalists, editors, designers, and photographers; and an installed base of subscribers who had been loyal for decades.

The problem? With this abundance of resources, in the form of sales and editorial teams, and a successful newspaper infrastructure, Knight Ridder sought to pursue this new internet opportunity without cannibalizing its current business model. New competitors at the time—startups like Google and Yahoo!—did not have legacy businesses to protect. They also did not have cost structures, hard assets, sales processes, and editorial traditions that inhibited new approaches that the internet demanded.

Knight Ridder telegraphed its focus on its legacy business in the way it described its new mission: to create an *online newspaper*. In the Harvard Business School case study on the company, Tony Ridder sums this up best: "Our Internet operations were really run by people who came out of the newsroom, so they were editors who tended to look at this more as a newspaper."[17] When they launched, Google, Yahoo!, and the other new resource-constrained startup entrants did not describe their mission in these legacy business terms. They were free to pursue this new opportunity in ways that the established leader, with all of its abundant resources, was not. This freed these startups to invent more personalized and more appealing ways of publishing and delivering content and therefore more targeted and more profitable advertising platforms.

It didn't help matters that not long before, Knight Ridder had sunk considerable resources into a product called Viewtron—which delivered news to a screen over a phone line.[18] Knight Ridder's leadership felt this new internet looked suspiciously like their failed Viewtron venture. Worse, they remember that Viewtron lost them $50 million. With the embarrassment of this failed experience still fresh in their minds, why in the world would they pursue this new opportunity that looked so similar?

It is tempting to assume that we are all smarter than Tony Ridder and his team. With the benefit of hindsight, we might assume that we would have seen how different the internet was compared to the inferior Viewtron. We would have learned from that previous failure. We would not have been burdened by our abundant resources and would have been brave enough to cannibalize our newspaper business in favor of new internet options. Perhaps. Looking backward it may be tempting to think you would have if you have never known a world without the internet.

The real question is not whether we would have made different decisions then. Today, with similar uncertainty in the face of established resources and promising breakthrough twenty-first-century technologies, the more important question is how will we behave now? If you are at an established company, will you recognize today's equivalent of the internet threat to your business? Or will your abundant resources burden you to protect them and miss the threat? Will your abundance make you feel overconfident to the point that you miss opportunities to innovate and use your resources to your entrepreneurial advantage? It turns out that you can adopt the process I will teach you in this book to pursue entrepreneurial ventures within legacy companies. This can make the difference between a newspaper business clinging to its old model and a Google or Yahoo! inventing a new one. More on this to come.

 CAUTION: HUMAN ERROR

Because we tend to think more is better, we cling, we covet, we accumulate, despite the benefits of scarce resources that I reference above.

The Definition of Entrepreneurship

This brings us to the question of what we mean by entrepreneurship. My definition borrows from a range of experiences and disciplines that I have bracketed below.

ENTREPRENEURSHIP

A structured process for solving problems without regard to the resources currently controlled

A structured process [this comes from engineering]

for solving problems [this comes from my own entrepreneurship experience + liberal arts + engineering]

without regard to the resources currently controlled [this comes from the classic Harvard Business School definition].[19]

How's that for a mouthful?

When I share this definition around the world, I see initial looks of surprise, and then heads nod with enthusiasm. It makes sense to students just starting out, to seasoned entrepreneurs, and to aspiring entrepreneurs within established organizations to define entrepreneurship as a method for solving problems, problems that I define as unmet needs. Solving problems and addressing unmet needs are at the heart of any entrepreneurial venture—in Steve Jobs's personal computers, Oprah Winfrey's diverse media products, Elon Musk's electric cars, Charles Schwab's individual investment platform, Jeff Bezos's inexpensive and convenient access to books (and now everything else). Grounding entrepreneurship in an ambition to solve a problem will keep you focused, will help clarify your next steps, and will motivate you to take them. Solving a problem under a specific condition of scarce resources will help you do so, more as a Bob Reiss who benefited from scarcity than as a Tony Ridder who was burdened by abundance. Embracing the structured *See, Solve, Scale* Entrepreneurial Process will help you learn, master, and then apply these three steps that stem from fundamental startup principles. Remember, you can't learn entrepreneurship as a spirit, and I can't teach a spirit. But as we work through *See, Solve, Scale* together, you will see this structure unfold.

PART 2

The See, Solve, Scale Entrepreneurial Process

When I first met Ben Chesler, he was an eager and confident Brown undergraduate already concerned about food waste. He could not reconcile that while millions of people were starving, more than 40 percent of America's food supply ends up in landfills. Or as the Natural Resources Defense Council puts it, "if the United States went grocery shopping, we would leave the store with five bags, drop two in the parking lot, and leave them there. Seems crazy, but we do it every day."[1] Ben knew that this waste made no sense, and research showed it was a large contributor to global warming. But he did not know how to diagnose in more detailed causal ways what contributed to this overwhelming problem or how to focus his passion and energy to solve it. For my course, every student is responsible for identifying a problem and developing a large-scale ($100 million in annual revenue) entrepreneurial solution. In Ben's case, despite his passion and confidence, he was so unsure at that time how to turn this unsolved problem into such a breakthrough solution that he and his team opted to tackle a much simpler, more mundane challenge for the class assignment.

Three years after he finished the course, I learned that Ben had applied the Entrepreneurial Process skills from the course to the problem we had discussed at Brown, cofounding a startup focused on reducing food waste. Here is how Ben's company, Imperfect Foods, describes itself:

> Imperfect fights food waste by finding a home for "ugly" produce [Unmet Need]. We source it directly from farms and deliver it to customers' doors for about 30 percent less than grocery store prices

[Sustainability Model]. Our subscription produce box is affordable, convenient, customizable, healthy, and delicious [Value Propositions]. But Imperfect is bigger than just the box. By eating "ugly," you're helping build a more sustainable and effective food system. You're helping fight food waste. You're ensuring farmers are rewarded for their full harvest with less wasted land, fossil fuels, and water. You're improving access to healthy food. You're creating fulfilling careers for employees. With every bite into a misshapen apple or crooked carrot, you're helping shape our world for the better.

Notice the three fundamental steps of *See, Solve, Scale* that I have bracketed: an Unmet Need, a Value Proposition, and a Sustainability Model.

When we connected by phone, the first thing that surprised me was to hear that Ben's startup—Imperfect Foods—had just closed a Series B round of venture capital financing. I say surprised because I had not heard about any prior rounds of funding, and Series B ("B is for Build") tends to be an investment north of $10 million, in this case $30 million. Closing a $30 million Series B venture round just three years out of college signaled that he and Imperfect Foods were moving quickly.

Imperfect's Series B funding was a significant milestone. This is the type of capital that a startup raises once it has identified a problem to solve, developed a small-scale solution to that problem, and created a model for having long-term impact beyond the resources Ben and his team controlled. It is the type of capital that signals that the entrepreneurs are thinking big. In this case, too, it signaled an approach of doing well by doing good.

When I probed a little, Ben disclosed that Imperfect had already passed the minimum year-five revenue target that I require Entrepreneurial Process students to project in their class business plans. "Danny, I can't disclose the details," Ben explained, "but let's just say that we have already surpassed your class revenue target." Ben was telling me that after less than three years, Imperfect Foods had passed the $100 million revenue mark. This was rarified air, as only a tiny percentage of venture capital–backed companies reach that mark ever, let alone in just the few years it took Ben and his team to do so.[2]

Ben emphasized that as a liberal arts student with no other prior entrepreneurship training, before taking my course, he had felt underqualified to start a new venture. Now, all three steps of *See, Solve, Scale* and especially the first step—using Bottom-Up Research to find and validate an unmet need—guide his approach to solving problems. In his own words, here is what Ben shared with me about the *See, Solve, Scale* process:

Ben Chesler on Starting Imperfect Foods

As we were looking to start Imperfect, we knew that food waste was an environmental problem, but we weren't sure how to validate that it was also a problem for customers and farmers. Unsure of where to start, we took a page straight out of the Entrepreneurial Process and went to visit farms. We stood in these massive facilities where produce was sorted, watching as apples and cherries whizzed by at high speeds before getting sorted into an endless array of bins depending on their shape, size, and color. "What's in that bin?" I remember asking as tons and tons of fruit were carried away on a forklift, to which we got a response along the lines of "Oh, that's the fruit that doesn't meet the standards for the grocery store." We knew we had found a problem to solve.

Now that we had a problem to solve, we set out to, well, solve it! After hearing the plant managers talk about the huge bins of produce that were going to waste, we asked them if they could give us the produce for free. "No, but we can sell it to you for a great price." Armed with this new knowledge, we set out to design a system that would provide real value to the farmers. From prior customer research, we knew that customers would buy this "ugly" produce as it was 30 percent cheaper than the grocery store. After doing the math, we realized we could meet customers' needs and also provide real value to the farmers. Imperfect Produce was born: An online grocery store that delivered farm-fresh yet "ugly" fruits and vegetables to your door for 30 percent less than the grocery store.

As we began to get traction with the business, we realized quickly that we were going to have to learn to scale, and we were going to have to do it fast. Given we were an online grocery business, which is typically relatively low-margin and capital intensive, we knew we were going to have to raise money in a "Series A" financing. At first we were hesitant—we would own a smaller part of the company and we wouldn't have full control of the business. That second point was very important to us because one of the reasons we had started the company in the first place was to solve an environmental problem. After much debate, we decided it was best to raise the money— better to own a smaller piece of a larger pie. We chose a mission-aligned investor, Maveron, the firm started by Howard Schultz, to lead our round. As you'll see below, that initial investment led to great things for Imperfect.

As we began to wrap up our call, Ben clarified what he and Imperfect would be using the Series B venture capital funds for. "We already have eleven distribution centers, and by the end of the year, we anticipate having a total of thirty nationwide. We now have over one thousand employees, and we are hiring as fast as we can find qualified people." Imperfect now has hundreds of thousands of customers across more than twenty-five markets and has rescued over one hundred fifty million pounds of food. It has donated millions of pounds of food to over one hundred food banks and nonprofits, and has supported over two hundred growers to ensure they're getting a fair price for everything they grow—even the curvy cucumbers and undersized apples.[3]

———

As a liberal arts student with no prior entrepreneurship or business background, but focused and determined to make a difference, Ben is an exemplar of one kind of entrepreneur whom this process can empower. I recognize that you may have different motivations or be starting from a different place. You may have been frustrated by an unsolved problem for a long time, and already have a clear sense of a problem you want to solve. Or you may have only a vague sense, and may instead be attracted to what you perceive as the excitement, independence, and glitz of an entrepreneur's lifestyle. If you are working within an established organization, you may be looking to arm yourself with a process to help your organization innovate and solve your organization's problems or those of your customers, clients, or other stakeholders.

Just so you don't think that all of my students walk into my class with Ben's confidence, or that you need to have it to start this process, let me share another example about Emma Butler. Emma is an example of what we might call a reluctant entrepreneur. Because some of her best friends had taken my course and encouraged her to do so, she enrolled. The first day, she was so nervous she was shaking. Why? She could not imagine that a visual arts and French studies concentrator belonged anywhere near an entrepreneurship course. But she soon found that her instincts were wrong.

After mastering this process in my course, Emma is now the founder and CEO of Intimately—an adaptive clothing company for women with disabilities. Emma had been aware of this general target area because of her mother's struggles with fibromyalgia, which causes widespread musculoskeletal pain. After I explained the importance of Bottom-Up Research, which you will learn in chapter 3, Emma listened to over 250 women with different disabilities to find and validate the diverse challenges these women face when they try to dress themselves.

Fast-forward a couple of years, and Emma has launched a growing company, has raised capital, has won several international pitch competitions, has developed a brand and a supply chain, and has been featured in *Forbes, Glamour,* and *Entrepreneur.*

When I asked Emma to share a little more detail about her trajectory, she responded with much more than I had understood, even about her experience in the course. Here is what she shared:

Emma Butler on Starting Intimately

During Danny's course I worked with other students on an augmented reality app that allowed big consumer brands to acquire Gen Z customers in a unique way. Whatever assignment we did for our project, I would go home and do the same task but for Intimately. If we did the financial model together in a study group, I did the financial model for Intimately in my dorm room that night. I did all the assignments twice. When we wrote the business plan for our app, I did the business plan for Intimately. I had a higher learning curve than the other kids in the class who knew what a financial model or even what a business model was (I had no clue what either of those were), but I kept working and reading and rereading and doing and redoing the assignments until I understood. Then finally, I could contribute and worked to create the entire business plan and pitch, and we ultimately got an A.

Two of Danny's lectures in particular stood out to me, one in the early phase: Bottom-Up Research. When we began doing research for our AR/VR app for the class, I started to think more about what I was interested in, adaptive apparel. I had my mother's experience as anecdotal data. But disabilities can be so diverse and differ from one diagnosis to the next. So in order to understand disability clothing, I had to chat with women with all different disabilities. I didn't show them a product or ask for feedback or do a focus group, I just tried to listen and understand their dressing routine. This way I could get a fuller picture of how women with disabilities get dressed and the similarities across all disabilities.

From all of these Bottom-Up Research interactions, I discovered two main pain points relating to dressing for disabled folks:

- We need to work on fastening technology (i.e., buttons, zippers, hook-and-eye). Why can we send someone to the moon but disabled women still have to fiddle with buttons or use scratchy Velcro?
- We need to redesign clothing openings for mobility purposes. For example, instead of putting pants on by bending over and sliding each leg through (which is impossible for someone in a wheelchair or with paralyzed legs), we could do side-opening pants that make it so users don't have to bend over to put on pants.

With these findings, I needed to find someone who is excellent in industrial design and could invent new closures to tackle the first problem, but also a team member who understood the construction of clothing in order to redesign the way we put on clothes. I built my product team knowing I needed two superstars for first hires in these two areas.

When I did all of the early Bottom-Up Research interactions and immersed myself in shopping as a disabled woman, I learned about the buying and discovery process of people with disabilities. If someone becomes disabled, let's say they are in a car crash and have a spinal cord injury, they go to the hospital. It's there that the doctors, occupational therapists, and physical therapists help inform the patient about their new life as a disabled person. They recommend wheelchair brands, what wheelchair accessible van to buy, the best support groups, and also adaptive clothing. Disabled shoppers aren't reading *Vogue* for their next clothing purchase. They ask their OTs and other disabled friends about products that work. That's why Intimately has since created strategic partnerships with OTs, PTs, and disability organizations across the country like the Christopher Reeve Foundation. Without talking to these women, I would not have understood how to access the disability community. I could have created a great product, but if I didn't act as an anthropologist and understand where and how they shop, I would miss my market.

It was also crucial for me to listen to these women so I could really get it right. I knew if I could really get it right, I could tap into this market of 600 million women worldwide with some sort of disability that affects the way they dress. If I was going to create something for this underserved and marginalized group, I needed to create a solution that mattered and helped them. I didn't want to be another "inspirational porn" social entrepreneur who took advantage of these people. I wanted to take an unmet need and solve it.

The second lecture I will never forget was the Landscape Exercise [Note: this exercise is covered in detail later in the book]. Danny told us to think really big and for the long term; envision out to 2050 and see the world we want to see and invent backward from there. Our class group did the assignment and thought about where we wanted our company to be by 2050. But the whole time I kept thinking about my company.

At the time, I thought Intimately would be an online retailer for bras and underwear for disabled women. I looked to other lingerie companies like ThirdLove, which raised $68 million, or True & Co (where one of my teammates in the class worked) that was acquired by PVH. But when thinking about what I wanted the world to look like in 2050, I realized I wanted a cultural shift in the entire fashion industry.

I thought about how the problem I had identified would evolve and where I wanted the disability community to be in 2050. I wrote out in my class notebook phrases like "I want to see a disabled president of the USA" and "world-class supermodels with disabilities" and "high employment rate for all people with disabilities." If we were to have disabled presidents or high employment rates for people with disabilities, they'd need something to show up to work with that actually fit them. These people should have choices in what they wear: from business casual, to preppy clothes, to boho chic. Alone, I couldn't create the thousands of clothing lines that would be needed to offer disabled people choices in what to wear. But what I could do was license my technology and work with big brands to provide adaptive clothing lines. We could work together to make systemic change in the fashion industry.

I also thought about 2050 and where I would be in my personal life. I thought about if I have a daughter or a son with a disability, what kind of world do I want them to live in? They deserve to have all the choices and opportunities that nondisabled people have, whether it comes to education, careers, or fashion.

If I have a disabled daughter, I never want her to know the difference between shopping as a nondisabled woman and a disabled woman. I want her to find adaptive options at all the biggest brands. Now, a few years later, in part thanks to that exercise, Intimately has pivoted to be a B2B brand that licenses our adaptive apparel technology and patents to large companies. I want to allow my future daughter to have all the options for dressing.

I'll admit it: the building blocks of this process, the stories I tell, and even the vocabulary I use tend to come from the world of entrepreneurial startup ventures. I also offer ample examples from the wide range of other contexts I have already mentioned. But rather than piling on to the stacks of books and other resources that focus on "corporate innovation," I offer hooks to apply *See, Solve, Scale* beyond the classic startup. I say hooks because although not every detail of the process is a precise fit, I describe unexpected examples like that of neuroscientist Chris Moore, whom I mentioned earlier, who realized that this process could enhance the way he did breakthrough research.

Having taught this process through workshops in established organizations, I know there is a thirst for a way to reignite the entrepreneurial spark. Employees and leaders are worried about new entrepreneurial upstarts unseating them. They want to regain their edge against this new competition. And they are eager to learn how to compete as a startup would. This book and this process will help them do that. As I hinted in the Introduction, this expanded view of entrepreneurship will also help investors to identify opportunities that their competitors may not even notice.

Being able to teach this process to all of the above categories of aspiring entrepreneurs in the broad sense of the word has been the most rewarding part of my professional career. I have sought to carry that through here, and doing so has required finding the right balance between telling the stories of entrepreneurs in traditional startups and those in other contexts. Regardless of where you work, though, I encourage you to read and think about all of the book's stories and lessons. Over the course of our careers, most of us work at a range of organizations and in a range of roles, and the ability to apply *See, Solve, Scale* in different contexts will help you excel in all of them.

———

One of the most important lessons I have learned throughout my own professional and teaching careers is that in order to be successful, entrepreneurs in any context need to care about the problems they are solving. This is such a critical feature of the process that I address it in detail in three sections of chapter 4: Passion > Drive; Purpose > Passion; The Rant. Those sections introduce a Japanese concept called *Ikigai*—an approach to living a purposeful life that combines four essential elements: **What you are good at** and **What you love to do**, focused on a **Need in the World** and, for many entrepreneurs, **What you get paid for**. In those sections, you will read about an entrepreneur who had checked all the boxes of the Entrepreneurial Process but failed because, in the end, he focused only on his financial potential.

Right before we start to dive into the process itself, I mention Ikigai here because if entrepreneurship is a structured process for solving a problem, it assumes that you have at least a vague sense of the space in which you want to operate and why this matters. You do not need a burning sense at the level of detail that Ben had. In fact if you do, I might even recommend that you relax that resolve so you can prevent your preconceived notions from deterring you from pursuing interesting opportunities. But neither do I want you wandering around aimlessly searching for any old problem to solve.

If you don't have a clue about even a target area on which you are motivated to focus, feel free to fast-forward to the Ikigai section at the end of chapter 4. Or at least take a few minutes to think through and write down **What you are good at, What you love to do**, and a general theme of a **Need in the World** that interests you. The general need that frustrated Ben, for example, was food waste. For Emma, it was the challenges her mother faced dressing herself. Knowing the general problem category helped them to find and validate specific unmet needs in the first, "See," part of the process. If we think of a few of the other entrepreneurs I highlight in the Introduction, other examples of the level of targeting I mean at this preliminary stage might be educational barriers on which Gwen Mugodi and Patrick Moynihan each focused, a broken distribution channel that piqued the interest of Casper founders Luke and Neil, and economic development, which May El Batran and Dan Stoian each identified as a pressing general problem facing Egypt and Bahrain.

Some of you will be starting out solo, while others will already be embarking on this process as a team. In chapter 7, I will have a lot to share about guidelines for building successful entrepreneurship teams and even mistakes to avoid in doing so. In short, the most important characteristic of a successful entrepreneurship team is diversity. For now, if you are already working as a team, I encourage you to read through the three *See, Solve, Scale* steps of the process together. If you are working solo, I want you to anticipate forming a team as you circle back and start to apply this process to your target area of interest.

Finally, although I am sharing a structured process, I will not be spoon-feeding you every detail. That room for flexibility will empower you to adapt the *See, Solve, Scale* steps to solving problems in different ways that different types of entrepreneurs require. After all, how could entrepreneurs apply every detail of this process in the exact same ways to a software startup and a research lab and every context in between?

Because, as I mention above, my definition of entrepreneurship incorporates a nod to engineering, I will end this brief introduction to the process itself with an anecdote about my father, who was a NASA chemical engineer. One time when I was young and riding my bicycle around the neighborhood with a friend, my bike chain popped off. When I asked my father to help me fix it, he approached the problem like a NASA engineer. He hauled out what looked like a hardware store's worth of tools that he laid out across our driveway. He went to work on the chain and the sprockets. And after what felt like forever to an eight-year-old, he finally had my bike working.

A few days later when the chain popped off again, I cringed anticipating another engineering operation that would require a detailed order of loosening and cranking and tightening. But then my friend, Michael, who had watched my father's detailed approach, grabbed my bike, turned it over, nudged the chain back onto the sprocket, and in a few seconds we were back on the road. With only love and respect for my father, whose attention to this kind of engineering detail was part of his charm that we all loved, I don't want to dictate to you every detail of this process. For some of you, my father's precise engineering attention to each and every step in order will resonate. For others, you will adapt the conceptual guidance I am providing and "fix your bike" like Michael did for me. When it is critical to follow all of the precise details of a particular step, I will say so.

CHAPTER 3

STEP 1
SEE: FIND AND VALIDATE UNMET NEEDS

The real voyage of discovery consists not in seeking new lands, but in seeing with new eyes.

—Marcel Proust

The world changes according to the way people see it, and if you alter, even by a millimeter, the way a person looks at reality, then you can change it.

—James Baldwin

How Do You Start This Process?

What is the first step you should undertake in this process? How do you start? If entrepreneurship is a structured process for solving problems, where can you find an opportunity—a problem to solve—and how can you validate it? As I advise above, it is important to have a general target area in mind (e.g., healthcare, education, nutrition) that resonates with what you care about. You might also keep in mind insight from Bill Sahlman of Harvard Business School, who says that "Opportunity is Everywhere: Every business problem. Every crisis. Every disgruntled customer. Every non-consumer. Every contextual shift. Every impossible. Every perverse incentive is an opportunity." But while that is true, Bill knows that saying so is not a magical incantation that makes those opportunities surface. And even if you can surface them and recognize them, how do you know that they are worth pursuing? These are some of the most challenging questions that entrepreneurs face when they get started. And these are what we are going to focus on as we take the first step in the process—See: Find and Validate Unmet Needs.

Top-Down Research

Most entrepreneurs I meet around the world tell me they start by doing Top-Down Research. They seek secondary research that someone else has packaged for them on the size of their chosen industry, and how quickly it's growing. Then, they seek a logical way to segment it, say into dog food, cat food, iguana food, equine food. They look at existing competition.

While this kind of research can be necessary, it is by no means sufficient. And it can even prove harmful when aspiring entrepreneurs stop there. They think that this kind of secondary research that an "expert" has conducted and compiled for them is all they need, and they never get to the kinds of creative inferences that successful entrepreneurs tend to make. This can be an expensive mistake.

Top-Down Research limits our thinking. Because it measures activity in an existing market, it points us toward what exists, not to what could or should exist. Because it comes from public sources and is available to everyone, it does not provide any competitive advantage.

Imagine if Luke and Neil of Casper had relied only on Top-Down Research statistics about the mattress industry. What would it have revealed? It was a $30 billion global market. It was growing by a couple of percentage points year over year. It was dominated by a few well-resourced veterans that had perfected a traditional sales and distribution method. All of that was information that the incumbent mattress companies and even other aspiring mattress entrepreneurs could access. This alone would not have provided Luke and Neil creative insight into unmet sleep needs or mattress purchasing needs. None of it would have given Luke and Neil insight into anything proprietary.

Remember Scott Norton who cofounded Sir Kensington's condiments company, which was sold to Unilever for a reported $140 million? What would Scott have concluded if he had relied on the top-down statistics telling him that the global ketchup market was $4.15 billion, it was growing at 3.8 percent, it was even more consolidated than the mattress industry, dominated by only a few players and one primary one, Heinz? Again, none of this prepackaged research that you and I could find within seconds on the web would have provided Scott insight into the problems that condiment consumers faced. Heinz, Conagra, Del Monte—all of the dominant players in the ketchup industry had access to this same data and much more, so none of it would have provided Scott any proprietary insights. If Top-Down Research does not provide a competitive advantage in this first step of *See, Solve, Scale*, what does?

Bottom-Up Research

If I had asked people what they wanted, they would have said faster horses.
—Henry Ford

Bottom-Up Research eschews secondhand analysis in favor of a first-hand method of observing and listening to consumers and others throughout the supply chain. It takes more than what consumers say they need to show us the problems they are facing. And it reveals what consumers *actually* need. As Henry Ford notes above, this is often different from what consumers say they need, as their current experience limits their perception. The Bottom-Up Research method also allows us to quiet the biases that we ourselves bring to this process.

Unmet, Strong, and Enduring Needs

Let's first be clear about what we mean by an "unmet" need. In this context, unmet can mean not met at all, and it can also mean partially met. In other words, we are looking for a need that is not fully satisfied. Part of what makes an entrepreneur is the ability to say "what if things were not this way?" Often, as I share in examples below, doing so requires seeing past a partially met need to imagine how things can be even better. To most people, it may look like a met need, but seeing with new eyes allows an entrepreneur to see it is not met.

In fact, let's qualify the type of need we should be looking for, as not all needs are created equal, and addressing some needs will have a better chance of resulting in entrepreneurial success than others. Here I am referring to *strong* and *enduring* needs.

Why strong? Veteran venture capitalist Thorne Sparkman likes to say that when he is looking to invest in a venture, he wants to find one that is addressing a "hair on fire" need. As Thorne says, "if your hair is

on fire, you are motivated to find a bucket of water to put it out." Like
most investors, Thorne would prefer to invest in a venture that is addressing a problem that its customers are motivated to solve. Among all the
other choices those customers have for where to spend their hard-earned
money, if you are addressing a strong need, they are more motivated to
pull out their credit card to spend it with you. Lorine Pendleton, a successful angel investor, and one of our center's Entrepreneurs In Residence,
emphasizes this point with a different metaphor saying that she would
rather invest in a startup that is selling aspirin than vitamins.

Why enduring? If we are going to put in all the effort *See, Solve,
Scale* requires—to find and validate an unmet need, to develop a Value
Proposition, to create a Sustainability Model—why not do so focusing
on a need that has long-term rather than short-term or faddish potential? Here is where a vitamin might have more long-term appeal than
an aspirin. So maybe the ideal is a vitamin that can also cure a headache!

Is this a hard-and-fast rule? Isn't it possible to launch a successful
startup focused on weak needs or even wants? Of course it is possible,
and we all can name good examples of entrepreneurial "successes" that
are addressing even frivolous wants. Anyone remember Pet Rocks? Cab-
bage Patch dolls? Pokémon Go? Bob Reiss's game startup was a good
example of a startup that capitalized on a short-term opportunity. In
general, I recommend that at this earliest stage of *See, Solve, Scale*, we would
be smart to keep our eyes and ears open for strong and enduring needs.

Be an Anthropologist

In 2009 I was asked to teach a summer course on "cultural entrepreneurship" with anthropologist Lina Fruzzetti. I did not know what cultural entrepreneurship meant, and it turned out that Lina didn't, either.
As we put our heads and pedagogical approaches together, I learned from
Lina that a critical part of anthropology was a kind of Bottom-Up Research called ethnography. Ethnographic research methods, study design,
training, and evaluation help anthropologists observe and listen to people
behaving naturally in their own habitats without intervening in ways that
would change that behavior. And as Henry Ford would have cautioned,
without asking them what they want.

Synchronize Your Hearts

You've got to start with the customer experience and work backwards to the technology. You can't start with the technology and try to figure out where you're going to try to sell it.

—Steve Jobs

The other shorthand way to describe Bottom-Up Research is empathy—putting yourself in someone else's shoes. When we are empathizing, do we mean *judging* someone else's shoes? Should we tell them, "Boy, your shoes are so 2016!"? Should we *pitch* them on a new and better pair of shoes? Of course not. At this point, at this first stage in this process, when we are looking to find and validate unmet needs, we need to be disciplined to avoid judging, to avoid rushing to conclude anything about a next step.

Other cultures employ different metaphors for empathy. A couple of years ago, when I was teaching a group of Japanese faculty members, they told me that in Japan they describe empathy as "synchronizing your hearts." Isn't that a wonderful way to convey what we are trying to do in this first step of our process? We are looking to feel what someone else is feeling, to behave as an anthropologist to observe and listen to the way people are behaving naturally—without changing their behavior—as a way to find and validate an unmet need and as a way to discover and define the problem we are looking to solve.

Why do I emphasize observing and listening, and caution us not to pitch? Let's face it, entrepreneurship can make us enthusiastic about solving problems. I know how challenging it is even at these earliest stages of this process to resist the strong temptation to pitch our idea, our proposed solution. It's understandable that when we feel we have even just thought about a solution to someone's problem, why wait to mention it? The answer is that at this earliest stage of our process, we have no solution, no product or service, or even more than a vague, unformed, un-validated sense of an idea that we have not yet converted into an opportunity. In short, we have nothing concrete ready to pitch. At best, we might have a solution in search of a problem, and that is an expensive and foolhardy approach to entrepreneurship. The value of *See, Solve, Scale* is that it avoids luck as the basis of success; it tips the odds in your favor.

Technology experts in particular often fall into the common trap of offering a solution in search of a problem. Think of Google Glass or the electric toothbrush that interfaces with your mobile phone. What problem were these trying to solve? Did the developers understand unmet needs before they invented them? Technologists more than others tend to rush past this first critical step of finding and validating unmet needs and fall prey to "technology push." Whether on your own, in an established organization, or in a lab, if you are a technology-focused entrepreneur, you can benefit from the discipline of behaving like an anthropologist and with empathy. Resist the understandable temptation of assuming too soon that your technology will solve an important problem.

You might be surprised to learn that the first point in Apple's early marketing philosophy was not state-of-the-art technology or design perfection, but empathy, an intimate connection with the feelings of the customer: "We will truly understand their needs better than any other company," Apple's philosophy emphasized. If that contradicts the popular image of Steve Jobs as the brilliant designer who imposed his inventions on customers, you might be even more surprised to read what Jobs knew he could learn from listening to them with empathy: "If we can rap about their needs, feelings and motivations, we can respond appropriately by giving them what they want."[1]

In step 3—**Scale: Create a Sustainability Model**—you will leverage these empathetic insights you gain through anthropological Bottom-Up Research even further as empathy also forms the basis of successful branding campaigns. They will also give you credibility when you are pitching to investors and other potential stakeholders.

Now let me share a few more caveats based on years of teaching this valuable Bottom-Up Research skill and seeing patterns of mistakes that entrepreneurs can make in deploying this approach. I am not talking about surveys or focus groups, and here is one caveat that may surprise you: asking for explicit feedback does not allow you to define needs.

No Surveys or Focus Groups

As online resources like SurveyMonkey have made conducting surveys easy and inexpensive, my students and workshop participants have often turned to surveys as part of their Bottom-Up Research approach. But surveys are not an effective way of observing and listening to people behaving naturally in their own habitats. They force us to respond to prepackaged questions on a computer screen. They bias us to focus on issues others want us to focus on. They motivate us to guess what the survey designers are looking for and to answer our questions in ways that we think will please them.

In short, surveys are a contrived and unnatural way of interacting. No one lives their life naturally by filling out a survey. In a survey, we cannot detect emphasis, witness body language, hear someone's anger or anxiety. As Steve Blank, author of *Four Steps to the Epiphany*, puts it, surveys do not allow us to see the pupils in someone's eyes dilate. There is nothing anthropological or empathetic about a survey process. I often see results of surveys at this earliest stage that make statistical conclusions. "87 percent of those we surveyed blah blah blah," and I cringe remembering the strong reminder from my P&G research training: qualitative well before quantitative. Even at P&G, we did quantitative research only well down the line, if at all, far into the product development process, and maybe only years after a new product had been released. When finding and validating unmet needs, resist the temptation, therefore, to succumb to simplicity and seeming efficiency—avoid surveys.

Similar to the concern about surveys, no one lives their life participating in a focus group. Doing so requires us to answer specific questions that someone has framed for us, it often motivates us to guess what the focus group is looking to conclude, it biases us to look for ways to please the facilitator, and the discussion dynamic is unnatural as often one or two participants tend to dominate and sway the group's opinion. In short, conducting a focus group forces participants to behave in contrived ways, rather than helping us to observe and listen like an anthropologist to how people live their lives. So avoid focus groups at this early stage, too.

No Feedback

Remember where we are in the process. Like an anthropologist, we are searching with empathy to find and validate *unmet needs*. We are not yet formulating any *solution* to them. Nevertheless, even in this first stage of the process, we may have random product ideas floating around in our heads. That is natural. The problem is that I see some entrepreneurs rushing to ask for feedback on these ideas. And like surveys and focus groups, asking for feedback on very raw ideas at this first stage biases and disrupts the otherwise natural interactions we are hoping will reveal problems for us to solve. Although we might ask for clarification on what we are hearing and observing, that is different from asking for feedback on product ideas that are way premature at this stage. So just as I warn above against pitching, at this earliest stage of the process, avoid asking for feedback.

Let's imagine what might happen if you could not resist and asked for feedback on a product idea that popped into your head when you should be observing and listening for unmet needs. In most situations, at this early stage in this process, you are likely to get one of two extreme responses: I love that random idea or I hate it. If we ask for feedback on that random idea in these early stages, many of us do so from friends and family and others who know us well. They know us so well, in fact, that they can detect our enthusiasm, and they do not want to rain on our parade. There is little upside in telling us our idea stinks—only the downside of hurting our feelings.

On the other hand, at this early stage, if we do have an embryonic idea, why might some people tell us it stinks? Maybe they do feel like we are pitching them and they get defensive. Guess what, at this premature stage, any random idea is so embryonic, at best, that it is not ready for feedback. So don't ask for it and refocus instead on finding unmet needs.

Observing Is Harder than You Think

The hardest thing to see is what is in front of your eyes.
—Johann Wolfgang von Goethe

Be a witness, not a judge.

—Buddhist teaching

It's not what you look at that matters, it's what you see.
—Henry David Thoreau

How hard could this Bottom-Up Research really be? All I am suggesting is that you observe people. I admit it sounds simple. On the other hand, in my experience, while simple to say it, it is not easy to do it. Observing, in fact, is harder than you think. Let me prove it to you.

Take a minute and watch this short video of a group of people passing basketballs. Half of the group is wearing white shirts, half is wearing black shirts. Your job is simple: focus on the players wearing white shirts and count how many times they pass the basketball to each other. The video is short and is going to go by quickly so be ready to count: youtube.com/watch?v=vJG698U2Mvo[2]

How many passes? Did you count correctly? If you are like most people with whom I share this, it is likely you got the right answer.

But it is also likely that you missed the gorilla. On average, the research from award-winning experimental psychologist and cognitive scientist Daniel Simons shows that over half miss it. The first time I saw this video, I missed it. In fact, I swore it was a trick. How can that be? How did I miss a gorilla walking right in front of my field of vision? Well, observing is harder than you think. I told you what to pay attention to, and that bias caused you not to see something that seems impossible to miss. We are all biased, especially when we think we know what we are looking for, when we are looking to confirm something we suspect to be true. We acknowledged earlier that as entrepreneurs we are excited to get out there and offer up our solutions to problems we are certain exist. Is it possible that our biased enthusiasm causes us to "miss the gorilla"? This phenomenon even has a fancy scientific name: "inattentional blindness."

Here is another example. Trafton Drew, while an attention researcher at Harvard Medical School, showed a slide of lung tissue to board certified radiologists and asked them to inspect the tissue for cancer cells.[3] These are the types of tissue slides that these doctors are experts in observing all day long. It is what they spend years in medical school and post–medical school training learning how to do. Here is a link to the slide, so take a few seconds to see whether you notice anything unusual: https://doi.org/10.26300/dcfq-m071

Now take a look at the upper right corner. Do you see the gorilla? You may be shocked to learn that 83 percent of these board certified radiologists missed it. As NPR captured Drew's conclusion, "This wasn't because the eyes of the radiologists didn't happen to fall on the large, angry gorilla. Instead, the problem was in the way their brains had framed what they were doing. They were looking for cancer nodules, not gorillas. 'They look right at it, but because they're not looking for a gorilla, they don't see that it's a gorilla,' Drew says. In other words, what we're thinking about—what we're focused on—filters the world around us so aggressively that it literally shapes what we see."[4] Remember the burden of abundant resources. If we are experts in a particular field, that abundance of experience makes observing without bias harder than we think.

The French biologist Louis Pasteur may not have been thinking of Bottom-Up Research, but he understood the importance of observation and of being prepared to do it when he said, "In the fields of observation, chance favors only the prepared mind." Part of being prepared is to acknowledge that observation is harder than you think.

 CAUTION: HUMAN ERROR

Overfamiliarity can cause us to miss what in retrospect seems obvious.

Not "Eureka!" but Rather "Hmm . . . That's Funny . . ."

Science fiction writer and biochemistry professor Isaac Asimov once said that "the most exciting phrase to hear in science, the one that heralds new discoveries, is not 'Eureka!' but rather 'Hmm . . . That's funny . . .'" You might feel this during your first critical step in this *See, Solve, Scale* process in ways that are different from how you might have expected. Just as this structured approach to entrepreneurship overcomes the bias that entrepreneurship is about exhibiting the right "spirit," doing Bottom-Up

Research belies the popular notion that like the mythical scientist, the successful entrepreneur will discover the key insight in a eureka moment. I have never seen that happen. Instead, like Asimov's scientific experience, in entrepreneurship, finding unmet needs requires noticing and paying attention to the gorillas walking in your field of vision. In those moments, we will not have any clue what the implications of those observations are. But pay attention and note when you feel that "hmm . . . something is funny" instinct. When you do, you will know that you are onto something—that you are likely noticing symptoms of an unmet need.

In *Where Good Ideas Come From*, Steve Johnson talks about the concept of a "slow hunch"—that in addition to collisions of smaller hunches, big ideas often take a while to germinate. They start with that "hmm . . . that's funny" observation that Asimov talks about, and become big ideas over time, evolving both on their own and by colliding with others.[5]

Invest in Bottom-Up Research

Moonshots don't begin with brainstorming clever answers. They start with the hard work of finding the right questions.
—Derek Thompson, "Google X and the Science of Radical Creativity"[6]

Albert Einstein cautioned, "If I had an hour to solve a problem and my life depended on the solution, I would spend the first 55 minutes determining the proper question to ask . . . for once I know the proper question, I could solve the problem in less than five minutes." Einstein's insight helps to clarify the critical importance of this first step in *See, Solve, Scale* and conveys why you should spend so much time and effort on it. I empathize with the temptation to rush past this first step. I understand that you might be eager to get out there and deliver a product to market. But in Einstein's same metaphorical hour in which to do so, spend the first 55 minutes finding and validating an unmet need to address. Because once you nail that first step, designing a solid Value Proposition to address that need will flow. Without a valid unmet need, you are wasting your time. Or you better hope you will get lucky.

Proof That Bottom-Up Research Is Critical

A few years ago, I came across some research on the reasons that start-ups failed. What might you guess are the top reasons? Lack of sufficient capital? Team friction? Competition? Regulatory challenges? All good guesses. But in fact the #1 reason is Ignoring Customers and the #2 reason is No Market Need.[7] Huh? First of all, it is hard to imagine that any serious entrepreneurs would ignore their customers. There are times when we should not accept what customers are telling us, but ignoring them is not a great recipe for entrepreneurial success. More about this to come. And no market need? That jumped off the page as a perfect endorsement for Bottom-Up Research. If you want to tip the odds more in your favor, Bottom-Up Research is a great way to inoculate your startup against these two most common causes of startup failure.

I hope I have convinced you that it is important to spend time up-front finding and validating unmet needs. Start that process by defining the problem we want to solve. Otherwise, we are a solution in search of a problem. I know from the hundreds of courses and workshops I have led, however, that stories help to reinforce these concepts and will help you to remember them. My oldest course and workshop alumni smile when they see me and ask whether I still share the Bottom-Up Research stories that I shared with them years ago. Even if they do not remember the precise rationale for doing Bottom-Up Research the way I recommend, they remember the details and nuances of these few mini–case studies.

Tide

I can't believe what you say, because I see what you do.

—James Baldwin

My students' favorite story involves one that I have come upon in so many different contexts, I consider it P&G lore. It involves the stewards of a beloved and successful brand, Tide, a detergent you may have used. At the time this story takes place, Tide was a powdered detergent that came in a cardboard box. It had been around for approximately thirty years, and the people in charge of the brand wanted to learn what Tide consumers thought of the packaging. As experts in this bottom-up approach, they asked these consumers open-ended questions that allowed them to tell their story in their own way. They avoided closed-ended questions that would have restricted the range of answers and would have felt more like a survey. They followed what I refer to now as my "Warshay litmus test": they did a good job of listening at least 80 percent of the time. The consumers claimed to be happy with the cardboard packaging.

But the Tide team did not take at face value what they were hearing. Listening at least 80 percent of the time means talking less than 20 percent and perhaps 0 percent, which means fully observing. So they asked some of those same consumers for their permission to come to their homes and to observe them using Tide—as they do naturally, in their own habitats. In short, these Tide brand team members behaved like anthropologists. As this P&G lore goes, one woman who had said she was happy with Tide and who had invited the brand team into her home, unpacked the box, put it on the counter, pulled open a drawer, pulled out a sharp knife and *stabbed* the box, bore a little hole and started to pour the powdered detergent into a measuring cup. The Tide brand team that was watching was *horrified*! What was this crazy woman doing stabbing the side of their box? The woman herself looked a little confused. "This is the way I have been using your product for thirty years," she said. "And I'm happy doing so."

According to this Tide lore, that insight led to the development and launch of not only a different package, but also a new form factor in a product called Liquid Tide. That did not happen overnight in the fairy-tale form I am describing here. It took much more confirmatory research, as well as significant product development, testing, and marketing. The key for us here is that it all began with Bottom-Up Research—observing and listening to people behaving naturally—to find and validate an unmet need.

My three children who have heard me tell this story many times tease me about how I tend to lean in when telling it. But even if it is partly lore, I love this story because it holds several critical lessons for anyone looking to master this first part of *See, Solve, Scale*.

First of all, it is important to note that the Tide brand team found this unmet need *thirty years* into Tide's history. Thirty years! Bottom-Up

Research isn't valuable in just the earliest stages of a new venture: it will continue to deliver value through the life of a product or service. P&G brands never stop doing Bottom-Up Research, and neither should you.

Second, the Tide brand team did a phenomenal job of listening well. But just asking the consumers and listening to what they *said* was not good enough. It took *observing* like an anthropologist would in the natural habitats of Tide consumers to discover an unmet need.

Third, and most important, the consumer herself did not know that she had a problem. And it is not her responsibility to recognize that she does. Nor is it her responsibility to solve that problem. As Steve Jobs put it: "Some people say 'Give the customers what they want.' But that's not my approach. Our job is to figure out what they're going to want before they do."[8]

Dawn

According to a similar piece of P&G lore, when the Dawn dishwashing liquid brand team wanted to understand how their consumers enjoyed using their product, they used the same approach: they listened to them and then they observed them in their own homes. In big numbers, they noticed something unexpected: consumers were using Dawn dishwashing liquid . . . to wash fruits and vegetables. There is nothing on the label that indicates that anyone should use Dawn for this purpose. These Dawn brand team members knew more about their product and about dishwashing than anyone in the world. Yet they had no idea that anyone was using Dawn for this purpose. It took observing consumers who were using this product in their own habitats—not in contrived ways—to find this unmet need.

These dishwashing experts might have ignored these consumers. "Who are these crazy people using our dishwashing product to wash broccoli?" They might have ignored the gorilla walking right in front of them. But they did not. They did not know at the time what to make of that insight, but they noted it, and they noticed a trend. That insight led to the development of a new P&G brand called Fit, which is a soap designed and marketed for washing fruits and vegetables.

Premama—You Don't Have to Be P&G

This kind of research does not occur only at large companies. Consider the case of one of the teams from my Brown undergraduate course. For the course, students form teams, and they go through every step of this *See, Solve, Scale* Entrepreneurial Process, including pitching to venture capital investors at the end of the semester. Toward the beginning of the course one year, a group of students—four men—approached me to say they had hit an impasse. They knew they wanted to launch a product in the field of nutrition, but they were having trouble finding a specific problem to solve. I encouraged them to do more Bottom-Up Research and suggested that they hang out in the nutrition aisle at the nearby Whole Foods Market, observing consumers and perhaps asking a few open-ended questions to get them talking about their experience in their own words. After a few hours, they came rushing back to me excited to share what they had observed. "We think we found something," they gushed. "We spent a few hours watching consumers in the nutrition aisle, and we noticed a pattern of pregnant women pulling bottles of vitamins off the shelf."

They shared that these women looked unhappy, annoyed, and disappointed. The women disclosed that they were at Whole Foods to shop for something called prenatal vitamins, which these four guys learned pregnant women and even women trying to get pregnant had to take for the health of their babies. These women shoppers were unhappy because these vitamins came in large "horse pill form" that were tough to swallow, they tasted bad, and they exacerbated the nausea the women were already experiencing, made them constipated, and advertised to everyone around them that they were pregnant.

None of these four guys was going to be a consumer of these prenatal vitamins. Yet this team did an excellent job of observing and listening to responses to their brief open-ended questions *empathetically* to find and validate an unmet need. After they found this problem that women in big numbers were facing, I put them in touch with a product development expert named Manny Stern, who helped them reformulate these vitamins into convenient patented powder packs that women could tote around discreetly and dispense conveniently into any beverage of their choice. This new form provided the same nutrition as the standard pill form, it was easy to consume, it tasted great, and it did not make them nauseated or constipated.

Fast-forward, and their venture—Premama— won the Rhode Island Business Competition. It has now raised $10+ million in angel funding and venture capital, its prenatal products are selling better than established brands, and having diversified their team they have now used more Bottom-Up Research to find and validate additional unmet needs among these same women consumers to launch several additional nutritional products in new categories.

Before we move on to the next step in *See, Solve, Scale*, let me offer two additional recommendations for when you begin to apply this Bottom-Up Research approach. First, although the three examples I have shared focus on consumer-facing products, you can apply this same approach to service businesses and to business-to-business ventures. You can also apply it to contexts way beyond business as the details below about neuroscientist Chris Moore illustrate.

South African Shampoo, or Don't Let Perfection Be the Enemy of the Good

As I hope the anecdote about my father fixing my bicycle chain emphasized, sometimes you don't have to follow every detail of a process. In fact, sometimes you are not able to even if you want to. To reinforce how you can still apply the general concept of Bottom-Up Research, I will share a quick account from when I was asked to provide this training to a personal care products company in South Africa. I urged them to start with finding and validating unmet needs using the bottom-up approach I just shared with you. They were hooked. One woman in charge of the company's shampoo brands raised her hand and told me and everyone in the room that she couldn't wait to try it. There was just one challenge: how could she observe her consumers using her product when they did so naked in the shower? I had to admit that she had a point. But we "work-shopped" the challenge, and a few minutes later another woman raised her hand and said, "You know, we offer a brand of shampoo that young mothers use to wash the hair of their newborn babies, and I bet some of them would allow us to watch them." Everyone agreed that, although not what they were originally looking to do, they would give it a try.

Sure enough, they did get permission from several mothers and learned a number of important consumer insights. They learned, for example, that some of those same families also used their shampoo to wash down the basin and even the bathroom floor. Instead of telling you what they did with that bottom-up-discovered insight, let me challenge you to think through what you would do with it?

The main point of this example is to illustrate the value of doing even a less-than-perfect type of Bottom-Up Research. Don't let perfection be the enemy of the good. Even if, as in this South African shampoo example, you cannot apply Bottom-Up Research perfectly, do it in some "imperfect" way. Whether in a product, service, business to consumer or business to business context, remember to apply these foundational bottom-up principles:

- Be anthropological and empathetic and observe how people behave naturally.
- Listen to responses to your brief, open-ended questions.
- Avoid closed-ended questions that would feel like a verbal survey and would restrict the range of answers often to "yes" or "no."
- In this first step, when you are looking to find and validate unmet needs, resist the temptation to pitch or to ask for feedback on random product ideas floating around in your head.

Whether "perfect" or not, remember to tap into the entire supply chain, not just through observing and listening to consumers. Suppliers, manufacturers, distributors, competitors—all of these and other touch points in whatever general space that interests you can offer valuable opportunities to find and validate unmet needs.

———

It ain't what you don't know that gets you into trouble. It's what you know for sure that just ain't so.
                                    —Mark Twain (as quoted in the film *The Big Short*)

When I share this Bottom-Up Research technique with aspiring entrepreneurs, I often detect their impatience and sometimes even catch an eye roll. "Yeah, yeah, but I've already done some of that," I can tell they are saying. Or "yeah, but don't worry, I'm the rare entrepreneur who guessed right, and I'm really sure I already understand the needs of my customers." In these situations, I ask them to humor me and go do some Bottom-Up Research.

Here is what I tell them: Let's imagine you go out there, you do some more Bottom-Up Research, and you discover that you already knew 100 percent of what you observed and heard. Well, that's not a waste of time, because you will then feel even more confident, and you can share those extra anecdotes with others you are looking to recruit to your venture. But guess what? That never happens. One hundred percent of the time, those skeptics come rushing back to me and share even the nuanced ways in which they were wrong. Even if they were 80 percent right about what they had understood about the underlying needs, that means that they were 20 percent wrong. That final percentage can make all the difference between a successful venture and a failed one. Success rests on nuanced and subtle insights. Even if you feel confident that you have nailed this first step already, humor me. Go back out and do some more Bottom-Up Research in the way that I have described it here.

In Premama's case, for example, the unmet need for a new prenatal vitamin emerged from Bottom-Up Research. And yet Dan and his team did not stop at that initial insight. Premama's first product was called Priwater—a bottled beverage that contained a dose of prenatal nutrition. Additional Bottom-Up Research revealed a reluctance among its target consumers to tote around a bottle that was inconvenient to carry and that broadcast that they were pregnant. Listening to grocery managers also revealed the logistical challenges of manufacturing, shipping, and stocking heavy breakable bottles filled mostly with water. Those additional Bottom-Up Research insights led to a critical product pivot to much more convenient powder packets on which Premama filed a patent, launched, and scaled its business.

Unmet Needs Beyond Business

Earlier I promised to share more about why *See, Solve, Scale* is a methodology, not an ideology, and why it applies to a wide range of fields far beyond just business. On the very first day as executive director of Brown's newly launched Nelson Center for Entrepreneurship, I walked into the offices of Diane Lipscombe, the director of Brown's Carney Institute for Brain Sciences. I was hoping we could talk about collaborating, even though I was unsure what collaboration between a new Center for Entrepreneurship and a group of neuroscience researchers might produce. Because interdisciplinary thinking is a hallmark of Brown's culture, however, I suspected that combining the Carney Institute's "chocolate" with our "peanut butter" might produce something appealing. Diane also had an open mind, and during our brief conversation a couple of strong and related unmet needs emerged. Most notable was that, on average, it took seventeen years for a research idea to translate into a real-world clinical application. Before I knew it, we had agreed that I would do a Bottom-Up Research workshop for Carney's brain researchers.

These scientific researchers embraced the anthropological and empathetic approach and enjoyed the Tide, Dawn, and Premama stories. But let's face it, no matter how entertained workshop participants seem, what matters is how they apply what they learn and what impact it has. I never know that until well after that initial meeting.

A little while after that workshop, I got an email from a world-class brain researcher, Chris Moore, that would help me realize that the *See, Solve, Scale* Entrepreneurial Process had potential beyond what I had considered. Chris wrote to me: "Really great seminar: A very important connection to science is that scientists know how to use the 'scientific method' once they have the creative idea, but how to get the creative idea—the pre-period—is something that is surprisingly almost never trained." When I followed up to ask Chris to elaborate, he explained that researchers tend to form a hypothesis, test it through the scientific method, and prove it correct or incorrect. But they don't investigate enough up front whether that hypothesis will yield enough consequential clinical impact and whether it can reduce the seventeen-year path to the real world. "Your Bottom-Up Research training, Danny," he emphasized, "showed us that we tend to rush past the part where we determine what to test in the first place. And while I never would have imagined that an entrepreneurship workshop would have helped me see it, your training will now change the way we do brain research so it can have more relevant and faster clinical impact." *Wow!* At that point, I realized I was onto something much bigger than simply a structured approach to starting better businesses.

Hundreds of Entrepreneurial Process alumni have applied its three steps in a wide variety of contexts: in government, medicine, nonprofits, large companies, the military, the arts, startups, research labs like Chris's, and many others. No matter in what area you find yourself, and no matter what sort of challenge you are facing, you can use Bottom-Up Research as a first step toward addressing it. Remember, *See, Solve, Scale* is a methodology not an ideology.

I'm hoping that you will use Bottom-Up Research and in doing so identify an important problem. But how do you go from a bottle of unpleasant prenatal vitamin pills to an easy-to-digest good-tasting line of women-focused nutritional supplements? Read on.

CHAPTER 4

STEP 2
SOLVE: DEVELOP A VALUE PROPOSITION—MINDSET GUIDELINES

What Is a Value Proposition?

If in the first step of *See, Solve, Scale* you define the problem you are going to solve, in this second step you will begin to solve it. On a small scale—perhaps in a laboratory, a classroom, a spare bedroom or garage, a social enterprise accelerator, a makerspace, a corporate innovation space—you will begin to identify and pilot a solution. In this section, you will learn what a Value Proposition means, take a critical preliminary step of putting yourself in a creative frame of mind to develop breakthrough solutions, learn to use several valuable innovation tools, answer three clarifying questions, work through a structured Value Proposition exercise, and learn from an excellent Value Proposition example to help you formulate your own Value Proposition. These are all skills that no one is born with, but anyone can master them. They are what **Solve: Develop a Value Proposition** means.

Value Proposition is one of those terms that people often misuse. When I ask experienced entrepreneurs to use the phrase, they often stumble, with only some circling around the idea that it refers to the value offered to potential consumers. What they often miss is how critical it is to be able to communicate this value.

As my Brown colleague Angus Kingon defines it, Value Proposition is a "statement that ties the customer *needs* to the *benefits* of using your product or service in *economic* terms." Let's unpack the italicized words and make sure we know what we're talking about.

First, you may notice a word that should now be familiar—*need*. Remember what I said earlier and what the first step of *See, Solve, Scale* focuses on: finding and validating unmet needs. In fact, not any old needs, but *strong and enduring* ones.

Second, notice the word *benefits*. Benefits are what you promise to deliver to your customer in ways that will address their needs. Doug Hall, author of *Jump Start Your Business Brain*,[1] emphasizes that promised benefits should be *overt*. That means that they are clear to our prospective customers and they do not require those customers themselves to try hard to figure them out. Doug also emphasizes that in addition to these overt benefits, we need to communicate why our prospective customers should *trust* us to follow through on our promise to deliver these overt benefits and solve their problems. Finally, Doug reminds us that even if we promise overt benefits, and our prospects believe that we can deliver them, we need to be *dramatically different* from others who promise the same things. These three "laws of marketing physics," as Doug says, are critical for any startup success. In fact, whenever you see a startup faltering, reviewing these basics will often reveal some weakness in at least one of them.

In addition to being overt, credible, and dramatically different, it is important to distinguish between features and benefits. Features are a way to describe *what* you are promising—they describe the way your solution functions. Features may touch on the underlying technology or even on the science that supports the technology. But keep in mind that consumers do not buy a product because of its features, as cool as they might be. Apple knows that its consumers don't buy the newest laptop because of its new advanced chip, for example. They buy it because of its benefits—it makes their work more efficient and reliable.

As artificial intelligence gains traction in a wide range of industries, its proponents often emphasize the "cool factor" of its features. That's why venture capital investor Rocio Wu warns entrepreneurs not to rely on the siren call of AI features to lure customers and instead to focus on the benefits of what AI provides: "Customers are not looking for technology per se. They want solutions to solve problems. Positioning your service or product as 'AI for health care' or 'AI for sales' is not nearly specific enough. . . . Business leaders want to know you understand their problems and opportunities intimately, and that your solution is tailored for their situation. Artificial intelligence should enable better solutions."[2]

If features focus more on functions and answer the key question of *what* your product does, then benefits focus on the ways in which your product or service will address your customers' needs. In short, benefits answer the key question of *why*: Why should I care and why should I buy your product?

I love the way former Harvard Business School marketing professor and editor of the *Harvard Business Review*, Ted Levitt, distinguished between features (what) and benefits (why) by reminding us that "people don't want to buy a quarter-inch drill bit, they want to buy a quarter-inch hole." Benefits inspire our prospective customers to take action because they address a strong and enduring fundamental need. They solve a problem for customers by touching them psychologically. You are closing in on a benefit if you can describe how your solution changes not only what they do but also the way they feel.

In his inspirational TED Talk that I share with all my students, and in his book, *Start with Why: How Great Leaders Inspire Everyone to Take Action*,[3] Simon Sinek has a powerful reminder: "People don't buy what you do; they buy why you do it." Sinek cites examples from business and beyond: the Wright brothers, Steve Jobs and Steve Wozniak, and Martin Luther King Jr. "Their goals were not different than anyone else's," he reminds us. "And their systems and processes were easily replicated. . . . [Yet] they are members of a very select group of leaders who do something very, very special. They inspire us." Benefits answer the question *why*, and when we start with and emphasize the *why*, we inspire. We tap into the fundamental psychological needs that underlie the surface features or functions, the *what*.

Finally, in as focused and precise psychographic and demographic language you can use, be explicit about who your product or service will benefit. The classic mistake I see here is not being precise enough about who you are targeting as your customer. That will be a problem in Step 3: Create a Sustainability Model when you deploy your limited resources to target a market, to build a brand, and to acquire customers. Even at this earlier stage, this means you also need to start defining who is *not* your target customer.

For now, remember that in your solution to the problems you have found and validated, you need to think in terms of three fundamental questions:

Why: benefits
What: features
Who: who your product or service will benefit

Mindset Guidelines for Developing a Breakthrough Value Proposition

In the first step of the *See, Solve, Scale* process—See: Find and Validate Unmet Needs—I asked you to focus on "what is." Observing and behaving like an anthropologist and acting with empathy means to see the way things are. That's difficult because it is challenging to relax our biases. Observing how things are is harder than you think.

In this next step, Solve: Develop a Value Proposition, I ask you to see things for how they "could be." That is difficult in a different way. Unless we stretch our minds first, our perception of how things are will limit our ability to see how things can be different. My friend from the Royal Society of the Arts, Scott Burnham, has written a fantastic book about this phenomenon called *This Could*.[4] Scott summarizes a classic experiment that demonstrates the impact of this kind of mental stretch. Harvard psychologist Ellen Langer and her colleague, Alison Piper, conducted an experiment in which they illustrated the impact of what she calls conditional thinking. Two groups of participants performed a task using a pencil in which they made mistakes. The participants in one group were given a rubber band and told, "This is a rubber band." When told to correct their mistakes, 3 percent of that group realized that the rubber band could also be used as an eraser. When the participants in the other group were given a rubber band, they were told, "This could be a rubber band." Forty percent of that group realized that it could also be used to erase their mistakes.[5]

Hearing what something *could be* rather than *what it is* was all it took to stretch the minds of the second group to see the potential of a rubber band differently. When we start this step of developing a Value Proposition—a solution to the problem you identified in step one—we need to shift our mindset away from *what it is* toward *what it could be*.

Two of my good friends, and periodic teaching collaborators, are Bob Johnston and Doug Bate—founders of the Strategy Innovation Group and authors of *The Power of Strategy Innovation*. Bob and Doug have helped countless large companies and organizations transform into innovation experts. Throughout their successful careers, they have offered their clients several guidelines for developing Value Propositions. Think of these guidelines as mental warm-ups before you dive into specific Value Proposition problem-solving techniques.

To start these warm-ups, consider insights from the World War II–era creativity expert Ruth Noller.[6] An expert mathematician, Ruth communicated her advice in the form of a mathematical formula $C = fa(KIE)$, in which creativity is generated by the interaction between Knowledge (K), Imagination (I), and Evaluation (E). Most important for our purposes here, Noller emphasized that a crucial catalyst in this formula is one's attitude (a). She believed that without the right attitude, no amount of knowledge, imagination, evaluation, or any other factor can lead to creative outcomes.[7] In other words, you have to be open to the possibility of a new idea.

Diverge Before You Converge

The best way to have a good idea is to have lots of ideas.
—Linus Pauling, two-time Nobel Prize winner

You cannot dig a hole in a different place by digging the same hole deeper.
—Edward de Bono, lateral thinking and creativity expert

Often, in the early stages of any creative process, we tend to rush toward a conclusion. We might feel that we have too little time to mess around with "process" and are anxious to get to the "product." We might feel like we know the "right answer," so why not get right to it? We might feel embarrassed among our peers and among our superiors to push ideas beyond the limits that feel appropriate. One of the most common tendencies of startup entrepreneurs is overconfidence[8] which can reinforce rushing toward a conclusion. I am sure you can add a number of other reasons or excuses for our tendencies at times to narrow our focus too early in a creative process.

I am including this caveat here to help you avoid these tendencies during the development of your Value Propositions. Bob Johnston and Doug Bate warn us to resist these natural tendencies and instead to diverge before we converge. That is, at first take a wide and broad approach. Think as expansively as possible, include all ideas without editing them, knowing that later you'll have the chance to identify which are the best alternatives.

Diverge means to generate ideas without regard to practical limitations, and without judgment, evaluation or criticism. Wharton Organizational Psychologist, Adam Grant, puts it in even more concrete terms when he warns that "your first 20 ideas are actually less creative than your next 15. And that if you want to max out on creativity, you actually need 200 ideas on the table before you hit the highest point of novelty." In short, diverging will surface unexpected breakthrough solutions you would miss if you converged too soon.

 CAUTION: HUMAN ERROR

Our enthusiasm for solving problems can cause us to converge too early on a potential solution, rather than forming a portfolio of options.

Create a Portfolio of Ideas to Mitigate Risk

One specific approach to diverging is to develop a *portfolio* of potential opportunities, which we can then test in an iterative process. After all, at this early stage of the process, how could we possibly know which one idea is the right one to pursue? By using an iterative process through which we test, learn, and adjust we can begin to zero in on which idea or ideas have the best chance of succeeding. We may hit fatal flaws along the way for some of our ideas. According to research conducted by Gerald Hills and Robert Singh, the *number* of ideas is one of the most important aspects of idea generation or opportunity recognition. According to their research, more than 82 percent of nascent entrepreneurs generated between one and five ideas before selecting the eventual opportunity to pursue.[9,10] Carrying forward a portfolio of ideas through the next steps in the process is the practical part of diverging before we converge. As you begin the process of developing a solution to the problem you have identified, be sure to keep your mind open to multiple potential solutions, rather than falling in love with one.

It Is Easier to Make an Innovative Idea Feasible than a Feasible Idea Innovative

When Bob Johnston said this to my class years ago, it hit me like a bolt of lightning. I had never thought about it quite that way before. Picture yourself in a meeting in an established organization. You muster the courage to offer a suggestion, and someone (everyone?) jumps all over it to criticize how unrealistic it is. "But we don't have room for that in our budget." "It doesn't fit in anyone's department." "Our technology is nowhere near ready to do that." Startup entrepreneurs can relate to this hesitancy as well: "We don't have the funding to afford that approach." "We haven't invented that part of the solution, yet." "No one on our team knows how to do that." As we discussed above, one of the reasons that successful startups seem to innovate more is that they have a less rigid sense of what their established capabilities are.

At this stage of Value Proposition development, see if you can resist those significant temptations to evaluate your fragile, early ideas with concerns about feasibility. Why? Isn't it more efficient to trim ideas that will never work? Yes and no. Yes, in the literal sense that it might seem more efficient, but efficiency is not what should govern this part of the process. There will be time later to trim, pare, revise, even eliminate. At some point we might have to consider budgets and technology constraints. At this early stage of this creative process, however, it is important not to evaluate on the basis of what we might consider feasibility concerns. Resisting that normal tendency will help everyone on your team feel more comfortable about voicing their ideas.

Embrace Wild Card Ideas

Despite this warning to resist the tendency to focus on feasibility, if you are like most people, you will probably do so anyway. It is for this reason that when Bob and Doug visit my class, they force students to include at

least one "wild card" on their list of ideas—one that is unrealistic and that
no one has any intention of implementing as is. To force the matter, they
begin by asking their clients to make a list of ideas that are "illegal, immoral, or would get you fired."

A few colorful examples from class include a pill to prevent sunburn,
a marijuana breathalyzer, drone tree seed planting, a power router that
recharges personal and household devices through the air, a device to
recycle glass back into sand to reverse beach erosion, a normally func-
tioning window that also has air-conditioning capabilities, ethical female
pornography (student teams pursued the last two, and they were the best
ventures that semester). Crazy wild card ideas force us to relax our feasibility filters. They make us laugh and help our creative juices flow. In
many cases, these absurd ideas come to fruition in ways we never might
have expected.

Bob and Doug enforce this wild card concept through a well-known
story of innovation. One day, a group of innovation consultants was fa-
cilitating an idea generation process for a team in the candy division of
General Foods. The division needed new ideas to refresh its product line.
Despite all of the above guidance to diverge and to choose innovative over
feasible, this team was not producing any breakthrough ideas. When the
consultants required them to include several wild card ideas, someone
blurted out, "What about talking candy?" Everyone laughed. Who ever
heard of talking candy?

After a few seconds of silence, one of the food technologists spoke up
and said, "You know, we don't have talking technology, but we do have
a sugar and CO_2 formulation that in your mouth pops and crackles and
makes funny sounds." You have probably guessed that this led to the development of the Pop Rocks candy line, which became a marketplace sen-
sation for years.

Beware the Forces That Inhibit Entrepreneurship

If you are looking to apply *See, Solve, Scale* in an established organization, you may recognize and should be extra sensitive to three fundamental forces that can work against you. They are forces that push us to
converge, filter out ideas that do not seem feasible, and limit our willing-

ness to embrace wild card ideas that can help us expand our range of opportunities and lead to dramatic possibilities.

If you are looking to apply this process in more of a small startup environment, don't tune out. These concepts apply to you, too. No matter the specific context, I am warning you about these forces here so that you can prevent them from inhibiting your own Entrepreneurial Process.

Corporate Gravity

The first of these forces is what Bob and Doug call Corporate Gravity. As they say in their book, *The Power of Strategy Innovation*, "just as NASA rockets need to escape the earth's gravitational field to reach new planets, [entrepreneurial] teams must escape the force of "Corporate Gravity" in order to discover new opportunities."[11] They define corporate gravity as "an invisible force that prevents employees from venturing too far from the current business model." In other words, "that's not the way we do things." Corporate Gravity reflects implicit assumptions about how both the company and the market work that inhibit new approaches. This produces evolution rather than revolution.[12] None of us can live without gravity; just be sure it does not restrict your creativity as you embark on this Value Proposition development process.

Corporate Myopia

A related source of entrepreneurial blockage is what Bob and Doug call Corporate Myopia—"a condition where the urgency of today's business supersedes the importance of the future business, resulting in a nearsighted perspective."[13] Leaders of established organizations have two fundamental responsibilities: to sustain the fortress and to invent the future. As you know if you are in charge of an established organization, it is tough to do both.

This tendency to maintain the current business is another excellent illustration of the burden of abundant resources. Companies that have current lines of business to maintain may at first believe they hold an advantage over new startup entrants. Those companies experience Corporate Myopia and have to spend effort and resources maintaining those businesses or "sustaining the fortress." Knight Ridder, discussed above in the abundant resources section, struggled to move beyond its successful newspaper identity to capitalize on new opportunities that the internet provided. Startups—like Google and others that competed against Knight Ridder—have no legacy businesses to maintain, established markets to defend, or fortresses to sustain. Instead, they can devote all of their scarce resources to inventing the future. Beware the urgent calls of today's demands as they distract you from inventing the future.

Corporate Immune System

A third force that works against entrepreneurship in established organizations is what Bob and Doug call the Corporate Immune System—"the role played by current corporate systems and processes to 'repel' anything that threatens the current stability of the overall business." Different from the implicit assumptions in Corporate Gravity, a Corporate Immune System comprises explicit systems or processes such as compensation incentives or return on investment thresholds. While a Corporate Immune System repels things that threaten the organization, it also acts to repel things that could improve it.[14]

An example that Doug shared with me involves a well-known over-the-counter pharmaceutical company. Their sales were creeping along every year, and they needed new product ideas to increase their rate of growth. Bob and Doug worked with them, and they came up with quite a few interesting new product options to grow the business, but did not implement any of them. What scared them off was the short-term effect that a new product's launch would have on their company's profitability and, by extension, its stock price. So the strong financial results and unwillingness to jeopardize them (even for the longer-term, stronger revenue growth of a new product/brand) created an immune system response that prevented new products from ever seeing the light of day. That was the project that led Bob and Doug to define the concept of the Corporate Immune System.

Another example concerns the heads of manufacturing who did not want to produce a new product because they would have to stop production of other products, reset the machines, and do smaller runs of a new product. This would change the productivity goals they were given for their area for the year, which would in turn affect their bonus—another circumstance where statistical goals to ensure corporate efficiency and predictability ward off new product introductions.

Corporate Immune Systems are the most insidious of these three forces because they do have value. In fact, many of these systems and processes are essential for the survival of an established organization. This organizational immune system is of course a metaphor based on our biological immune systems that are necessary for us to survive. Without them, bacteria and viruses would infect us, and without those defenses, we would die. However, our own immune systems can malfunction, overheat, or become too aggressive. They can even target our own organs as pathogens and turn on them. These autoimmune tendencies are insidious because we cannot get rid of our immune systems or we would not survive. Similarly, when organizational immune systems become too aggressive, we cannot just get rid of them or the organization might not survive. In *The Innovator's Dilemma*, Clayton Christensen puts it a different way:

> One of the dilemmas of management is that, by their very nature, processes are established so that employees perform recurrent tasks in a consistent way, time after time. To ensure consistency, they are meant not to change—or if they must change, to change through tightly controlled procedures. This means that the very mechanisms through which organizations create value are intrinsically inimical to change.[15]

While useful in some ways, Corporate Immune Systems and the processes to which Clayton Christensen refers inhibit our ability to think through solutions to the problems we invested so much time and effort in our first step of *See, Solve, Scale* to reveal.

 CAUTION: HUMAN ERROR

We rely too heavily on "Corporate Immune Systems," which reject not only actual threats but also valuable innovations that compete with existing ways of operating.

Aparigraha: Becoming Unattached from Abundant Resources

We need much less than we think we need.
                                        —Maya Angelou

This trick that we do in the show is not the trick that I thought we were going to do. But it is the trick that was calling out to me.
                                        —Teller, of Penn & Teller

We are showered every day with gifts, but they are not meant for us to keep. Their life is in their movement, the inhale and the exhale of our shared breath.
                                        —Robin Wall Kimmerer, *Braiding Sweetgrass*[16]

As I walked into Sunday yoga class one morning, I saw that my teacher, Shannah, had written on the board the Sanskrit word *aparigraha*—one of the five universal yogic codes of ethical behavior that reminds us of the importance of non-possessiveness or nonattachment. Through the years, Shannah has tended to remind us of nonattachment around December holidays when it is so tempting to cling, to covet, and to accumulate. Aparigraha is a mental discipline that acknowledges that what we have is enough and that we do not need what other people have.

Here is what Shannah herself recommended when I asked her for practical guidance to achieve aparigraha discipline in an entrepreneurial context:

- Pay attention to your breath. Let the simple act of inhaling and exhaling teach you about the fullness of breathing life in, without the need to hold on to it. If we were only to inhale, we would get to a point where we can't go any further, so we *must* exhale (let go) in order to make space for the next inhale. Newness is the next right thing. In other words, life is a continual filling up and emptying, and the breath is a wonderful metaphor for that. Journal about your observations and experience.
- Look at the physical things you have surrounded yourself with. Do these things make you feel free and light or do they have a hold on you and make you feel heavy and encumbered? Remember, what you cling to clings to you. Too much of one thing creates

a maintenance problem and ends up keeping us imprisoned. Experience the difference between enjoyment and attachment.

- Notice where you impose your expectations on people, places, and things, demanding that they give you the usual fulfillment and comfort. Notice how those expectations keep you limited and often disgruntled.
- Just as we have muscles in the body, we also have a "muscle" of the mind that we forget is there. We are biased toward a "holding on" muscle and need to develop a stronger "letting go" muscle. We get our mind in shape by using this muscle more often, practicing with little things first so we are prepared when the bigger things come along. Notice when you cling to anything—emotions, thoughts, beliefs, habits, things—then give your "letting go" muscle some exercise.

As Oprah Winfrey says, "Breathe. Let go. And remind yourself that this very moment is the only one you know you have for sure."

Doing these aparigraha mental exercises can give an entrepreneur with scarce resources the confidence that those resources are enough, and as we say above, that they are even preferable to having too many resources. Aparigraha can help us embrace that last part of our entrepreneurship definition we covered at the beginning of the book: *without regard to the resources currently controlled.*

If we have abundant resources, what should we do to avoid letting them get in the way? Rather than thinking we have to jettison them in order to be entrepreneurial, the mindset of aparigraha can prevent those abundant resources from impeding us.

Remember the last part of our entrepreneurship definition. Whether scarce or abundant, aparigraha allows us as entrepreneurs to behave without regard to the resources we currently control.

Aparigraha also emphasizes impermanence. Like the Buddhist principle of nonattachment, aparigraha allows us to see things beyond how they are now. It allows us to let go of how we have grown accustomed to the way things are and to begin to imagine how they might be. It acknowledges that entrepreneurship is about changing convention, breaking rules, and creating new ones. As a metaphor for aparigraha, like yoga and meditation often do, Deborah Adele in *The Yamas and Niyamas* looks to the breath: "Like the breath when it is held too long, the things that nourish us can become toxic. Aparigraha invites us to practice divine play, experience full intimacy and contact with the moment, and then to let go so the next thing can come."[17]

Right after graduation from business school, I spent two weeks in Alaska with two classmates. We spent one week rafting down a remote section of the Copper River and the other sea kayaking in Blackstone Bay. One of the challenges of that adventure was literally going with the flow of the river, the bay, and of the inevitable challenges that we confronted along the way: weather, animals, gear, food, and the like.

Our guide, Kevin, had a wise, quiet demeanor that influenced three brash MBAs who thought they knew everything. At one point, Kevin noticed how attached we were to organizing and protecting the condition of our gear, our food, and our raft. His advice? "Get your boots wet and sit on your lunch. That way you will have nothing left to worry about." I loved that then and I love it now, as it is such an insightful commentary on the price of obsessing about and trying to protect what we have. He did not say throw your lunch and boots overboard, but he did suggest that we get over our worry and our attachment and move on to enjoy the trip. In *See, Solve, Scale*, I do not suggest that we abandon whatever resources we have. But I do suggest that we follow Kevin's suggestion to find a way to stop them from dominating our thinking.

As Robin Wall Kimmerer, Native American botanist and author of *Braiding Sweetgrass* puts it, "Scarcity and plenty are as much qualities of the mind and spirit as they are of the economy."[18]

Expiration Date

As I have emphasized through "caution callouts," an important theme of *See, Solve, Scale* is that it helps us overcome the cognitive biases that get in our way and that I have cautioned against throughout the book. Bottom-Up Research helps us to relax the biases that we all bring to human interaction. Caution against pitching or even asking for feedback early in the process acknowledges that we tend to latch on to a random product idea too quickly. Aparigraha is a mindset that helps us overcome our human tendency to cling, to covet, and to accumulate abundant resources. Aparigraha, however, is elusive. It challenges even the most experienced yogi, and it takes a lifetime to master.

Sometimes it is necessary to institutionalize ways to acknowledge and overcome these natural tendencies. When it was founded in 1997, the Olin College of Engineering in Needham, Massachusetts, set out to reinvent engineering education and to differentiate itself from other better-known engineering schools. Recognizing that it would not discover all of its students' unmet needs at the start of this process, it acknowledged that it needed to iterate its Value Proposition before it invested resources to scale. Now, Olin is famous for its innovative engineering curriculum, which without distinct academic departments is interdisciplinary and focuses on design and innovation. Its pedagogy emphasizes team-based projects.

Despite its initial success in the early 2000s, every few years, the school's faculty came together to examine and in some cases rewrite parts of its curriculum from scratch. Olin did not leave an evolution of its curriculum to chance, to the brilliant insight of future leadership, or even to a mental discipline that would compel that leadership to behave as if it did not have such abundant resources. It did not hope that Olin would overcome the gravity, myopia, or immune system forces inherent in the established resources that it amassed over time. Just like a manufacturer does, Olin established limits on how long any of its programs could continue—in other words, it set expiration dates. Olin's strict discipline forced many of its resources to disappear so that it could reinvent them anew. It forced the college to behave as if it had scarce resources: to find and validate unmet or partially met needs again, and to restart the process of developing its Value Proposition. I like to say that this approach forced Olin's leadership to see with new eyes.

Passion > Drive

I have no special talents. I am only passionately curious.

—Albert Einstein

Nobody cares how much you know, until they know how much you care.

—Teddy Roosevelt

Successful entrepreneurs tend to love what they are doing and revel in their entrepreneurial identity.[19] In the rare cases where aspiring entrepreneurs try to launch something for which they do not have passion, they fail. Entrepreneurship is not easy. Far from it. You are looking to change the world, solve problems that have challenged or befuddled or even plagued us for a long time. You are taking risks by blazing a trail, and that is difficult. Despite the academic credibility behind what I am sharing with you here, *See, Solve, Scale* cannot be an academic or intellectual endeavor. You cannot go through the motions of this process without the emotions. Whether you are in a lab, makerspace, social enterprise accelerator, hospital, military base, museum, government agency, big company, or any other problem-solving context, a critical ingredient in your success is passion.

I saw this when I was a venture capitalist focused on the consumer health and natural products industry, reading hundreds of business plans and meeting with dozens of entrepreneurs, each dripping with passion for their entrepreneurial mission. Although their expression would vary based on their different personality types, I could feel that their passion would motivate them to move beyond, around, over, or through the inevitable obstacles that would get in their way. Some with medical training and many without were convinced that they had discovered a natural substance that would cure cancer and were not going to let a little thing like working through FDA requirements get in their way. Others were looking to commercialize new diets that they believed were the key to longevity. As sixty-year-olds who looked more like thirty, they were determined to be living proof of the efficacy of their diets. And increasing numbers of technology experts from outside this world were licking their chops to apply their skills to this natural products industry, the retail and distribution infrastructure of which was lagging behind the times. The passion of these earnest entrepreneurs alone was never a sufficient reason for me to invest, but it was necessary. And as an investor, I was not alone. The research of HBS professor Jon Jachimowicz has concluded that not only do entrepreneurs who demonstrate passion in their pitches receive more investment offers, this relationship is sensitive. Even "a one standard deviation increase in the expression of passion is associated with a 40.4 percent increase in the likelihood that the entrepreneur received funding."[20,21]

In my own investment experience, while most entrepreneurs I met demonstrated passion, rare exceptions stood out. One particular aspiring entrepreneur had an impressive pedigree: elite college and business school, and experience at a consulting firm that taught him how to analyze a market. He came armed with a fancy top-down analysis of every natural food category in the grocery aisle, leading to his conclusion that there was an unmet need for all-natural Italian food. This was early in my venture capital experience, and I have to admit I was seduced by his credentials, as well as by his ability to quote statistics about growth rates, margins, and manufacturing and distribution strategies like a walking business school case study. He checked all of the boxes. And beyond that, he had what Silicon Valley veteran Randy Komisar calls *drive*, which Randy defines as a force that "pushes you toward something you feel compelled or obligated to do."

But as the meeting went on, something else became clear. Sure, his spreadsheets and charts revealed classic "hockey stick" revenue projections. His manufacturing analysis promised profit margins that would make any MBA smile. He quoted industry experts about impressive growth rates in the specialty food markets. But it was clear that his brain and wallet were dominating our conversation and his heart was nowhere to be found. Yes, he appeared good at understanding the dynamics of this industry. But this did not seem to be an opportunity he cared about. And he was not making the case that the world would be better off if he did this. In other words, he did not have passion "which pulls you toward something you cannot resist."[22] Reflecting back on my own entrepreneurship experience and remembering how difficult it often was to overcome the challenges we faced, I passed.

This is not to say you should abandon a project if you don't feel overwhelming passion at the outset. In fact, sometimes a journey through *See, Solve, Scale* can reveal and help you express a latent passion. Finding a problem that you are excited to solve, developing a Value Proposition that begins to do so, and envisioning and developing a Sustainability Model— all of these steps can both reflect a dormant passion and provide meaningful ways of expressing and amplifying that passion.

One of the most striking qualities of Dan Aziz, founder of the prenatal vitamin startup Premama that I mentioned earlier, is his passion for helping someone experiencing a medical need. As one of the biggest Premama investors put it, he invested in Premama because of Dan and in particular because he knew that Dan had so much passion he would "go through a wall" if anything got in his way. Premama is a good example of the dual-sided passion vehicle I am talking about. On that Bottom-Up Research visit to Whole Foods, finding and validating the unmet need that pregnant women faced revealed a latent passion that Dan and his startup team may have only intuited at first. In launching and scaling Premama, Dan's continued pursuit of a Value Proposition and Sustainability Model has clarified even further the breadth, depth, and reach of this passion. It has provided a vehicle through which Dan can nurture that passion and continue to express it on a larger scale.

It is not always easy to assess or strike the perfect balance between rationality and passion. As Eva de Mol notes in her *Harvard Business Review* piece entitled "What Makes a Successful Startup Team," balance that includes shared entrepreneurial passion is the basis for superior entrepreneurial team performance.

> When we talk about this balance between team member experience (hard skills) and passion and vision (soft skills) there's a sweet spot where stellar teams seem to live. If team members are supersmart and experienced, but they don't feel like sharing this knowledge due to a lack of alignment about the vision for the company, their knowledge is useless for the business. Instead, these differences in passion and vision make teams perform worse.[23]

Purpose > Passion[24]

When you walk with purpose, you collide with destiny.
　　—Bertice Berry, sociologist, author, lecturer, and educator

When you find the job or vocation that feels easy, it brings the most goodness to you and the world. If you're lucky enough to be in that space, that's what success is.
　　—Chinedu Echeruo, Serial Entrepreneur, Hopstop Creator

As necessary as passion is for initiating motivation, and as preferable as passion is to sheer drive, I do want to share a few cautionary notes about it. First, as positive an emotion as passion is, important research has demonstrated that it is possible for too much passion to hinder an entrepreneur's progress. As Melissa Cardon and her research colleagues indicate in their article "The Nature and Experience of Entrepreneurial Passion," "passion that is too positive or intense can limit an entrepreneur's creative problem solving . . . because the entrepreneur is resistant to exploring alternative options, fearing that doing so may dilute and distract the intense positive experience."[25]

Second, although investors are more likely to support entrepreneurs who demonstrate passion when they pitch, you can't fake it. While investors tend to invest in ventures whose founders express authentic passion, they are *less likely* to support entrepreneurs who express passion insincerely.[26]

Third, what's even more important than passion for sustaining entrepreneurial motivation is purpose. Passion alone does not foster resiliency or the internal fortitude to follow through on noble, long-term goals. Passion is an emotional state, and emotional states, by their very nature, are fleeting. Purpose, on the other hand, is a sense of well-being and more of a state of mind that includes passion as well as other important ingredients. Passion is self-oriented, it is about how you feel about something, while purpose is the intersection of goals that are both meaningful to you and important to others.

One way to amplify beyond passion alone is to define purpose as pursuit of something that is both meaningful to you and consequential to the world.

Yes, while it is important for whatever we are pursuing to reflect our own priorities, we need to consider the impact we are having on the world around us, too.

In more specific terms, remember that purpose is the confluence of **What you are good at** and **What you love to do**, focused on a **Need in the**

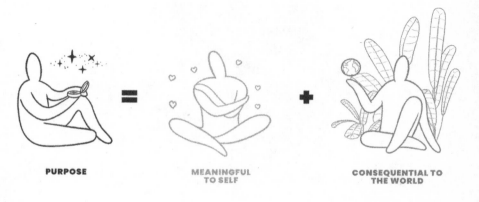

PURPOSE   MEANINGFUL   CONSEQUENTIAL TO
                 TO SELF   THE WORLD

Courtesy of Wayfinder

Courtesy of Wayfinder

World. Did you notice that word "need"? Yes, need is an important link to *See, Solve, Scale*. Purpose focuses and channels our passion for what we love to do and what we are good at toward addressing a need. For many entrepreneurs, another important link is to incorporate **What you get paid for**. As I mentioned earlier, the Japanese word *"Ikigai"*—an ancient approach to living a purposeful life—emphasizes the harmony of these four critical elements. This graphic illustrates where that sweet spot is:

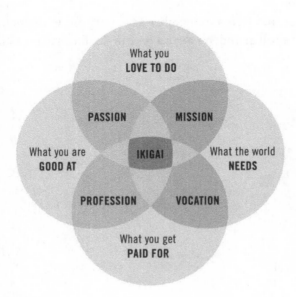

Thinking again about Dan Aziz of Premama, when his team found and validated an important need in the world, why was meeting that specific medical need for pregnant women meaningful to Dan? Why has Premama become an expression of more than his passion and risen to the level of his purpose? Was there something from Dan's past that motivated him? As a young teenager in Canada, Dan excelled at hockey, and he seemed destined to play in the National Hockey League. One hot, sunny summer day while he was wakeboarding at a friend's vacation house, the rope got caught around his neck, and the motorboat pulled him violently and help-lessly in its wake. Dan ended up paralyzed facedown in the water. Fortu-nately, someone nearby knew enough to right him gingerly and keep him breathing. An ambulance rushed him to a hospital, and he had a lifesaving operation and recovered. Dan was no longer able to play a contact sport like hockey, but was able to return to sports to row crew for a Brown team that won a national championship.

Through his athletic endeavors, Dan had developed the type of raw *drive* that would push him "through a wall." The *passion* to start a new venture catalyzed a love for entrepreneurship that became an important part of his identity. After experiencing a near-death, Dan developed an acute level of empathy toward health-care problems, and therefore *purpose* for solving them. If passion catalyzed his initial entrepreneurial interests, his purpose for solving certain medical problems that pregnant women face has sustained those interests.

As much as purpose can motivate and channel our passion, it also has an effect on our health. Adults with a purpose in life report higher levels of psychological well-being, flourishing, hope, resilience, and life satisfac-tion. Furthermore, purposeful people have been found to live longer and have significantly lower incidences of heart attack, Alzheimer's disease, and stroke.[27,28]

Purpose can even protect entrepreneurs from the negative emotions that high-stress entrepreneurial lifestyles can cause.[29] University of Cal-ifornia–San Francisco research faculty member and entrepreneur Blake Gurfein summarizes a body of research that indicates "at least some en-trepreneurs appear to be protected from negative health effects associated with high pressure and stress. This likely stems from the high degree of autonomy [that] purposeful entrepreneurs have."

Entrepreneurial stress aside, if entrepreneurship is a process for addressing a need that is an essential component of purpose, and if purpose causes us to flourish, reduce stress, and even live longer, that is quite an endorsement of the value of entrepreneurship for ourselves and for the world we can influence through it.

In *Monk and the Riddle: The Art of Creating a Life While Making a Living,* Randy Komisar warns against living the deferred life plan:[30] "I will take that consulting job only for a little while, I will sock away a bunch of money," they promise, "and in a few years, then I will pursue my life's purpose." Too many of these deferred life plan adopters have what Randy calls drive but no passion, let alone a sense of purpose for what they do in the meantime. Worse, many never get back to what will make them happy and what will be consequential to the world.

Even those who do take an entrepreneurial plunge may live a deferred life plan if they think only about the financial results of their entrepreneurial pursuits. That very smart would-be Italian food entrepreneur had aligned all of the dominoes that he thought would fall in the direction of making a culinary fortune. What he lacked was *why* this mattered to him, and *why* it would be consequential by meeting a strong and enduring need over the long term.

The Rant

May we do work that matters.

—Gloria Anzaldúa[31]

Your time is limited, so don't waste it living someone else's life.

—Steve Jobs[32]

With every class at Brown, I share what my students have come to call "the Rant." I am not, by nature, given to ranting. But when I saw so many of my entrepreneurship students, who had headed like lemmings to Wall Street and consulting firms, bemoaning their lack of happiness, passion, and purpose, I had to do something to help reverse that trend. Each semester, as students approach me for advice about their banking or consulting interviews, I know it is time for the Rant.

I start by drawing a graph on the board that shows where Brown entrepreneurship students enter school as some of the most open-minded eighteen-year-olds in the world, yet somehow over their next four years, they conclude that there are only two things that a Brown grad can do: consulting and banking.

This tendency confuses me since almost all of these students write in their personal statements to be admitted to the course that they would like to become an entrepreneur. Yet, when they are on the cusp of job hunting, many rationalize their "deferred life plan" by saying that consulting or banking will be good training for their ultimate entrepreneurial ambitions. I break it to them that these are not places where you learn the skills that are essential for entrepreneurship. For entrepreneurship you need to master the skills related to assembling a diverse team, creating a product or service, developing a brand, selling, and raising money. Although you learn other things, these entrepreneurship skills are not the skills that consulting and banking teach you.

It takes persistence to get through to some students. Sometimes I resort to a sports analogy: let's imagine you want to become the starting shortstop for the Boston Red Sox and you tell me that to prepare, you are going to run the food concessions at the stadium where the Triple-A minor league affiliate of the Boston Red Sox plays. "Food concessions?" I resist. "To become a major league shortstop, you need to learn to hit for power, to turn a double play, and cover second base on a steal." "No," the student responds. "You don't understand. I'm going to be serving hot dogs, sodas, and pretzels to baseball fans. I'm going to be talking baseball lingo. I'm going to be around baseball players." These students fixated on banking and consulting are going to be around entrepreneurs, talking entrepreneurship lingo. But they are not going to be in the entrepreneurship game or in other contexts honing their entrepreneurship skills.

Entrepreneurship—solving important problems without regard to the resources you currently control—in all the various contexts we have discussed is one way to develop those skills. After you read this book, you might dive in and do just that. You can also join an entrepreneurial venture and contribute to it and learn from it. Venture for America (VFA), for example, is a wonderful organization started by Brown graduate and former presidential candidate Andrew Yang that will train you and place you in a startup in one of over a dozen cities looking to add value to their entrepreneurial ecosystems. VFA fellows become part of a cohort of other current fellows and a valuable network of VFA alumni. They receive ongoing mentorship and professional development training, and they contribute to local startups and community organizations.

Jeffrey Bussgang's book *Entering Startupland: An Essential Guide to Finding the Right Job*[33] is an excellent guide for finding a job in a startup where you can contribute something meaningful and gain valuable and relevant entrepreneurship experience. It's also possible to learn entrepreneurship skills in some existing companies and other established organizations. The key is to find one that will provide opportunities for you to learn the kinds of things that entrepreneurs need in their own startups. Remember, I learned the rudiments of what I call Bottom-Up Research at P&G. Working in a product- or project-management job will train you in scoping out a solution to a specific problem and hold you accountable to meeting budgets and deadlines. Being in an environment in which you hire, manage, and maybe even fire others will train you how to do these things before you need to do so in your own startup. Most of this kind of learning you will do on the job. Look for organizations that offer explicit training. The training itself is of course often valuable, and so is the signal that helping you learn is a priority.

The good news is that "the Rant" has preempted many students from succumbing to the seductive siren call of consulting firms and investment banks, when their true calling lies elsewhere. When disillusioned bankers and consultants return, I point them back to Randy Komisar's *The Monk and the Riddle*, which they were assigned to read for the last day of class. Komisar is clear on the hazards of living a deferred life plan: dedicating yourself to something that does not make you happy or feel fulfilled or at least does not advance your long-term vision, and feeling like you sold out in ways that violate your values.

As Stanford psychology professor Bill Damon says, "The biggest problem growing up today is not actually stress; it's meaninglessness." Do yourself a favor: read Randy Komisar's book.

CHAPTER 5

STEP 2
SOLVE: DEVELOP A VALUE PROPOSITION—TECHNIQUES

With your mind stretched beyond "what is" to "what could be," it is now time to dive in further to Step 2: Develop a Value Proposition. As you recall, this step begins to answer the questions What, Who, and, most important, Why. I say "begins" because this part of the process tends not to be linear. It is iterative in that it requires you to approach the problem you identified in step 1 from more than one angle. In this chapter, therefore, I am going to share a number of different techniques that will help you devise solutions and answer the three Value Proposition questions. Reflecting back on the anecdote about my father fixing my bike chain, you may want to dive into each of these techniques and apply them in detail to your situation. Or you may prefer to get the gist of certain techniques and move quickly through them.

The first technique I will introduce—being a Geographic Follower—may surprise you: you do not have to invent something from scratch. Rather, you can build on a solution that someone else has developed elsewhere and reapply it to your own circumstance. Second, just as *See, Solve, Scale* benefits from its structure, so will Systematic Inventive Thinking (SIT), which structures and in some ways limits our creative thinking to a few common patterns. Third, the Nominal Group Technique is a structured alternative to brainstorming. Fourth, Open Innovation will build on the Bob Reiss approach of leveraging the expertise of others that led to his successful trivia game venture. And finally, the adage, "Don't fall in love, fall in like" will help you benefit from quick and inexpensive failures.

Geographic Follower

The future is already here—it's just not evenly distributed.
                              —William Gibson, science fiction writer

While the whole world was having a big old party, a few outsiders and weirdos . . . saw the giant lie at the heart of the economy, and they saw it by doing something the rest of the suckers never thought to do. . . . They looked.

                              —*The Big Short* prologue

Many aspiring entrepreneurs—especially those in the tech world—believe you have to invent something from scratch to be legit. But it turns out that many successful entrepreneurial ventures draw on the insights and successes of precursor ventures that have addressed similar problems in other geographies.

Bob Reiss, the game creator whose story we discussed in chapter 2, made his fortune in trivia games, but he did not invent the genre. In fact, he saw Trivial Pursuit starting to thrive in Canada and thought he could bring that concept to the American market. Throughout his career, Bob had developed an acute pattern recognition of the migration of concepts from Canada to the United States. He knew that products tended to sell ten times as well in the much larger US market. The germ of Bob's venture came not from a lab or a makerspace, but from his experience noticing concepts in Canada. As Bob himself shared when he visited class, "This is something like adding letters to the beginning or end of an existing word on a Scrabble board and earning credit for all the letters. There's no shame in piggybacking on someone else's formula for success."

None of this excuses us from developing a differentiated Value Proposition, one that is dramatically different from the competition. The trivia game that Bob Reiss and his team developed, while inspired by the precursor Trivial Pursuit, was different in both its format and execution. Bob improved his version of the game and even its manufacturability and marketability. He partnered with *TV Guide* to capitalize on its recognizable brand and circulation of 17 million subscribers, calling it *TV Guide's TV*

Game. Keeping his eyes open in Canada was the key to Bob developing a Value Proposition in the first place.

Many years I host a group of Chinese students from Peking University during their visit to Brown, and when we discuss the R&R trivia game company, the idea that an entrepreneur does not have to invent something from scratch blows their minds. They are hungry to learn about *See, Solve, Scale,* and many of them hold that same bias as my engineering colleagues: they think that the first step needs to be inventing something. When we get to this part of the R&R discussion, and we talk about what Bob Reiss actually did if he did not invent the trivia game concept, I say that he did something that is not all that complex: he kept his eyes open. I then urge these Chinese students while they are in town to do the same. I caution them against spending all of their time on Brown's campus and instead I recommend visiting the Providence Place Mall downtown or Whole Foods Market down the street and do what Bob did: keep their eyes open.

They see things that they do not have in Beijing, concepts they might replicate there. They also notice that they have things in Beijing that we do not have here which they might replicate in the United States. To be clear, I am of course not talking about stealing someone's concept or infringing on their intellectual property. I am talking about noticing trends whose popularity you can leverage elsewhere. In short, I am referring again to seeing with new eyes.

Sounds easy, right? Yet, just like doing Bottom-Up Research, observing in this way involves developing a new set of muscles. Bob Reiss was not the only person who observed the growing popularity of Trivial Pursuit in Canada. Thousands of consumers had already purchased that board game. Bob drew on his prior experience in this industry to notice this early trend and to see its potential to do ten times the sales if he brought the concept to the American market, and he knew how to leverage his scarce resources to make it happen.

This concept of paying attention to a trend somewhere else is one legitimate source of developing a Value Proposition. It is called being a **Geographic Follower**. Replicators create value by discovering and refining a business model, by choosing the necessary components to replicate that model in suitable geographical locations, by developing capabilities to routinize knowledge transfer, and by maintaining the model in operation once it has been replicated.[1] If you worry that you do not have the tech chops to invent something, this may open up for you a different way of thinking about entrepreneurship, in general, and of developing a Value Proposition, in particular.

If you do have those tech chops, this concept can also work in your favor and relieve you of the bias that you might have to use those chops to invent something from scratch. One example of such an entrepreneur is a Brown chemist named Christoph Rose-Petruck, who had made many breakthrough discoveries in his lab. When he participated in a daylong Entrepreneurial Process workshop and told me he wanted to learn how to translate his research into entrepreneurial ventures, his biggest breakthrough came at this juncture of the R&R discussion. As Christoph realized, "one does not have to make a groundbreaking new discovery before becoming an entrepreneur. Repurposing an existing concept can be a winner." This insight led Christoph to look at other technologies that he had not invented, and that he could reapply to a novel purpose. For decades, X-ray phase contrast imaging, which provides much better image quality and image detail than conventional X-rays, had been a common technology in many other physics and chemistry labs, for example. Through a new startup, Research Instruments Corporation, Christoph looked at this imaging technology in new ways and began applying it to new fields such as medicine and manufacturing.

In *Range*, David Epstein points out that "scientists who have worked abroad . . . are more likely to make a greater scientific impact than those who have not. The economists who documented that trend suggested that one reason could be that migrants 'arbitrage' opportunities, the chance to take an idea from one market and bring it to another where it is more rare and valued."[2]

Systematic Inventive Thinking

"You mean you're comparing our lives to a sonnet? A strict form, but freedom within it?"

"Yes." Mrs. Whatsit said. "You're given the form, but you have to write the sonnet yourself. What you say is completely up to you."

—Madeleine L'Engle, *A Wrinkle in Time*[3]

As we saw in the Tide, Dawn, and Premama Bottom-Up Research examples above, sometimes entrepreneurs find themselves in positions where the problem they are looking to solve stems from insights they have gathered from an existing product or service. The woman who revealed she had been stabbing the side of the laundry detergent box for decades demonstrated that her problem was not with washing her clothes, but with the way the current box operated. Users of dishwashing soap revealed that they had a problem washing fruits and vegetables in ways that the current product was not formulated to address. Dan Aziz and the other Premama founders discovered not the fact that pregnant women had to provide essential nutrients to their babies, but rather that there were flaws in the delivery mechanism of the current prenatal vitamin lines. Reinventing existing products or services is a powerful source of Value Proposition.

One of the challenges to doing so is what in the early twentieth-century German psychologist Karl Duncker called fixedness—a cognitive bias or a mental block against using an object in a new way that would help us to solve a problem.[4] In his famous candle experiment, he gave participants a box of thumbtacks, a candle, and a book of matches, and asked them to attach the lit candle to the wall in a way that would prevent the wax from dripping on the table below. Most tried to tack the candle to the wall or to use the melted wax to glue it to the wall and failed. The key was to see past the box as a container for the tacks and to tack it to the wall as a stand for the lit candle. The key was to break your fixedness to see past the box as a container for the tacks.

The Systematic Inventive Thinking (SIT) methodology is an approach to doing just that. It helps us to identify and then break our fixedness to develop new value or to deliver existing value in a new valuable way. Like *See, Solve, Scale* overall, SIT may seem counterintuitive when it asks us to structure and even limit our creative thinking to a few common creativity templates. Based on twenty-five years of research and experience with many different types of entrepreneurial teams in a wide range of creative processes, Jacob Goldenberg, Roni Horowitz, Amnon Levav, and David Mazursky observed and detected recurring patterns that most innovations follow. They realized that structuring and disciplining a creative team's process to follow these common patterns will yield breakthrough ideas and successful results. In Amnon's words:

At the heart of SIT's method and innovation toolkit is one crucial idea: that inventive solutions share common patterns. Focusing not on what makes inventive solutions different, but on what, if anything, they might have in common, led to the development of the five Thinking Tools that form SIT's core.[5,6]

The SIT structured invention approach defines five Thinking Tools: Subtraction, Multiplication, Division, Task Unification, and Attribute Dependency.

One of the reasons I include SIT in the Solve stage of this process is that Goldenberg and Mazursky's research identified an asymmetry in two groups of highly innovative products. In the products that eventually became successful, a high percentage could be explained by one of these five SIT patterns, while in the unsuccessful product group a high percentage could not be.[7] Imagine the power investors would have if they bet on companies whose products or services conformed to these five SIT templates. If you are in a large organization, SIT will empower you to judge which new products or services deserve internal resource support. And if you are in a startup, SIT will empower you to invent or perhaps reinvent products or services that have a higher likelihood of success.

An important clarification that Drew Boyd, coauthor of *Inside the Box: A Proven System of Creativity for Breakthrough Results*, shared with me is that this is not a design technique. SIT is a creativity technique whose tools help move us past our fixedness so that we can solve the problem we have identified. SIT is an insight and benefit generator. After you have broken your fixedness, then you can focus more on the design of a new product or service.

 CAUTION: HUMAN ERROR

We suffer from fixedness—a cognitive bias or a mental block against using something (e.g., an object, an idea, a service) in a new way—which often inhibits our ability to see solutions to a problem.

Subtraction

Subtraction, the first tool, involves removing an essential component from an existing product or service and finding beneficial uses for the new arrangement of the existing components. "Instead of trying to improve a product by *adding* components or attributes, you remove them, particularly those that seem desirable or even indispensable." Just like Bob Johnston cautions us to avoid criticisms of feasibility early in the process, here too Drew Boyd cautions us to focus on the benefits of this new product or service, not on how it will work. Remove the legs of a high chair, for example, and eventually you see the benefit of it becoming a more portable baby chair that you can attach to the table.[8] Subtract the bank teller, and you have an ATM; subtract the frames on glasses, and you have contact lenses. Leonardo da Vinci understood this when he observed that "a poet knows he has achieved perfection not when there is nothing left to add, but when there is nothing left to take away."

The reason I start with subtraction is that this is another of those areas where our intuition leads us astray. As Gabrielle Adams, an expert in organizational behavior, and her colleagues at the University of Virginia demonstrated across eight experiments, we tend to default to adding things that tend to make products more complicated, rather than to subtracting them, which often yields simpler and better solutions.[9,10]

As I write this under the COVID-19 quarantine, I am experiencing a form of subtraction. Just before the pandemic, Brown surveyed its faculty and learned that less than 20 percent were willing to consider teaching online. Just a few months later, with no warning, 100 percent were doing so. The pandemic forced us all to subtract the physical infrastructure of Brown's campus, something we had felt was indispensable just weeks before. It left us with no choice but to leverage online platforms like Zoom to teach our courses and to deliver our center's programming.

For some, with little time for preparation, this posed a significant challenge. For others, it freed us of the constraints of a physical location and enabled us to teach in different and in some ways more effective fashions. Online features empowered us to poll our classes, divide into breakout rooms, and invite more remote guests to join us. Like aparigraha, you might think of subtraction as a method of experimenting with the benefits of scarcer resources than you might have thought possible to help yourself overcome your tendency to accumulate.

 CAUTION: HUMAN ERROR

In a creative process, we tend to add things, which often makes products more complicated, rather than subtract things, which often yields simpler and better solutions.[11]

Multiplication

Multiplication, another prevalent innovation pattern that SIT identified, does the opposite of subtraction: to an existing product or service, it copies a component and changes it in a qualitative way. The copied component should be changed in some way that often will not make sense at first. The two keywords for this tool are *more* and *different*. Copy one or more of something that already exists in the product, while changing the components according to some parameter that makes it different. A double-bin trash can that allows users to separate their garbage into disposable and recyclable goods is an example of multiplication. You have copied and changed an existing component—an extra bin—giving it a new beneficial use. Another is Gillette's double-bladed razor. Adding an extra blade to provide one more shaving surface would not suffice, as SIT defines it. But copying the existing blade and setting it at a different angle, which raises whiskers so the other blade can cut them better, does.[12]

Division

This third prevalent innovation pattern cuts and rearranges a product's or service's components to form a new version. As Drew reminded me, humans are natural dividers, so this technique feels natural: desks into drawers, drawers subdivided further by hanging folders. Separating print cartridges from the computer printer and even subdividing them further as print cartridges for black, cyan, yellow, and magenta. Using this division tool forces consideration of different structures, either on the level of the product or service as a whole or on the level of an individual component. Remote controls are an example of "functional division" in that they move channel changing, volume adjustment, and device selection into a more convenient and portable device. Airlines that have empowered passengers to check in, check luggage, and save their boarding passes from home are experiencing a form of division.[13] Dividing a product into its components gives us the freedom to reconstruct it in new ways—it increases our degrees of freedom for working with the situation. The old hi-fi, with its speaker and turntable integrated in one cabinet, gave way to modular speakers, tuners, and CD and tape players that allowed users to customize their sound systems.[14] I love Drew's example of a drone, which illustrates two different division approaches: *location* because the aircraft is separated from the pilot, and *time* because the flight is often preprogrammed at an earlier time and executed much later. When using division, rearrange at first without knowing why you are doing it and ask what would be the benefit.

Task Unification

Giving an existing resource (a component of a product or service or something else in the immediate vicinity) an additional task is a fourth prevalent innovation pattern that the SIT team discerned. Thomas Edison reconstructed his gate to connect it to a nearby water pump so that anytime someone entered or exited they would also be pumping water. We often find this occurring in resource-constrained environments, where people use the Task Unification approach to wring every last bit of use out of things. For example, the Bedouin use camels for a large number of different tasks: transportation, currency, milk, skin for tents, shade, protection from the wind, and burning feces for fuel. More resource-rich societies tend to use specific resources for each task. Face lotions that have the added function of protecting us from sunburn are an example. And we might also consider the dishwashing liquid example above a form of Task Unification when consumers used it to wash fruits and vegetables.

Drew cautions us to avoid thinking of Task Unification as bundling (e.g., a Swiss Army Knife that simply bundles otherwise separate features together) or as repurposing. The new product or service has to become more valuable by doing additional work.

Attribute Dependency

Windshield wipers that change speed based on the pace of rainfall are an example of a product following the fifth common innovation pattern, Attribute Dependency. Rather than focusing on product or service components as the other SIT patterns do, Attribute Dependency involves *properties*—characteristics that can change within a product or component (e.g., color, size, material, function). You can spur innovative thinking by trying to create new relationships for product characteristics where they do not ordinarily exist and to modify or dissolve relationships where they do. As one thing changes, another thing changes. These can be two internal attributes of the product or service, or as in the variable windshield wiper example, an internal attribute and an attribute of the environment. Attribute Dependency does not work if both attributes are environmental (e.g., time and weather) since you cannot control them.

Take a standard pair of eyeglasses. There is no dependent relationship between the color of the lens and external lighting conditions. By creating a dependent relationship between color of the lens (internal attribute) and sunlight (environmental attribute), you come up with a transitional lens that changes color when exposed to sunlight, eliminating the need to buy a separate pair of glasses for sunny days.[15] Happy hour is a service example: the price of drinks (internal attribute) drops as the time of day (environmental attribute) changes. Lots of recent innovations that create smart, adjustable products (e.g., different key fobs that adjust the seat and other car settings) are good examples of Attribute Dependency.

SIT is a little like haiku. Every haiku must consist of three lines, the first of which must have five syllables, the second seven, and the third five. While we might believe that restricting our approach to this template would limit our poetic creativity, those limits in fact produce dramatic results. Here, for example, is what is often regarded as the most famous haiku by Matsuo Basho (1644–1694):

Furuike ya
kawazu tobikomu

mizu no oto
Old pond
A frog jumps in—
The sound of water

Similarly, we might believe that restricting our thinking to these five SIT structured templates would limit our creativity. Instead, following SIT's approach can get your team's creative juices flowing, especially when you have found and validated unmet needs about an existing product or service.

Amnon and his team tend to follow the adage that "function follows form." To help their clients break their fixedness, they start by having them use these five approaches to modify the form of their products to create new functions. As you know, I focus first on finding an unmet need, and I worry about creating solutions that are in search of a problem. The balance in the *See, Solve, Scale* approach is a blend. In cases where your Bottom-Up Research has found and validated unmet needs related to existing products or services, I recommend considering the five SIT templates as tools in your Value Proposition development arsenal.

When Dan Aziz and his Premama team encountered women unhappy with their prenatal vitamin capsules, for example, they used a form of Subtraction to reinvent the vitamin delivery mechanism: they identified the capsule as an "essential component" and imagined the product without it. As a next step, I put them in touch with Manny Stern—the food development expert who worked with them to explore what a "non-capsule" vitamin could be. In addition to creating a format that was easier to swallow, the team formulated various flavors that tasted good and masked some of the challenging ingredients (like zinc). The result was a powdered form of prenatal vitamin that gave pregnant women more value by losing a component that they now no longer viewed as essential.

Dear Kate's Task Unification

Here's another example—Julie Sygiel, a Brown chemical engineering student, had no entrepreneurship exposure before taking my Entrepreneurial Process course back in 2008. Over the semester in the course, Julie and her class venture team found and validated an unmet need that challenges half the population—menstrual leaks and stains—and proposed a special type of underwear to solve that problem.

Because I belong to the other half of the population, I was uncertain about whether Julie and her team were thinking big enough when they proposed solving this problem. "Is this a *big* opportunity?" I remember asking. "Maybe you could go back and find a comparable company that is doing something in the women's undergarment space to demonstrate that these kinds of companies can have impact in a significant way." Undaunted, Julie and her team came back with Spanx, the women's underwear company that had developed revolutionary shaping briefs and leggings, that was already doing $250 million in revenue at the time. After more Bottom-Up Research, involving interactions with women of all ages about their periods and even posting open-ended questions on the inside of campus bathroom stalls, they used a form of Task Unification to develop a line of underwear that would embed the functionality that women find in separate panty liners, pads, and other menstrual protection products. They launched the venture, and here is how the company describes its Dear Kate product on its website:

> Our superior leak resistant and stain fighting Underlux™ technology is built into all Dear Kate undies and activewear.
>
> We bleed. We sweat. And we don't let anything hold us back.
>
> Gone are the days of late night tampon runs and ruining clothes you once loved. Dear Kate products fit perfectly into your cycle and hold up to two tampons' worth, meaning you can wear them as coverage on your lighter days or as backup on your heavy days.

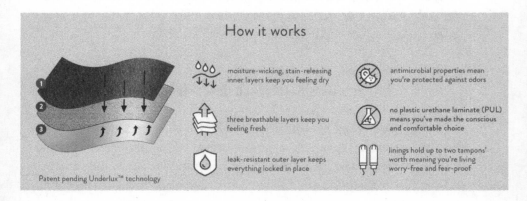

How it works

moisture-wicking, stain-releasing inner layers keep you feeling dry

three breathable layers keep you feeling fresh

leak-resistant outer layer keeps everything locked in place

antimicrobial properties mean you're protected against odors

no plastic urethane laminate (PUL) means you've made the conscious and comfortable choice

linings hold up to two tampons' worth meaning you're living worry-free and fear-proof

Patent pending Underlux™ technology

Open Innovation Engages and Motivates Experts to Solve Challenging Problems

SIT is one of the most effective techniques I know for a team to innovate. But how can you expand your access beyond your team? Open Innovation contests, an approach to engaging and motivating experts from diverse backgrounds to solve challenging problems, are a twenty-first-century Value Proposition tool that you should have in your arsenal. In their *JAMA* article "Use of Crowd Innovation to Develop an Artificial Intelligence–Based Solution for Radiation Therapy Targeting," for example, cancer researchers describe a contest they posted on Topcoder.com—a commercial platform that hosts online algorithm challenges for a community of more than one million programmers. This particular contest solicited solutions to a complex lung cancer–related problem and offered a total of $55,000 in prizes. The top five entries developed AI approaches that were as good as the clinical services offered by oncologists. This meant that these AI algorithms could improve cancer care globally by transferring the skills of expert clinicians to under-resourced healthcare settings."[16]

So what is the explicit connection of Open Innovation to *See, Solve, Scale*? These cancer researchers were able to mobilize far more creative problem-solving resources than the resources they directly controlled: one million programmers on the platform, 564 contestants from sixty-two countries who registered for this particular cancer challenge, thirty-four actual contributors who submitted a solution, and the top five who won the prize money. What's more, these contributors reflected the diversity that I will discuss in detail in chapter 7 as being essential for a successful entrepreneurial team, as many of the Topcoder participants regularly compete on imaging problems from all fields and across all industries. Even beyond diverse, the Topcoder platform "specifically recruited non-domain experts"[17] who, like Luke and Neil in the Casper mattress startup, benefited from their scarce knowledge base, in this case of this particular cancer domain.

You might be wondering what motivates the contributors to participate. Harvard Business School professor Karim Lakhani notes that "the main motivation is financial, but other factors contribute. Some contestants like belonging to a community. Others like recognition via ranking on the platform or beating 'the best of the best.' Most people lose contests, yet people continually compete."[18] Now that platforms like Topcoder make it easy to get started, crowdsourcing solutions through Open Innovation is becoming a popular, efficient, and in our terms entrepreneurial approach to solving problems.

Value Proposition Exercise as a Venture Blueprint

At this stage in the Value Proposition process, we have focused on having the right mindset to overcome lots of human tendencies that inhibit innovative solutions to problems. We have begun to formulate preliminary solutions through Systematic Inventive Thinking and other creative innovation techniques. Right now, to help you reinforce the components of your Value Proposition and to provide structure for communicating them, let me share an exercise that helps my students and workshop participants clarify the essential elements of their Value Propositions and start to communicate those elements. You will notice that it draws on the Value Proposition components shared above.

Write one sentence using the following format and words (starting with "For") that focuses on overt benefits:

[WHO]

- For (target customers quantified)
- who (quantified statement of the need or opportunity)

[WHAT]

- the (product/service name) is a (product/service category-features)

[WHY]

- that (statement of benefits)

Now write a second sentence about real reasons to believe:

- Customers will trust our ability to deliver these benefits because (real reasons to believe)

Write a third sentence about dramatic differences:

- Unlike (the competition), our product (quantified statement of difference)

If you were doing this exercise as part of a semester-long Entrepreneurial Process course, I would give you feedback and you would iterate your work several times. This is one of the few exercises in which I tend to be a bit pedantic and in which I will ask you to follow the precise instructions. If you get sloppy at this stage, the rest of the process suffers, and you will end up having to return to this stage anyway. If you are not clear about whose problem you are solving, you will be inefficient when you try to target and acquire customers. If you are imprecise about what problem you are solving, your marketing messages will not work, and worse, you might become a solution in search of a problem. If you cannot answer why your target consumer will want your product in language they would use, you may be selling a drill-bit feature and not the benefit of a ¼-inch hole. Follow these instructions to the letter. If your first sentence does not start with the word "For," for example, you are on the wrong track.

Second, make your benefits overt, your reasons to believe real, and your differences dramatic.

Note that I ask you to quantify the ways in which your product or service is different from the competition. Listing qualitative reasons tends to be pretty easy. Doing so with numbers requires you to dig deeper to understand the extent of our difference. That quantitative extent is often the source of the drama in a dramatic difference (e.g., this vacuum cleaner sucks up sixteen times more dirt from your carpet than the competition's). When it comes time to communicate the difference in an investor pitch or marketing message, doing so with numbers is more persuasive.

Example Value Proposition

Here is an example of a strong (even if not perfect) Value Proposition from a Brown class venture project:

For restaurants that want to increase profits and to reduce food waste, "Achilles" is a predictive analytics service that tells restaurant owners when to purchase certain foods to reduce purchase costs and inventory holding costs. We will be able to deliver these benefits because our team's extensive software engineering experience will allow us to build an intuitive platform that is convenient to use. Furthermore, our team has experience in the food services industry, which will allow us to connect with customers. Unlike relying on the restaurant owner's intuition or prior connections, our product aggregates and processes food price data to give restaurant owners a 20 percent cost advantage versus the competition.

Here is the Value Proposition Exercise I completed for this book:

For the millions of aspiring entrepreneurs who do not adhere to narrow business and tech stereotypes, See, Solve, Scale *empowers a large and diverse set of problem solvers. Readers who have never considered themselves entrepreneurs will trust Danny Warshay's ability to teach them this process because for the past sixteen years he has taught over three thousand mostly liberal arts students at Brown University, MBA students at Yale and Tel Aviv University, and professionals throughout the world. Danny's own entrepreneurial successes began when he and a team of fellow Brown undergraduates sold their software startup to Apple. But instead of random and often irrelevant anecdotes that other successful entrepreneurs teach and publish,* See, Solve, Scale *weaves together a wealth of academic research with case studies from Harvard Business School and the ventures of many of Danny's students. Unlike the other books that tell us that entrepreneurs are cut only from a narrow cloth, are creative geniuses from birth, and conform to a certain personality type,* See, Solve, Scale *empowers millions of aspiring problem solvers who may not even know they are entrepreneurs with a structured process that anyone can learn, master, and apply.*

This Value Proposition Exercise is itself something that requires iteration. It is a litmus test for whether you have solid Value Proposition elements, and if not, it will reveal those weaknesses. That is okay as long as you now circle back to reinforce where needed. You might need to do more Bottom-Up Research, for example, to understand the problem you are solving more clearly or to clarify more precisely who is experiencing that problem. You might want to look around for solutions in other geographies that you can repurpose in yours. You might want to look beyond your own team to engage others through Open Innovation. You may want to think again through the five SIT patterns to achieve a dramatically different solution. If you cannot quantify the difference, circle back and try to do so.

Think of the results of this exercise as a blueprint for your venture. If you were building a house, it would be so much more efficient to make revisions on the blueprint than to do so once you had begun building (and way worse if you had already finished building).

A Structured Alternative to Brainstorming

One of the challenges early-stage venture teams face during the Value Proposition development process is how to manage group dynamics to ensure that all of the members of the process are heard. Nominal Group Technique (NGT), originally developed by André Delbecq and Andrew H. Van de Ven, is a structured alternative to brainstorming that promotes contributions from everyone who is participating, including introverts, and helps groups arrive at consensus.[19] A simple Google search will reveal thousands of descriptions and resources for doing NGT, so I will not replicate those in too much detail. For easy reference, here is a list of the basics compiled in the *Journal of Extension*.[20]

1. Divide the people present into small groups . . . , preferably seated around a table.
2. State an open-ended question.
3. Have each person spend several minutes in silence individually brainstorming all the possible ideas and jot these ideas down. Remember Adam Grant's caution in chapter 4 that you may need as many as two hundred ideas to achieve a novel breakthrough.
4. Have each of the small groups collect the ideas by sharing them (one response per person each time), while all are recorded in key terms, on a flip chart. No criticism is allowed, but clarification in response to questions is encouraged.
5. Have each person evaluate the ideas and individually and anonymously vote for the best ones (for example, the best idea gets 5 Points, next best 4 Points, etc.).

6. Share votes within the group and tabulate. A group report is pre-pared, showing the ideas receiving the most points, to share with the larger group.
7. Allow time for brief group presentations on their solutions.

Don't Pour the Concrete Too Early

At this early solution stage, after we have crafted three sentences in the Value Proposition exercise, we should remember that the second word in "Value Proposition" suggests we are *proposing* something. We do not yet know how it is going to be received. Rather than immediately pouring a sidewalk in concrete, for example, we should confirm our understanding on a small scale regarding where our proposed customers walk and create bare patches on the lawn. Before we apply our scarce resources to launch-ing our venture, let's confirm that we are on the right track.

In recent years, an increasing number of entrepreneurs have turned to an approach that Eric Ries called Lean Startup, and that builds on the smart teachings of a veritable entrepreneurship guru named Steve Blank. Steve and Eric focus on developing what they call a minimally viable prod-uct (MVP) very early in the process as the basis for soliciting qualified feedback from early customers.

When Steve spoke at our center, I found that our approaches to entre-preneurship had a lot in common. I like Steve and Eric's use of MVP. It captures the imperfect and even crude version of our proposed solution that at this Value Proposition stage we are trying to develop. Once we have used Bottom-Up Research to find and validate an unmet need and have developed a clear and persuasive Value Proposition, we should test our assumptions with potential customers. As mentioned above, many overly confident entrepreneurs roll their eyes when we suggest first testing our assumptions. "Why delay? I know I've nailed it, and I'm eager to attract additional resources to scale up."

Investors will want to see proof that your assumptions are accurate, and you should, too. While Bottom-Up Research will go a long way to-ward convincing them that you have clarified the problem, you will need to provide similar evidence that you have developed an effective solution. Investors and anyone else whose resources you are looking to attract—

cofounders, advisers, employees, others—will embrace your plan to expand if you can demonstrate that as your rocket is built and is leaving the launching pad, all it needs to get into orbit is more fuel. If it is still unproven that you should be building a rocket in the first place or that it will get off the launching pad, you would be well served to prove it to everyone—especially to yourself—that you have developed an effective Value Proposition.

One way my approach differs a bit from Lean Startup is in how much Bottom-Up Research you should do before starting to build or sell anything. In my view, it is wise to start by finding and validating the problem to solve before building the product, while Lean Startup puts more emphasis on customer interactions once you have developed an initial product. The Lean phrase "customer development" has some limitations because it sounds like something the sales department should be doing, even though this early stage of the process is not about generating sales at any large scale. It is about making sure we are on the right track and putting us on it if and to the extent we are not. Although I cautioned against asking for feedback during Bottom-Up Research, it is an essential part of this iterative Value Proposition stage. I just sometimes worry that those familiar with Lean Startup may fall into the bad habit of what I described earlier as "technology push" though I know that that is what Steve and Eric want to help you avoid.

The MVP approach is also another reminder that developing strong Value Propositions requires an iterative approach. *Minimally* Viable underscores that realistic insight; *Maximally* Viable would not. Creating the perfect product or service right out of the gate would require a crystal ball or at least a large dose of luck. Because that never happens, don't even try. Instead, create a first attempt knowing it is flawed, and then learn and iterate.

Pivot: Don't Fall in Love, Fall in Like!

Iterative means that this process is not linear; it often takes steps backward before it moves you forward. At each iteration, you have three choices: if your minimally viable product validates your hypotheses, to *persevere* by proceeding in the same direction; if your MVP rejects your hypotheses, to *perish* by deciding to throw in the towel and abandoning; or to *pivot*, which is a term that Steve, Eric, and the Lean Startup movement have popularized to mean use what you have learned in the prior iterations to change some elements while retaining others.[21]

Rhode Island School of Design (RISD) student Alicia Lew and Brown math concentrator Grant Gurtin teamed up in my class to start Fanium, which became the first all-mobile fantasy football game. Eventually sold to CBS Sports, it got there only after a number of pivots. Grant shared what that progression looked like:

1. Game in which users would compete against their Twitter followers to see how well they could predict the winners of sporting events.
2. App that leveraged Twitter to find relevant sports tweets from experts (this technology was acquired by CBS Sports and is still used in the CBS Sports app). Reason for pivot: the app we created as a side feature was more compelling than the game itself. Though we struggled to build consumer traction for the product, we were able to develop a business to business relationship with CBS Sports that led to their acquiring us.
3. App that leveraged Twitter to find information relevant for fantasy sports players. Reason for pivot: We tested using our technology for fantasy sports as part of a development contest, and the product gained more traction (users and time on-site) than our previous product so we altered our area of focus.
4. An all-mobile fantasy football game. Reason for pivot: We decided being a news aggregator would not be a large enough business so we decided to leverage our technology to create the best fantasy sports experience on the market.

Using a golf analogy to emphasize iterating and pivoting, a friend and periodic collaborator, Dan Wyner, advises that rather than spending a long time lining up the perfect "one-putt" that no one would ever sink anyway, using a more rapid "three-putt" approach is more likely to put you further ahead in the process. Dan tends to apply this same "fail fast" iteration approach in other places, too. When Dan was in his forties, he enrolled in Brown's master's program in computer science. Even as one of the smartest people I know, Dan was a little curious how he would perform among his classmates who were less than half his age. The last time Dan had taken a computer science course, he practically had used punch cards.

In the final project for his computer robotics course, Dan's class was challenged to program robots that would play soccer against each other. The other students and even the teaching assistants tended to write complex programs designed to pinpoint the location of their robots on the "field," plan the best path to the ball, and then prepare to line up the perfect shot. Unfortunately all of that processing and planning required significant computing resources and time, and during that time, the status of the field would change, making most of that planning moot. Dan reasoned that the high-speed and instant reaction of a robot would allow it to kick the ball many times in roughly the right direction, in the time that his competition was still planning paths to approach and kick the ball perfectly. The results were a clear demonstration of fast, agile, iterative decision-making winning out against the slower, resource-intensive computational strategies, as Dan's robot decisively outscored all of the more elaborately programmed competitors.

I suppose we could say that Dan's robot embraced aparigraha. It did not cling to its last shot or obsess about lining up its next one. It remained unattached to the conventional rules that its competition clung to. Instead of becoming burdened by the abundant resources of hundreds of lines of code, it benefited from the scarce resources of just a few. By taking and missing shot after shot in the time it took its competition to take even one shot, it iterated, it failed fast, and it failed cheap.

As R&R's Bob Reiss likes to remind my students, falling in *love* is an emotional experience that causes many people to make ill-advised and out-of-character long-term decisions. This is also true in entrepreneurship, Bob emphasizes, which causes him to tell young enthusiastic entrepreneurs when discussing new ideas and early-stage ventures, "Don't Fall in Love, Fall in Like!"

Bandura Games as an Example of Like Before Love

I met Justin Hefter, CEO and cofounder of Bandura Games, in a series of workshops I led for entrepreneurs looking to solve problems that plagued various communities throughout the Middle East. Justin, along with his Israeli cofounder, Etay, and his Palestinian cofounder, Ammoun, describes Bandura as a "mobile game company that uses games as a medium for creating connections and empathy for people of different backgrounds from around the world." From the start, Justin, Etay, and Ammoun's primary focus has been to use video games as a platform for Palestinian and Israeli children to learn to cooperate with each other.

How Bandura evolved is an excellent example of "falling in like before falling in love." Justin admits that before the *See, Solve, Scale* workshops, he had approached entrepreneurship by making many of the classic mistakes. Biased by his consulting background, he relied on Top-Down Research of industry trends. He rushed past finding and validating explicit unmet needs. And because of his initial biases, Bandura was a solution in search of a problem. Rather than diverging first to consider lots of solutions, he converged to perfect his first solution—digital video games—and funneled his own resources and those from early investors into doing so.

Justin recalls a conversation in which I challenged him to imagine the cheapest, minimally viable way to prove (or disprove) his Value Proposition. At the time, this was a video game in which Palestinian and Israeli children would cooperate with each other to win the game together, rather than competing against each other. Doing so in a scaled-up digital version was expensive, so instead—applying *See, Solve, Scale*—his team designed a crude board game version of a well-known video game called *Temple Run*. The analog equivalent of video points was a supply of 1,000 pennies. They created two versions: one competitive, in which the players competed against each other, and one cooperative, in which players cooperated with each other. Justin and his Palestinian partner, Ammoun, tested these minimally viable versions with a few hundred students in two Palestinian schools in East Jerusalem and one in Ramallah, Palestine. Justin and his Israeli partner, Etay, tested these MVPs in several after-school programs in Israel.

"We were nervous even about the basic premise of the game, that a cooperative theme would appeal to children," Justin reminded me. "Using this Value Proposition step of the Entrepreneurial Process to help us pilot, iterate, and validate before moving on to creating our Sustainability Model was a huge breakthrough for Bandura. We had our doubts about how these children would react to such a crude analog version of what we anticipated creating. But the kids did not know what we were imagining for the future. All of them were excited about playing an American game in any condition. Eighty percent of them preferred the cooperative version. And they were very excited about the idea of playing an eventual version with other kids around the world."

Justin recalls that much of this insight they gathered was unsolicited. One Palestinian student, for example, unprompted said, "I felt much closer to my partner in the cooperative version, and it would be very cool if there were a way to play with other kids all over the world." The Bandura team also learned the bureaucratic challenges of selling into and working in schools and decided instead to market its games through a wider range of global distribution channels. Even while iterating to scale up the digital version, Justin, Ammoun, and Etay ran a crowdfunding campaign on Indiegogo and offered the board game version.

This discipline that Justin's Bandura team used to strip away the details of a "finished product" and to use a crude version instead will help you focus on the core innovation that more developed details can obscure.

Parenting Magazine and the "Walking Around Money" Catalyst

After our first snowstorm of the season one year, I needed to clear our driveway and sidewalks. I pulled our snowblower out of the garage, I set the choke, and I primed the gas line. But instead of pressing the primer the suggested three times, I figured since it was the first start of the season, more fuel would be better, and I primed it a bunch more. When I pulled the starter, nothing happened. I had flooded the engine with too much fuel. Before you get to the third step in *See, Solve, Scale*, where you will raise money and other significant resources to scale your solution over the long term, be careful not to "flood your engine." To avoid overwhelming your minimally viable product, at this Value Proposition stage, inject a minimal amount of financial and other resources.

To scale her startup, *Parenting Magazine*, Robin Wolander had projected that she would need to raise $5 million and started with a first-round target of $175,000. Struggling through seventy investor meetings, she managed to raise only $125,000. After all of that, her reward was that she had to cut her salary and her own personal equity stake. That alone holds many eye-opening lessons for any aspiring entrepreneur, including that it ain't easy. Entrepreneurship is often much more difficult than the romantic version many would have us believe, and it is good for you to know that up front. It is rewarding to solve problems that have baffled others to date, and because no one has solved them so far, doing so requires different approaches and often greater effort.

Doing so also requires persistence, which tests our confidence in our venture and even in ourselves. Robin knew from both Bottom-Up and Top-Down Research that she had found and validated an unmet need: young, well-educated, wealthy parents needed access to parenting information that other resources were not providing. Through Bottom-Up discussions with new parents and her observations at local newsstands, she concluded that the leading magazine, *Parents*, was unsophisticated.[22] That left a "white space" gap in a large and growing market that Robin, an experienced media executive, could fill. Yet, even with data to validate the opportunity and a minimally viable solution, investors were not beating a path to her door.

Imagine Robin's frustration when she was on investor meeting sixty-eight out of seventy. What if at mile 24 of 26 of a marathon, I asked you whether you had the energy to complete the race? My bet is that no matter how tired you were, you could muster the effort required to finish those two remaining miles. Now imagine at mile 24 I didn't tell you how many more miles you had to run to finish: 2? 20? 200? Forever? How would you feel then? "Exhausted. Unmotivated. Anxious," is what students say. And who can blame them? Not knowing how long the race is and how much more you have to run can make it impossible to motivate yourself to keep going. Yet Robin persisted. And that is a quality successful entrepreneurs demonstrate throughout this process.

Well before getting anywhere near meeting seventy and hitting the $125,000 mark, and at one of her very first investor meetings, Robin met with someone named Arthur Dubow, who gave Robin $5,000 of what he called "walking around money." It is not clear what strings it had attached to it or what Arthur meant by "walking around," and what the heck was the purpose of Arthur giving Robin $5,000 when she needed a thousand times that—$5 million? What purpose could $5,000 serve? "Well," you might suggest, "it could put some food on Robin's table and some gas in her car's tank. It could enable her to fly to meet other potential investors or to do some more Bottom-Up Research." In other words, there might very well be some practical value to that first $5,000. If you remember what we pointed out earlier about the value that an investor can provide beyond the cash they are providing, you might point out that Arthur, who had previous experience with the kind of company that Robin is launching, can add value to Robin's, too.

You might also point out that even that small amount of funding can give Robin confidence that someone else believed in her and in her venture. Going from no one believing in you to someone believing can make all the difference. When you are at meeting number twenty-six, you can say even to yourself, Arthur had confidence in me, so I should have more confidence in myself and in my Value Proposition. If that small investment can raise our own confidence level, then what might it signal to other prospective investors? That effect is binary. What happens now when a prospective investor asks whether anyone else has invested? Before Arthur's "walking around money," we had to answer, "No one." Now, we can say that someone else has broken the ice, has sized me up, has assessed my venture's potential, and has written a check.

If you studied biology or chemistry, you may remember that a catalyst is a substance that increases the rate of a chemical reaction or in some cases enables a reaction to occur in the first place. A catalyst is a tiny amount of that substance, and that tiny amount has an enormous, disproportionate impact. You might think of Arthur Dubow's "walking around money" as a catalyst. Without it, it is possible that Robin might not have had enough fuel in her car to drive around and might have had to find a job, might not have been able to look other investors in the eye when they asked who else had invested, might not have been able to have enough confidence in herself if she had remained her only cheerleader. Arthur's $5,000 did much more than enable Robin to "walk around." Just like a catalyst has enormous effect on a chemical reaction, Arthur's small amount of capital had disproportionate impact and catalyzed the rest of Robin's venture.

Student teams from my class and our center have experienced this dynamic when they have entered and won business plan competitions. They will tell you that if they had not won, say, $25,000 in the Rhode Island Business Competition, they very well might not have had the confidence and energy to pursue their ventures.

Eric Hjerpe, a successful venture capitalist, says that he is looking for a glimmer of greatness. At the same time, he admits that first he looks for a toehold. The "bare patches in the lawn," an MVP, walking around money, a catalyst—these are all evidence of the type of small-scale Value Proposition toehold that Eric is looking for.

———

If you retain nothing else from chapters 4 and 5, I hope you will remember that the *Solve* step is essential because it does not expect that your first attempts will achieve an ideal solution. On the contrary, *See, Solve, Scale* assumes that even if you embrace all of the many guidelines and recommendations I've described throughout these last two chapters, you would be lucky if your first attempts perfected an ideal solution. Every successful entrepreneur I know, including Justin at Bandura and Julie at DearKate from this chapter and all the others I share with you elsewhere, and definitely me in all of my startups and even in writing this book—all of us know that solving problems requires an iterative approach.

Ignoring this inherent iterative feature of *See, Solve, Scale* and leaping from finding a need directly to scaling an initial solution dooms many first-time entrepreneurs. Corporate Immune Systems promote this kind of premature scaling and doom entrepreneurship in large established organizations, too. High revenue hurdles, for example, rush an initial proposed solution into scaling mode. It's like printing thousands of copies of a book's first draft.

Rushing to scale an unvalidated initial proposed solution reminds me of the joke in which someone notices they are lost, and the driver comments, "Yeah, but we're making good time." Before you move to the next step **Scale: Create A Sustainability Model**, be sure you have iterated enough to develop a Value Proposition that is worthy of the investment you will need to make to achieve long-term scalability. To avoid "making good time" and ending up in the wrong destination, be sure you have pointed the car in the right direction. And if you have taken a successful test-drive down the street, it's time to take the car on the highway. Let's now move on to this next step in *See, Solve, Scale*.

CHAPTER 6

STEP 3
SCALE: CREATE A SUSTAINABILITY MODEL

You have defined your problem in step 1, and have iterated to begin to solve it in step 2. It's now time to start thinking big. The third step, **Scale: Create a Sustainability Model**, empowers you to have big and long-term impact toward solving the problem you have identified in the first step. In this chapter, you will learn the definition of a Sustainability Model and see how it is more valuable to you than its narrower cousin, the business model. You will see why a preliminary step of thinking big is critical, and you will use a powerful exercise—the Landscape Metaphor—to help you do so. You will add one more essential question of *How* to the Value Proposition questions What, Who, and Why; and this section will arm you with tools to help you answer that fourth question. You will learn why iterating in this more public-facing part of *See, Solve, Scale* feels more like failure than creativity and also learn to embrace that failure as a means to eventual success. Finally, no matter what kind of entity you form (for-profit, nonprofit, government agency, educational institution, or any others), you will demystify and master fundamental approaches to raising financial resources.

Sustainable Means Having Long-Term Impact at Scale

If a solution isn't enduring, it's not really a solution.
—Maggie Walker, the first African American woman
to charter a US bank and serve as its president

If your entrepreneurial venture has made it this far, you have already accomplished a great deal. You used Bottom-Up Research to find and validate an unmet need. You developed and iterated a Value Proposition, and you may even have released an MVP. What's next? How do you now move the needle from perhaps a few pilot users, to 1,000 to 1,000,000 and more? As important, how do you maintain that growth for years or even decades?

Those two qualities—scale and long-term impact—are what we are now looking to achieve. The word "sustainable" can imply lots of different things in other contexts—environmentally sustainable, for example. In our case, sustainability relates back to the two qualities of unmet needs we found and validated in the first place: *strong* and *enduring*. Scale addresses the strength of the need, and doing so over a long period of time addresses its enduring nature. If entrepreneurship is a structured process for solving problems, really solving the problem means doing so on a large scale over the long term.

You've heard the phrase "business model." One reason I use "sustainable" instead of "business" is that a business model does not always create long-term viability or long-term impact at scale. In my approach, small business is not an expression of entrepreneurship unless it is a precursor to a larger version through which it can have scalable and long-term impact.

Another reason I use "sustainable" instead of business model is that you may be envisioning or are already running something noncommercial (e.g., a nonprofit, a government agency, an educational or research institution). *See, Solve, Scale* applies to all of these types of entities, and the word "sustainable" is designed to include and empower all of them. There is nothing wrong with business, and in fact below I will share some research about the benefits of for-profit models. But remember, entrepreneurship is not just for business anymore.

Think Big

We're not thinking big enough.
            —Freddie Mercury, Queen, *Bohemian Rhapsody* movie

My Entrepreneurial Finance professor at Harvard Business School, Jeff Timmons, wrote in his classic *New Venture Creation* that "one of the biggest mistakes aspiring entrepreneurs make is strategic. They think too small . . . The chances of success are lower in . . . small, job-substitute businesses. And even if they do survive, they are less financially rewarding." I realize that may sound counterintuitive because often it appears that the way to mitigate the inevitable risk of starting a venture is to keep it small, tidy, and easy to get your arms around, and to control all of its variables. As Jeff reminded us, however, and as he demonstrates in the failure rates he cites of smaller ventures versus larger ones,

> Smaller means higher failure odds . . . Who are the survivors? The odds for survival and a higher level of success change dramatically if the venture reaches a critical mass of at least 10 to 20 people with $2 million to $3 million in revenues and is currently pursuing opportunities with growth potential. . . . One year survival rates for new firms increase steadily as the firm size increases. The rates jump from approximately 54 percent for firms having up to 24 employees to approximately 73 percent for firms with between 100 and 249 employees.[1]

If you think about it, that kind of threshold makes sense. Larger ventures face different risks and challenges, but think of all of the early-stage risks and challenges that they have overcome and put behind them. Actuarial-based life expectancy predictions work this way too: to a point, the older you are, the even older you are then predicted to get.

This can be a difficult concept to digest. During my first year teaching the Entrepreneurial Process at Brown, even after sharing Jeff Timmons's data about thinking big, I found that many of the ventures my student teams proposed were the size of a café. To many students, that was thinking big, and who could blame them? A café doing a few hundred thousand dollars in annual revenue sounds big to most of us, especially when we're in college. To help them overcome this "think small" mindset, I had to force them to think much bigger—in all the years since, I require all of the class ventures to credibly project at least $100 million in revenue in year five. As arbitrary as that is, it helps the students to think way beyond their risk-influenced comfort zone and the limitations of their own personal experience.

When Luke Sherwin and Neil Parikh came back to class to share their Casper mattress experience, Luke mentioned almost in passing that the company had reached over $100 million in sales within its first eighteen months of operations. As soon as he said that, I looked around the room, and I saw light bulbs going on. It took one of their peers, a recent graduate of that same course, saying it for them to believe it.

⚠ CAUTION: HUMAN ERROR

Many entrepreneurs have a hard time thinking big as they believe that the way to mitigate the inevitable risk of starting a venture is to keep it small, tidy, and easy to get your arms around. This tendency gets in the way of scaling over the long term.

Long-Term Impact at Scale

The way I describe the purpose of this third step in *See, Solve, Scale*— Create a Sustainability Model—is "to have long-term impact at scale." By that I indicate something a little different from Jeff Timmons's "think big" concept in *New Venture Creation*. While he offers a practical reason for thinking big—survival—I emphasize impact. If you are going to put in all of the effort required to launch your venture, why not do it in a way that can affect the lives of more than a few people, in a way that can improve the way many people live?

This emphasis also reinforces the liberal arts, problem-solving approach to entrepreneurship. Jeff Timmons's size emphasis is a good raw measure of survival and the potential returns to us and perhaps to our investors. Impact is a way of measuring how our venture affects others, in particular those whose problems we are looking to solve. Looking inward to our own motivations is not enough to ensure entrepreneurial success. Remember Simon Sinek's insight that successful leaders "do something very very special. They inspire us" by focusing on the *why*, which is about impact. This is similar to the distinction I drew earlier between passion and purpose.

Around the time we were launching our new entrepreneurship center at Brown, our star assistant director, Liz Malone, walked into the School of Public Health, where she had worked for several years, to meet with her former colleague and assistant dean of the school, Don Operario. The way Liz tells it, Don was polite to his former colleague, but skeptical about what entrepreneurship had to do with his public health research. Undaunted, Liz asked Don to update her on what he was up to. Don said that he had a team of researchers in China developing an app to help connect Chinese AIDS patients to Chinese medical resources. Liz perked up and said, "Don, you're an entrepreneur!" "I am?" Don replied, a little confused. When Liz explained my definition of entrepreneurship as a structured process for solving problems and the three steps in our process, Don got it.

Like many people, Don had maintained the misconception that entrepreneurship was only about starting businesses, but Liz helped him to see that not only did entrepreneurship have lots to do with what he and his public health colleagues were already looking to achieve, collaborating with our center to learn more and to develop insights and entrepreneurship skills could improve the impact they were looking to have. In Don's words, "If we see entrepreneurship through a lens of problem identification, product development, product assessment, and product use by the audience or the user community that needs it, we can see a methodology that harmonizes with the mission of public health."

As he thought further, Don realized that they were pretty good at the first step of finding and validating unmet needs (defining the problem) and even at the second step of developing a Value Proposition (iterating to solve the problem on a small scale). Where he admitted they needed some help was at this third stage of creating a Sustainability Model (having long-term impact at scale). "We want to identify what will spread like wildfire throughout a community or throughout a broader population," Don said. By the end of Liz's meeting with Don, they had planned out a series of workshops called *Solving the World's Public Health Problems Through Entrepreneurship*, which we have been leading together ever since.

I like to call Don a "zealot of the converted" as, everywhere he goes, he evangelizes about how entrepreneurship is the key to solving the world's health problems. How credible it is when Don—a converted skeptic from a different field—says so! And we see again that this structured process for problem-solving is more inclusive than other approaches to entrepreneurship. No matter what field you are in, no matter what occupation you have, no matter what problem you are looking to solve, arming yourself with this *See, Solve, Scale* process will enable you to solve it on a large scale over the long term.

The Pussyhat Project—Why Sustainability Requires More than Scalability

I describe this third step of *See, Solve, Scale* as a Sustainability Model because it empowers all entrepreneurs—not only those thinking about creating a business—to use a range of models to have impact at a big scale. Jayna Zweiman's Pussyhat Project is a fabulous example of developing a creative Sustainability Model intending to do just that. Not allowing her head injury, a short time frame, and limited funding to deter her, and instead leveraging her physical condition and other barriers (benefits of scarce resources), Jayna set two objectives: to create a large visual impact (inspired by the 1987 AIDS Quilt) and to create a scalable distribution model to enable many others to participate in the Women's March despite their barriers to access.[2] A third objective that emerged as Pussyhat started to scale was to leverage its mass involvement to lay the groundwork for future political participation. From her architecture background, Jayna knew that she could make something powerful out of basic components; she also embedded viral elements in her model to help it scale.

First, in order to foster a virtual community, whoever knitted a hat was encouraged to enclose a note to connect with the marcher wearing it. This also allowed those knitters who could not attend the march to express themselves. As Jayna puts it, "it's not just the people who showed up to

DEAR WEARER OF THIS HAT,
THIS HAT IS MADE BY: _____
                      (NAME)
_____   _____
(CITY)   (STATE)
A WOMENS ISSUE I CARE ABOUT IS:
_____
_____
_____
_____

IF YOU WANT TO GIVE YOUR HAT
WEARER AN OPPORTUNITY TO
RESPOND, PLEASE PUT YOUR
CONTACT INFO HERE: _____
_____
_____

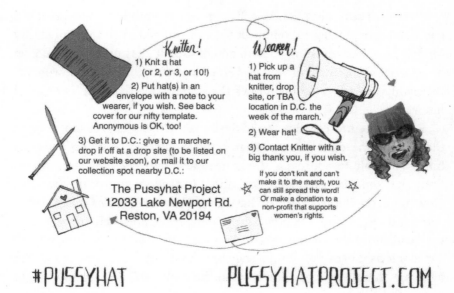

Knitter!

1) Knit a hat (or 2, or 3, or 10!)

2) Put hat(s) in an envelope with a note to your wearer, if you wish. See back cover for our nifty template. Anonymous is OK, too!

3) Get it to D.C.: give to a marcher, drop if off at a drop site (to be listed on our website soon), or mail it to our collection spot nearby D.C.:

The Pussyhat Project
12033 Lake Newport Rd.
Reston, VA 20194

Wearer!

1) Pick up a hat from knitter, drop site, or TBA location in D.C. the week of the march.

2) Wear hat!

3) Contact Knitter with a big thank you, if you wish.

If you don't knit and can't make it to the march, you can still spread the word! Or make a donation to a non-profit that supports women's rights.

#PUSSYHAT   PUSSYHATPROJECT.COM

the march; it's all the other millions of people behind the scenes who made a hat, who took someone somewhere, or who took care of kids while someone else went and marched."

Second, Jayna partnered with 175 yarn stores across the country, making it easy for people to participate. From conception to the march itself, where over a million participants wore Jayna's Pussyhats, was fifty-nine days. Here is a photo that illustrates this impact at scale.

Photo credit: Brian Allen/Voice of America

The quick scale that the Pussyhat Project achieved is impressive. But has it had enough long-term impact to be considered a valid Sustainability Model? Jayna herself thinks that in and of itself it has not. Still, as an icon of a particular moment of women's empowerment, Pussyhat is a wonderful example of thinking big and of the initial scale that was its original intent.

Pussyhat reinforces that a valid Sustainability Model needs to be more than viral, it needs to do more than achieve quick scale. It needs to have impact at scale to address a *strong* need and over the long term to address that *enduring* need we talked about in the first step of this process. How might the Pussyhat Project have long-term sustainable impact? What could it do to continue to grow? Emma Butler of Intimately suggests that we recall and embrace Bob Reiss's warning, "Don't fall in love, fall in like." "As iconic as it became," Emma suggests, "this might mean pivoting after a certain initial scale, and ideating on the pink hat." Perhaps that might mean using the tools I am sharing with you in this chapter to expand beyond Jayna's impressive initial Value Proposition to envision even the evolution of the problem, and a longer-term solution. How might the problem—challenges to women's rights—change over the next decade or two? Jayna approached the problem with an initial solution, but longer term, what else might she do to leverage the hundreds of Pussyhat knitting groups and the broader movement she has developed to channel their political energies?

Jayna's talent as an entrepreneur is in launching a series of campaigns that use crafting as a political and artistic collective statement to effect change. She has translated the lessons of Pussyhat into Welcome Blanket, for example. It has mobilized her crafting community to raise awareness about immigration issues by making Welcome Blankets for new refugees coming to the United States. And during the COVID-19 pandemic, Masks for Humanity provided a way for people to help make handmade masks for vulnerable groups and to raise awareness about the political and societal impact of the pandemic. Jayna's broader Sustainability Model is in her words a "movement of craftivists who are always looking for new projects, and who get tired of making the same object over and over. So the novelty of the Pussyhat might not have sustainability, but the design approach of the Project does."

Landscape Exercise: A Mental Stretch

Que la terre est petite à qui la voit des cieux!
(How small is the earth to him who looks from heaven)
                    —Jacques Delille, eighteenth-century French poet[3]

Seeing the Earth from a distance has changed my perception.
                    —Apollo 11 astronaut Michael Collins[4]

"Metaphorical ontology" is the use of figures of speech to go beyond science, history, and poetry to indicate the deepest, divine, heavenly reality. Because the vastness and richness of reality cannot be expressed by the overt sense of a statement alone, metaphorical ontology is necessary.[5]
                    —Jeffrey Burton Russell, American historian

As I have learned from my students and workshop participants, it is challenging to think big and envision long-term impact. The Landscape Exercise will help you overcome this resistance. Its primary purpose is to help you shift your mindset so that you can be more receptive to growing your Value Proposition into a large-scale solution with impact far into the future. You might think of this exercise as a mental stretch. This stretch will help you move beyond the near-term mental limitations we all have and will help you to think bigger and to consider the long term.

The Landscape Exercise consists of three parts:

1. Draw a picture of a *metaphorical* road and the landscape around it to depict the problem you are looking to solve roughly twenty to thirty years into the future.
2. Draw another picture of your Value Proposition in the form of a *metaphorical* vehicle that can navigate the road you have used to depict your problem.
3. Reexamine your Value Proposition at that distant point in the future and then envision how you can reinvent it backward through time until you reach today.

In the Landscape Exercise's first step, you envision the problem you are looking to solve as it evolves many years into the future. This forces you to envision what might happen if you do not solve this problem: how it could fester, grow, and become even stronger and more enduring. If you are feeling any hesitancy or even judgment from others about the significance of the problem you are looking to solve, this step alone can help you review, feel and reassess its significance. It is important that you envision the problem at least twenty to thirty years in the future, depending on the type of problem you are tackling. Envision far enough into the future that you are forced to rely less on current facts on the ground and more on your imagination, so far that your biases about what you know to be true today won't limit what you might imagine. Remember that what you are doing here is a mental stretch, so don't worry about how factual or linear or realistic any of this is or even feels.

To give you a sense for the limited level of "artistry" we are looking for, this is the landscape drawing of an entrepreneurship team from Instrumentation Technologies—a Slovenian hardware company with whom I have been working on its *See, Solve, Scale* process. The participants in this Landscape Exercise were supersmart, left-brain-dominant physicists who had to get over their artistic inhibitions to complete this first step. Once they did, even this initial step got them to start thinking beyond their near-term executional challenges, to begin to envision contextual issues

that they had not considered before, and to imagine how the unmet needs they had found and validated might evolve over time. Truth is, I have no clue what the metaphors in their drawing mean, and they are not going to win any art contests. That is not the point, though. The purpose of this first step of the exercise is to start to envision how the problem they are looking to solve could evolve and grow over time.

This first step focuses on context—everything that happens around your venture that it has to contend with, but which you cannot control. The political environment, the economy, regulations, interest rates, big tech shifts like AI, watershed events like 9/11 or the 2008 financial crisis, the COVID-19 pandemic—all of these are critical contextual issues that we all should be considering as we look to think big and for the long term and create a Sustainability Model to have significant impact. This first part of this exercise alone is helpful to make sure we consider these contextual influences out into the distant future. Most of all, this first step helps us to review the strength and endurance of the problem we are looking to solve over the long term.

Why all of this emphasis on the distant future? For one thing, if we are looking to solve strong and enduring problems, our solutions need to endure. Second, this focus on the distant future draws on the ground-breaking research of UCLA professor Hal Hershfield. In his work, Hershfield discovered that the key to influencing young adults to save more for retirement was to get them to envision their future selves at the time they would need their retirement savings. In Hershfield's words, "when people are confronted with their 'future selves' they experience an emotional sense of connection that can influence long-term financial and ethical decision-making. . . . Anything we can do that will increase how concrete and salient our future self is can help us make better decisions."[6] When he showed college students digitally altered images of their faces of how they would look thirty years into the future, on average they committed to save 30 percent more than the students who were shown pictures of their current selves. Similarly, this first step of the Landscape Exercise moves us beyond our current experience to envision what the problem we are working to solve could become. We understand the context around it, and we make an emotional connection to it.

In the second step of this exercise, focus on your Value Proposition. Envision a metaphorical car (or spaceship, or other vehicle) that can navigate the future road and landscape you have depicted. The point here, remember, is a mental stretch, to expand your thinking beyond where you had gotten in the Value Proposition step. Envision how parts of the vehicle can represent various parts of your Value Proposition, and anticipate the contextual issues you have identified in your future. Jayna and her Pussyhat team, for example, might depict and label the steering wheel as the feature that helps direct a large-scale women's empowerment movement, the horn as a communications strategy, the muffler as the part that dampens the political opposition, and the gas tank as the revenue-generator that Pussyhat's initial Value Proposition lacked. Maybe the vehicle is a metaphorical bus that Jayna's knitting teams drive, or maybe it's even a convoy of trucks which accounts for the growth of her future supporters.

Most teams to whom I have introduced this exercise have found it useful in expanding the potential impact of their Value Proposition. It accounts for potential future contextual influences they had not considered when they crafted their original Value Proposition, and doing this decades into the future without having to consider executional details frees them from worrying too much about near-term constraints.

Instead of relying on a forecast created by projecting incremental growth from Year Zero, this exercise will help you develop a more expansive, creative, and mature Value Proposition that better accounts for contextual issues many years into the future. You are trying to envision the "mature forest" first rather than only the "seed" that you have today. Remember the part of our definition of entrepreneurship that says *without regard to the resources currently controlled*. If all we do is focus on our little seed, we are doing the opposite and focusing only on our current resources.

In the third step of this Landscape Exercise, you will convert this metaphorical depiction of your future-focused Value Proposition into something that will enhance your current one. That requires starting with your future-focused version and inventing backward. Remember that creating a Value Proposition far into the future cannot rely on current technology or other known inputs. This forces you to be more creative than you may have been during the previous Value Proposition process. Now envision stepping backward toward today year by year and envisioning what you will need to do to achieve your future solution. When you reach today, I assure you that your revised Value Proposition will be more creative, bolder, and less encumbered by current feasibility than it was before this exercise. It will reflect bigger thinking, and it will envision bigger impact.

When you examine your refreshed Value Proposition, it may also seem less feasible. That's okay. As noted, big impact requires a focus on innovation more than on feasibility. If you do not have the complete range of technology required to execute your Value Proposition, that's okay. If you do not have sufficient financial resources to execute your Value Proposition, that's okay. If you do not have sufficient talent on your team to execute your Value Proposition, that's okay. Remember, entrepreneurship is a structured process for solving problems *without regard to the resources currently controlled.*

Airbnb is a striking example of a company that used the inventing backward process to spectacular effect. In 2008, RISD graduates Brian Chesky and Joe Gebbia set out with Harvard grad Nathan Blecharczyk to solve a problem they themselves had encountered regarding short-term rentals. They did a good job doing Bottom-Up Research. As Harvard Business School professor Thales Teixeira puts it, they thought like customers— both property owners and property renters. They empathized and learned the needs that alternative listing sources such as Craigslist did not address. They also did a good job of testing and iterating based on customer experience with their MVP.[7] But that took them only so far. What propelled Airbnb to scale for the long term was when they "made the unusual move of envisioning a perfect experience . . . *and working backward* to see what needed to be changed to meet that vision."[8]

Seeds of Peace and the Hazard of Thinking Small

I've made the point that entrepreneurship is not limited to companies driven by a profit motive. In fact, the Landscape Exercise worked beautifully for one nonprofit organization whose motive was to bring peace to a troubled part of the world. I work with a wonderful group called Seeds of Peace, originally a summer camp founded in the early 1990s for the purpose of bringing together Israeli and Palestinian teenagers, in the hopes that this would lead to greater connections and dialogue. Most of these teens had never met anyone from "the other side," and this summer camp experience broke down barriers that had seemed insurmountable. The early days of the Seeds camp demonstrated that experiencing a summer together could in fact begin to break down barriers. Feeling that the basic concept of dialogue could be scaled to do more, Seeds asked me in 2015 to lead workshops for its alumni. In Jordan, London, and East Jerusalem I trained Seeds alumni to use *See, Solve, Scale* to achieve even bigger visions of what the camp had sought to achieve.

An early encounter in London with a group of these Seeds alumni called Seeds Fellows made me realize that the Landscape Exercise offered particular promise for this group. I had been prepared to lead my typical Bottom-Up Research training until I chatted with a few of the Fellows at breakfast and learned a bit about their entrepreneurial visions. As I listened to them describe their ventures, I was struck by how small they seemed to be thinking: for example, an Arabic/Hebrew singing group, a support group for Israeli Arab women in high tech, a group that promotes volunteerism in Israel, an employment agency in Gaza for technology graduates, and a website that sells women's fashion.

As inspirational as they were, these Seeds Fellows seemed to be trying to keep their ventures small, tidy, and easy to control. It became more and more obvious that I had prepared the wrong workshop. They needed to learn how and why to think big. After that breakfast, I had to break it to my wife that we had to put our planned London sightseeing on hold.

In the workshop itself, I challenged the Fellows and even the Seeds leadership by pointing out that the seed metaphor they had adopted, while a vivid metaphor for the movement they were trying to grow, was limiting them. The problem was that a seedling would never grow into the forest that represented the scalable impact they would need to disrupt the generations of cultural and political tension plaguing Israelis and Palestinians. I had to get them to think beyond the near-term contextual friction that caused them to think that any fundamental, big shift was impossible.

This led me to the Landscape Exercise. I had to pick a time frame that would help them escape the negativity and cynicism that would accompany any effort to solve what felt like an intractable problem in the near term. And so I picked the longest time frame I have ever used: envision the problem you are looking to solve *in 2055*. The immediate response was striking: Hagit, a brave, creative Israeli educator who had recruited Arab and Jewish parents in Jaffa to establish a bilingual, binational, multicultural public educational system for 150 children, blurted out, "But I'll be in my eighties then; I can't even think that far into the future!" Exactly. That's the point. Projecting yourself so far into the future that you cannot be held back by known thinking, known conventional wisdom, known political resistance, known governmental policies, known cultural norms, and all of the other known hurdles is what we were trying to achieve. It was then—projecting herself forty years in the future—that Hagit could start to think big.

The other resistance I heard was from one Seeds Fellow named Micah Hendler who had founded the Jerusalem Youth Chorus, whose members are both Palestinian and Israeli teens. Micah expressed concern that he had no artistic talent and could not draw the types of metaphorical images I had asked him to draw. "I could never draw those pictures my kindergarten teacher asked me to and have still never been able to draw anything," he resisted. It took a few minutes, but he inhaled a deep breath, dove in, and did a great job on the exercise, which helped him to think much bigger about how he could have more scalable and long-term impact. Here's how Micah put it when I caught up with him:

> I started the Jerusalem Youth Chorus to improve relations between Israeli and Palestinian youth in Jerusalem. Doing the Landscape Exercise challenged me to think bigger. It was super-intimidating at the time, as I was barely able to keep my small chorus together, let alone think about doing more. But it helped me broaden my focus to other contexts and conflicts that need tools and spaces for healing and building trust. That has now taken the form of a creative culture change company called Raise Your Voice Labs, which helps groups all over the world to move in new directions, together. I even did the Landscape Exercise again in 2020 with my cofounders, and it helped us clarify and magnify our impact.

The Haitian Project Becomes the Haitian Network

My Brown classmate Patrick Moynihan is a Catholic deacon who has devoted his career to building and running the Louverture Cleary School in Haiti, which is dedicated to educating young Haitians from very poor families. Over 90 percent of the school's alumni are either studying or working in Haiti, earning on average fifteen times the per capita income of Haiti just a few years out of university, supporting themselves and their families and giving back to their country. What Patrick has done through this school is breathtaking, and for most people it would represent a career's worth of good work. In this case God's work.

When we launched our Center for Entrepreneurship at Brown, Patrick came to meet with me to update me on his progress. Usually, Patrick glows with the idealism that has motivated him to run Louverture Cleary School for over twenty years. This time, he looked frustrated. He had been meeting with some very wealthy people in the hopes of raising money to improve the school, and although they appreciated the impact the school was having on its students, they were not stepping up to donate. "No one doubts that we are changing the lives of these students. These guys could cut a check for hundreds of times of what I was asking for, and yet they don't. Why not?"

I told Patrick that I suspected it was because he was thinking too small. He had done a great job of finding and validating unmet needs. And he had evolved a strong Value Proposition to address those needs. But he had not taken the third step of developing a "think big" Sustainability Model, instead falling into the trap of thinking that framing the opportunity as small would reduce its risk. In fact it was the opposite. His prospective donors, I told him, could choose among an unlimited number of worthy organizations. They were looking to make maximum impact. Patrick's school educated only a few hundred students in a given year. In order to move the needle at the scale that they would find meaningful, he would need to help many more. Just as financial investors look for investments to grow financially, charitable donors also look for their investments to scale. And they would be looking for a donation opportunity that could justify a much bigger investment than what Patrick was requesting.

What did I recommend to Patrick? I challenged him to think big. "Instead of $100,000, what would you do with $10 million? Instead of educating a few hundred Haitian students at a time, what would it take for you to educate thousands? What model could you envision that would transform the entire country?" Patrick's eyes lit up. "Yes, I can bet that vision would motivate some of the donors who I can't get to cut a check. But how do I create that vision?" he wondered. After I walked him through the Land-scape Exercise, I introduced Patrick to one of my former Brown students, Daniel Breyer, who at the time was one of our center's Peer Entrepreneurs In Residence (PEIRs). Daniel worked through *See, Solve, Scale* with Patrick for several months, and I monitored their progress. I was excited to learn that Patrick and his team had used the Landscape Exercise to overhaul the School's Value Proposition and had developed a "think big" Sustainability Model. Here it is right from their website:

It's Time to Put Education First in Haiti

After three decades of incredible results and hundreds of successful alumni, the Haitian Project is expanding the impact of its Louverture Cleary School (LCS) by building a national network of schools across Haiti.

The Louverture Cleary School network will be a system of ten tuition-free, Catholic, coeducational secondary boarding schools—one in each diocese of Haiti—providing 3,600 students with a quality education steeped in service and 1,200 alumni with scholarships to Haitian universities each year.

While the LCS network will be a huge step forward for Haiti, the Haitian Project envisions it not as an end unto itself, but as an opportunity to inspire a shift in the focus of philanthropy toward education in Haiti and around the world.

The
Louverture Cleary
Schools Network

Guess what the reception was when Patrick circled back to the wealthy donors who had refused to cut a check? They leaned forward, expressed much more interest, and donated at levels that were unprecedented when Patrick was building one school. The Louverture Cleary Schools *Network*, building on the success of the initial one-school Value Proposition, is now on its way to transforming the educational and economic system of Haiti.

Here is how Patrick describes how this worked in his own words: "At the very moment Danny said the word 'landscape,' asking the question, 'What is your vision at its final state?,' I had the solution. I had the answer: the Network. I felt like Billy Beane in *Moneyball*."

To help reinforce the perspective that thinking big requires, I want to share a few other approaches for stretching your mind that remind me of the Landscape Exercise. Design Fiction, which artist and technologist Julian Bleecker developed, asks us to shed our concerns about feasibility and to write in a science fiction format to envision the future. In his 2009 manifesto, Bleecker writes that "like science fiction, Design Fiction creates imaginative conversations about possible future worlds." If you are looking to solve a problem in a large organization, note that Bleeker advises, "This is especially valuable in the belly of a large organization with lots of history and lots of convention.[9]

Charlie Cannon, a RISD Industrial Design Professor with whom I collaborate, has shared a similar exercise with my students designed to help them envision the future: depict yourself and a headline on the cover of *Time* magazine years into the future. And then work backward to plan how you will get there.

Ken Cox was a NASA scientist charged with envisioning the planning that would be necessary to launch missions to other planets. Those missions might take not only many years, but several generations, meaning that the team that arrived at the destination would not be the team that departed our planet. When Bob Johnston and Doug Bate come to class and challenge our teams through their version of the Landscape Exercise, they have them try to put themselves in Ken Cox's shoes to envision that kind of long-term mission.

And the most far-reaching approach I have ever seen is from an organization called Long Now. Its members are trying to envision so far into the future that they have adopted another significant digit in their dates, anticipating the Y2K-like challenge they will face in another eight thousand years! Its foundation website describes its mission like this: "The Long Now Foundation was established in 01996 to . . . become the seed of a very long-term cultural institution. The Long Now Foundation hopes to . . . make long-term thinking more common. We hope to foster responsibility in the framework of the next 10,000 years." Just as the Landscape Exercise intends, Long Now cofounder and computer scientist Daniel Hills indicates "it is time for us to start a long-term project that gets people thinking past the mental barrier of an ever-shortening future."[10]

Finally, astronauts who have orbited the Earth report experiencing a mental shift that has changed their perception of our planet and of their potential for impact. Known as the Overview Effect, this phenomenon has enabled these astronauts to place our human problems into a more expansive perspective. Similar to our Landscape Exercise, the Overview Effect creates a cognitive shift, a mental stretch that allows you to see the Earth as a planet moving through a star-filled universe. Most see that there are no borders or boundaries on this planet, except those created by us humans. Many of these astronauts returned to Earth with an "altered point of view about possibility, collaboration, and the future of our species. Some of them considered the experience to be transcendent and life-changing."[11]

Like all of these other mental stretches, the Landscape Exercise forces us to step away from our current experience and to question life as we live it today. It compels us to imagine ourself in the future looking back and asking the question, "Can you believe that we used to . . . ?" Before we begin to formulate the specifics of our Sustainability Model, it helps us envision bigger opportunities with longer-term impact than our near-term biases had previously allowed.

How?

We have discussed the three key questions that drive our Value Proposition: **Why**: benefits; **What**: features; **Who**: will use our product or service. When we address our Sustainability Model, we can answer a fourth key question: **How.** How are we going to fulfill our promise to deliver the value we are proposing in a way that is repeatable and scalable over the long term?

Even if we embrace Simon Sinek's suggestion to start with Why, at some point we need to consider How. How are we going to fulfill all that we have promised in our Value Proposition? How are we going to replicate and scale the minimally viable solution? How are we going to do all of this over the long term to the point that we can fully solve the problem we identified? How are we going to pour the sidewalks in concrete?

RUNA

RUNA is a venture launched by five students in my Brown 2008 class. None of them had any business or entrepreneurship experience. They were all classic Brown liberal arts students with academic concentrations ranging from Literary Arts to Public Policy. One of the students, Tyler Gage, had lived in the Amazon and developed an interest in the expansive botanical knowledge of the native communities. When the group met up to develop a portfolio of ideas to explore, Tyler tossed out the idea of finding a way to commercialize one specific Amazonian leaf called guayusa (pronounced "gwhy-you-sa"). Though it had never been produced in any commercial capacity, research had shown that guayusa contains as much caffeine as coffee, a large amount of polyphenol antioxidants, and no tannins, so the flavor is clean and smooth. Together, the team imagined how they could build the world's first supply chain for this ingredient and use Fair Trade agreements and sustainable farming practices to benefit the native communities who grow guayusa.

After the course ended, Tyler and his team launched a company based on guayusa, raised over $25 million in investments from social impact investors, celebrities, and even the Ecuadorian national government, and sold the company called RUNA to Vita Coco. They also generated millions of dollars of direct income for thousands of farming families in the Amazon and planted over 1.2 million trees. But what kind of company was it that enabled their team to capitalize on the long list of benefits that Tyler had known guayusa delivered? In short, what was its Value Proposition and even more, what was its Sustainability Model? RUNA's Value Proposition at first seemed clear:

- **What**: a leaf called guayusa that grew in Ecuador and contained caffeine that could rival coffee, antioxidants that could rival green tea, and a compelling taste.
- **Who**: "Reluctant Red Bull consumers" and millennials looking for a cleaner energy beverage, in addition to the local Ecuadorian families who could plant and harvest the crops.
- **Why**: "Clean energy from a leaf not a lab"—a smooth and long-lasting energy boost, a tasty way to quench your thirst, and the most important component for the RUNA team: a method of empowering these local Ecuadorian families to raise their standards of living.

The key question facing this team of students was **How**. How would they act on the insights that Tyler had about this valuable herb in a way that they could have long-term impact at scale?

Tyler tells his How story in his book *Fully Alive: Using the Lessons of the Amazon to Live Your Mission in Business and in Life*. As Tyler recounts, the very early steps that they took in the course, when they were working through the challenge I had posed to create a Sustainability Model that would enable them to change the world,

> . . . our first idea was simple: work with a few indigenous families in Ecuador who would farm the guayusa that we would then sell out of a loose-leaf tea house. Danny shook his head when we ran it by him. "Think bigger," he ordered. Our plan sounded like a lot of work to sell a few thousand dollars' worth of tea every month. He was hyper-focused on challenging his students to craft ideas that could be scaled into large [ventures].[12]

Tyler, Dan MacCombie, Charlie Harding, Aden Van Noppen, and Laura Thompson embraced my imperative to "think big" as well as any team I have ever had in the Entrepreneurial Process course. In thinking through various Sustainability Models, they considered farming guayusa in Ecuador, wholesaling the guayusa ingredient, distributing guayusa tea, and a few others. Because none of these models added meaningful value to the guayusa supply chain, it did not look like any of these proposed Sustainability Models would have long-term impact at scale.

At one point, as Tyler's book recounts, Charlie asked, "What about just making an actual energy drink?" After processing the idea for a few minutes and overcoming some initial skepticism with some quick Top-Down Research, they learned that there was $3.2 billion of energy drinks sold in the United States alone and that the market was forecasted to grow by 9 percent annually. The team identified an opportunity to bring a simple, natural energy drink to market made "from a leaf not a lab" and enter a much larger market than they had imagined. This nascent RUNA team leveraged Tyler's Bottom-Up Research among indigenous communities who were used to drinking guayusa and created a Sustainability Model that focused on the consumer-facing energy drink part of the value chain.

As the RUNA team considered these various Sustainability Models (How), the underlying Value Proposition (What, Who, Why)—guayusa's long list of benefits to both consumers and Ecuadorian farmers—did not change. What did change was the potential for this venture to grow big and to have long-term impact at scale. This impact included empowering over four thousand Ecuadorian farming families on a fair trade basis that allowed them to support their families to an extent they had never been able to achieve before. It also meant reforesting large sections of the Amazon.

RUNA is an excellent example of the catalytic impact I describe earlier that a small amount of early capital can have on the long-term viability and trajectory of a new venture. Tyler and Dan will tell you that if they had not won $25,000 in the Rhode Island Business Competition, they would not have taken themselves and the RUNA opportunity seriously enough to launch the company. As they scaled, they had to raise large amounts of money to build their supply chain in Ecuador and compete with the likes of Red Bull, but it was that first $25,000, their "walking around money," that got RUNA on its way. In Tyler and Dan's case, "walking around money" meant packing their backpacks and buying one-way tickets to Ecuador the day after graduation. It was choosing the right "think big" Sustainability Model that made all the difference.

Cacao

Alan Harlam, who for many years was director of Social Entrepreneurship at Brown, also worked with the RUNA team. At the time RUNA was tossing around various approaches, Alan shared with me a similar example that helped clarify how the choice of Sustainability Model can be the difference between a tiny venture and long-term impact at scale. Alan's students had studied a group of cacao farmers in South America who were struggling to move their families and communities beyond subsistence level. No matter how they tweaked and improved the efficiency of their planting, harvesting, and selling of raw cacao beans, it did not provide enough income for these farmers to support their families. Then the students studied the next level up the value chain where the beans were fermented. When some of the families moved up to that level by learning how to ferment the beans, they were able to sell those value-added beans for disproportionately higher margins that produced enough of a return for them to support their families. Selling the fermented beans rather than unfermented raw ones was the key. That shift in Model (the How) earned its label of Sustainability.

One of the critical choices you will need to make after developing a Value Proposition, therefore, is where in the industry map or supply chain to focus your venture. Some, like RUNA's original idea of selling loose-leaf tea, would have struggled to launch at all, let alone to scale. And the raw cacao farmers would never grow beyond subsistence level. Examining sustainability alternatives can lead to a model that enables you to think and become big.

ProfitLogic

ProfitLogic[13] was a company whose founding CEO, Michael Levy, had identified a strong and enduring problem that large retailers faced when they marked down their products to sell more quickly. Retail merchandisers relied on imprecise gut feel to determine product pricing, and with billions of retail sales dollars at stake, their inaccurate qualitative approaches were letting hundreds of millions of dollars slip away. Michael, a Ph.D. rocket scientist, hired others who, like him, had deep analytical skills.

Their small consulting firm analyzed large amounts of retail sales data by hand and advised its retail clients on how to optimize their markdowns.

Among all of the ventures we study throughout a semester course, ProfitLogic's Value Proposition is the most quantifiable. Michael and his Ph.D. colleagues are able to boost their retail clients' gross margins by 16 percent. Some of ProfitLogic's retail clients have billions of dollars in annual revenue. If, like most mainstream retailers, their gross margin is around 50 percent, the value that ProfitLogic can deliver is enormous: tens if not hundreds of millions of dollars. The crux of ProfitLogic's decision, therefore, focuses not on the What (markdown optimization), Who (large retailers), or Why (hundreds of millions of dollars in incremental gross margin). It focuses on How the company could change its model to deliver this value in ways that will enable ProfitLogic to grow much bigger by leveraging new software technology.

But why grow bigger? Michael Levy was doing well running a small consulting firm delivering enormous value to a handful of retail clients. What is the impetus for changing that model? Michael realized that there was far more potential for applying his Value Proposition to many more retailers than his small team could do via consulting. What's more, ProfitLogic had raised money from venture capitalists who had seen the firm's potential, and they wanted a huge return on their investment. A consulting firm wouldn't cut it. It is not scalable. It required more and more brilliant rocket scientists in order to deliver more value. Even if Michael could find and hire them, they would walk out of the door every night, require salaries and benefits, and take time off when they were sick and for vacation, and who knows whether they would remain at the company for the long term. As a consulting firm, ProfitLogic would never have long-term impact at scale. Enter Scott Friend, who had worked in sales at IBM in the retail division, and who Michael hired as CEO to implement a new Sustainability Model that would enable ProfitLogic to grow and achieve its long-term potential.

As they aimed to scale ProfitLogic, Michael and Scott set their focus on a couple of different high-tech models that would allow them to collect, transfer, store, and analyze their retail clients' sales data far more efficiently. They considered several models, among them an Application Service Provider (ASP, which today we would call cloud computing) that would host their clients' data on a central server, and Licensed Software running locally at each retailer. As I mention above, regardless of the alternative high-tech models Scott and his team were considering, ProfitLogic's fundamental Value Proposition would remain the same: it empowers companies to use their sales data to optimize their product markdowns and generate enormous incremental profits. Whether ProfitLogic chooses to deliver its value via ASP or Licensed Software, the 16 percent boost in gross margin it provides remains constant, even compared to how it was delivering value as a consulting firm. The Who, What, and Why don't change. The How does and in dramatic fashion.

A critical lesson that ProfitLogic illustrates is the range of variables your choice of Sustainability Model will influence, including burn rate, cash flow, funding strategy, relevant talent, and even who you choose to be CEO. Each Sustainability Model that Scott and Michael considered required different levels of resources. In order to choose, they had to understand the relative tradeoffs.

Burn rate, a measure of how much cash you are consuming each month, is crucial to measure and track, because you cannot survive if you run out of cash. If you scuba dive, you know that you must keep a close eye on how much oxygen you have left and at what rate you are depleting it. Similarly, if you are an early-stage entrepreneurial venture, you have to keep an eye on how much cash you have left and at what rate you are burning it. As my HBS professor Jeff Timmons always warned, never be OOC—out of cash.

As a consulting firm, ProfitLogic grew as fast as its cash flows alone allowed without any outside investment. The more client cash it generated, the more it was able to hire more Ph.D. consultants. As ProfitLogic looked to transition the slow manual analysis of its capacity-limited Ph.D.s to fast computers with almost unlimited capacity, Michael, Scott, and their team needed to invest in this technology up front, before they started generating cash. Their monthly cash deficits or "burn rates" varied. One form of ASP that ProfitLogic would customize for each new client would create a burn rate of $500,000/month. If ProfitLogic standardized its ASP approach so that it could reuse much of the same technology for each new client, it would increase its burn rate to $750,000/month. And if it chose to develop software that clients would license and run on their own servers, it would increase ProfitLogic's burn rate to $1 million/month. Yes, $1 million per month! Here, too, notice that regardless of which burn rate the company was willing to stomach, its Value Proposition continued to remain steady.

To stay alive while burning this cash, ProfitLogic sought resources that others control—tens of millions of dollars—in the form of investments from venture capitalists. One of the nuances of these investments was that at first the venture capitalists themselves were attracted not only to the dramatic value that the company was able to deliver to its retail clients, but also to ProfitLogic's aspiration to pursue an ASP delivery model. ASP at that time was the Next Big Thing because its low up-front and low ongoing IT costs promised to revolutionize the way big companies managed their computer systems.

As any faddish trend might, ASP lost favor, and the venture capitalists became more attracted to the Licensed Software model. Likewise, the preference of ProfitLogic's clients varied—some preferred ASP, others Licensed Software. And just like the costs and burn rates varied by model, so did the revenues and cash flows. ASP provided less up-front revenue and more over time; Licensed Software provided the opposite—more up front and less over time.

Finally, when Scott had to decide whether to develop actual software, he realized that ProfitLogic did not have the right team because they needed software developers, not Ph.D. rocket scientists, to do so. Scott even faced his own Founder's Dilemma, which is a concept that we will explore in greater depth in chapter 7. He had to come to terms with the fact that he, himself, was not the right guy to run a software company because he had never led a team of software developers.

All of these elements—when and how much cash it receives from its clients, the different burn rates ASP and Licensed Software impose, what kind of talent the company needed to execute these different models, and even whether Scott was the right CEO—varied according to which Sustainability Model ProfitLogic would adopt. All of them affected whether, the degree to which, and how the company would fulfill its Value Proposition and have long-term impact at scale.

One of these elements that I want to emphasize is cash flow. The timing of when you have to spend money and when you receive it illustrates an essential financial adage that every Sustainability Model should consider: a dollar today is worth more than a dollar tomorrow. The timing of when you receive payment from a customer can matter as much as if not more than the absolute dollar amount you receive. When a startup is looking to operate without regard to the resources it currently controls, and when it otherwise would be raising capital from venture capitalists and other sources of cash, the value of cash it can attract from its customers before it has to spend it can be enormous.

Remember Casper founder Luke Sherwin's almost offhand mention of the fact that the company had reached $100 million in sales at the eighteen-month mark? Perhaps even more impressive was Casper's virtuous cash flow model. Casper received the cash from its online customers immediately, and it did not have to pay its mattress manufacturer until sixty days later. That positive cash flow enabled Casper to grow exponentially without having to raise much outside capital in its early days. As you think big about your own ambitions to have long-term impact at scale, you will develop experience and skills to detect ways to improve these kinds of free cash flow characteristics of your venture.

Scarce Resources Distinguish Entrepreneurship from Product Development

Occasionally someone who works in an established organization like a big company or a government agency will ask how *See, Solve, Scale* is different from a conventional product development process. On the surface, product development encompasses similar steps: define a problem; create a product solution that will address that problem; and then scale it. It feels similar to the first part of our definition of entrepreneurship: a structured process for solving problems.

It is the second part of the definition that distinguishes entrepreneurship from product development: *without regard to the resources currently controlled*. In large organizations endowed with lots of resources, going through the three steps of our process does not make what you are doing entrepreneurship. You need to do so in a context in which you have scarce, not abundant resources.

Doing so requires limiting access to too many resources, or said another way, it requires imposing a context of scarce resources, of *aparigraha*. Remember the Knight Ridder newspaper example above? It seemed counterintuitive, but it was *because* of the newspaper company's abundant resources—its publishing expertise, its substantial sales and editorial talent, its distribution network, its printing assets—that it did not behave as an entrepreneur—with one significant exception.

As I described earlier, in the early days of the internet, Knight Ridder CEO Tony Ridder might have looked at his high profit margins and at what had always been high barriers to entry and figured the internet wouldn't threaten Knight Ridder's newspaper business. The internet looked suspiciously similar to the failed Viewtron that had lost $50 million. So half-heartedly, Tony had Bob Ingle, executive editor of the *San Jose Mercury News*, looked into putting the newspaper online. I say half-heartedly because Tony didn't provide Bob with dedicated resources to do so. He did not excuse Bob from his current responsibilities, provide Bob more office space, or assign Bob salespeople and editors. Worse, Knight Ridder's institutional and cultural defenses—its Corporate Myopia, Gravity, and Immune Systems—were focused on maintaining its successful newspaper model. We see that, for example, when Bob tried to recruit newspaper editors to his online team. "When [Bob] asked for help from the newspaper desk editors, the response he received was, 'Get the hell out of here. I have a *real* newspaper to put out.'"[14]

Fail Fast, Fail Cheap

In many companies, a person like Bob would have given up in the face of institutional resistance and a lack of urgency to build on the company's core products. Bob's Bottom-Up Research indicated that its readers and advertisers were looking for more customized information and communication than a print newspaper could provide. And his Value Proposition was a new customized online medium (What) for self-developed communities and the advertisers who want to reach them (Who) to provide a more personal information experience and a more efficient advertising medium (Why).

In the face of this resistance and at an entrenched company with a culture that knows little about failure, Bob succeeded. He did get the *San Jose Mercury News* online! How? Not by throwing Knight Ridder's own substantial resources at the problem, which is often the typical way product development works at a big company. Instead, Bob capitalized on his lack of resources. Through a series of low-cost experiments, he followed the entrepreneurial adage that Dan Wyner's soccer robot embraced: to fail fast, fail cheap. "'To learn deeply the needs and adaptability of our customers,' Bob commented, 'we will first develop a handful and ultimately hundreds of low-cost, easily tested applications. We will adjust as we go.'"[15] An example of a valuable insight Bob learned from an initial mistake was the importance of local content and also local management. Like Justin at Bandura Games, Bob started with and then evolved a series of crude minimally viable products, not a well-resourced, fully scaled version such as one might expect from a big company.

So we don't have to feel bad that Bob Ingle didn't have more resources. Instead of limiting his success, his scarce resources enabled it. He had no choice but to experiment inexpensively rather than moving too quickly to scale and deploying significant and permanent resources in one direction. Doing so kept him off the radar of Knight Ridder's leaders who were more focused on sustaining the fortress of their legacy newspaper business than in inventing the future.

Not getting too committed to your beginning assumptions, developing low-cost, easily tested applications that allow and even encourage you to fail and learn—those sound like Bob's way of reiterating our adage of not pouring the sidewalks in concrete before you see the bare patches in the lawn, or of falling not in love but in like. As challenging as it might have been for him to have Tony Ridder limit his resources in an otherwise resource-rich environment, Bob followed a structured process for solving problems. And by failing fast and failing cheap, he did so without regard to the resources he currently controlled. In short, Bob was not a product developer. He was an entrepreneur.

Failing Your Way to Success

Failure is another stepping stone to greatness.

—Oprah Winfrey

To make mistakes is human but to profit by them is divine.

—artist Elbert Hubart

There is a crack in everything / That's how the light gets in.

—Leonard Cohen, "Anthem"

The secret to Silicon Valley's astounding multiple-decade boom is failure. Failure is what fuels and renews this place. Failure is the foundation for innovation.[16]

—Paul Saffo, Stanford engineering professor

I've missed more than 9,000 shots in my career. I've lost almost 300 games. Twenty-six times, I've been trusted to take the game winning shot and missed. I've failed over and over and over again in my life. And that is why I succeed.

—Michael Jordan

Institutionalizing Failure

If failing is such a valuable part of *See, Solve, Scale*, how can we overcome our human tendency to resist failure? In other words, how can we do more than utter the incantation, "Fail fast, fail cheap," hoping that doing so will have the right magical influence on our normal resistance to failing? How can we make it easier to fail our way to entrepreneurial success?

I pose these questions here because iterating during the **Scale: Create a Sustainability Model** step of our process may make us feel more vulnerable than we felt iterating a Value Proposition. After all, it is one thing to iterate small-scale solutions among our team and perhaps a few others. Regardless of how critical the Palestinian and Israeli schoolchildren might have been of Bandura's cardboard MVP, Justin was eager to learn from these creative interactions. Now, the stakes will feel a little higher as we start to get real market feedback and begin to invest more resources. In this step, because we might be tempted to frame negative market feedback as definitive evidence of failure, it is even more important for us to know how to embrace it.

Teresa Amabile, a professor at Harvard Business School and a coauthor of *The Progress Principle*,[17] has devoted her career to studying creativity. Her research identifies five key characteristics of any organization working on risky projects. As you begin to scale your venture, it is important to embed these characteristics in your growing team.

- **Failure Value**: a recognition that mistakes are opportunities to learn.
- **Psychological Safety**: a culture where it's safe to take risks and

fail, and to openly discuss mistakes, without fear of being ostra-
cized or ridiculed.

- **Multiple Diversities**—of backgrounds, perspectives, and cognitive styles—which I emphasize in the next chapter when I guide
you through forming a successful venture team.

- **Focus on Refining Questions**, not just on answers, and on stepping back to ask whether the problems your team is trying to solve
are the most important ones. I like this one because it reinforces
the first step of our process to find and validate an unmet need.

- **Financial and Operational Autonomy** which applies to teams
that are part of a larger organization, like Bob Ingle's at Knight
Ridder.[18,19]

Astro Teller is the head of X—the subsidiary of Google that aims to
"create radical new technologies to solve some of the world's hardest problems."[20] To do so, Astro has institutionalized failure to make it a standard
part of his team's process, and he has made it a normal part of the X culture. In his *Wired* piece "The Secret to Moonshots? Killing Our Projects,"
we can see Teresa Amabile's characteristics at work. Teller warns us that,

> You can't just command everyone to fail fast. People resist
> because they worry, what happens if I fail? Will people laugh at
> me? Will I get fired? . . . We work hard at X to make it safe to
> fail. We killed over 100 investigations last year alone. I didn't
> kill them. The teams themselves killed each one. And teams
> kill their ideas as soon as the evidence is on the table because
> they're rewarded for it. They get applause from their peers.
> Hugs and high fives from their manager. They get promoted
> because of it. We've bonused every single person in teams that
> ended their projects, from teams as small as two to teams of
> more than thirty.[21]

On X's own website, you can see the types of "think big" moonshot
projects this promotion of failure has encouraged: balloons that deliver
internet service to remote places, drones that change the way products are
delivered around the world, kites that generate electricity in unexpected
places, and beams of light that support the rapidly growing demand for
data.[22] The key is that not all of these are successful, and where they have

not been, Teller has done what he promised and awarded big bonuses and recognition to the teams that failed. The net result of this failing your way to success approach includes such Value Proposition and Sustainability Model breakthroughs as Waymo, the self-driving-car company that incubated at X for seven years. It is now worth $70 billion, more than the market cap of Ford or GM.[23]

Like Teresa Amabile advises, the Psychological Safety in Brown's grading system motivates students to take bigger risks, sample subjects out of their comfort zones, and reach higher. Because the lowest grade you can receive is a C, and anything lower will not appear on your transcript, no one ever knows if you fail a course. As it does in *See, Solve, Scale*, this system activates the cliché that we learn more from our failures than from our successes. What is most relevant to where we are in the process—Creating a Sustainability Model—is that because all of us feel uncomfortable failing, we have to institutionalize its benefits. Even Brown students who come with perfect records from competitive high schools have a hard time believing we are serious about wanting them to risk failure. And so like Astro Teller at X has recognized, institutionalizing requires us to communicate and demonstrate these benefits to our growing team.

St. Augustine: *"Fallor ergo sum"*—"I err therefore I am"

In *Being Wrong*, journalist Kathryn Schulz discusses why getting things wrong is essential to human beings' effort to make sense of the world around them.[24]

The liberal arts student in me loves her ability to put this into historical context: "1,200 years before Descartes said his famous thing about 'I think therefore I am,' this guy, St. Augustine, sat down and wrote 'Fallor ergo sum'—'I err therefore I am.' Augustine understood that our capacity to screw up is not some kind of embarrassing defect in the human system, something we can eradicate, suppress or overcome. It's totally fundamental to who we are. Because, unlike God, we don't really know what's going on out there. And unlike all of the other animals, we are obsessed with trying to figure it out. To me, this obsession is the source and root of all of our productivity and creativity."[25]

A Heavy Load

Why is it so difficult for us to deal with failing and being wrong? Schulz sums up well how being wrong, how not succeeding, makes us feel: "Error is associated not just with shame and stupidity but also with ignorance, indolence, psychopathology, and moral degeneracy."[26] Yikes! The emotional effects of failure can last a very long time. If these scars are the lasting remnants of failure, no wonder we work so hard to avoid failing.

Those enduring natural psychological effects of failure remind me of the Zen parable, "A Heavy Load," which tells of two traveling monks who reached a town where there was a young woman waiting to step out of her sedan chair. The rain had caused deep puddles to form, and she couldn't step across them without ruining her fancy robes. She stood there, looking angry and impatient. She was scolding her attendants. They had nowhere to place the packages they held for her, so they couldn't help her across the puddles.

The younger monk noticed the woman, said nothing, and walked by. The older monk quickly picked her up and put her on his back, transported her across the water, and put her down on the other side. She didn't thank the older monk, and just shoved him out of the way and departed.

As they continued on their way, the young monk was brooding. After several hours, unable to maintain his silence, he spoke up. "That woman back there was selfish and rude, but you picked her up on your back and carried her! Then she didn't even thank you!"

"I set the woman down hours ago," the older monk replied. "Why are you still carrying her?"[27]

Reveal Your Failures

The surprising news is that there are good reasons for entrepreneurs to reveal and share their failures. A team of Harvard Business School researchers tested the reactions of two groups of entrepreneurs listening to other entrepreneurs presenting their ventures in a pitch competition. Half listened to what they thought were fellow entrepreneurs talking only about their successes, and half listened to entrepreneurs who shared those same successes and also owned up to failures. The details here are so fascinating that I thought I would share some of the scripts. Both groups listened to this:

> Hi, I'm the founder of Hypios. I have a Ph.D. in computer science from Stanford and have started a company that uses my superior skill set to help companies solve their toughest problems. I have already landed some huge clients—companies like Google and GE. I've had AMAZING success, and in the past year I have single-handedly increased our market share by TWO-HUNDRED PERCENT.[28]

The second group listened to that and then also heard this:

> I wasn't always so successful. I had a lot of trouble getting to where I am now. I almost failed out of grad school because I wasn't picking up the course material as well as my peers. I was completely new to the academic world, and I struggled to demonstrate my potential to my professors and colleagues. Similarly, when I started my company, Hypios, I also failed to demonstrate why potential clients should believe in me and our mission. Many potential clients turned me down. But I persevered . . . I started out with a very low problem-solving success rate, and it almost killed my company. I had a number of failed efforts with my initial matching algorithm and some companies were about to give up on me. But I worked hard to fix those problems and now we have a success rate of almost NINETY-NINE PERCENT.[29]

Listeners characterized the first group of entrepreneurs as full of "hubristic pride"—they came off as arrogant. What about when the second group revealed their failures? Were they characterized as ignorant? Indolent? Psychopathological? Morally degenerate? Quite the opposite. As Dina Gerdeman summarizes the results of this study in her piece, "Why Managers Should Reveal Their Failures," "participants who heard the entrepreneur disclose previous failures believed the person had more 'authentic pride' and came across as confident rather than arrogant. They also got the impression that this entrepreneur put a lot of effort into overcoming obstacles, and . . . that brought out warmer, fuzzier feelings, with listeners not only believing the entrepreneur was deserving of success, but also feeling motivated to improve their own performance."[30]

In a more recent study, Taly Reich of the Yale School of Management, Daniella Kupor of Boston University, and Kristin Laurin of the University of British Columbia conclude that although individuals and organizations often fear that making a mistake in their pursuit of a goal will lead others to judge them as less likely to achieve that goal, the reverse occurs. Observers infer that others who make—and correct—a mistake while pursuing a goal are more likely to achieve that goal than others who prevent that same mistake from occurring in the first place. The reason observers make this inference is interesting: "although observers construe prevention to mean that a goal pursuer has been consistently vigilant, they believe mistake correction requires more effort than prevention (even when it does not)."[31]

Respecting those who reveal their mistakes has been true in my own entrepreneurial experiences, on both the venture side and as an investor. No one is perfect, and anyone looking for me to join or support their team who claims to be perfect is not being honest. They are hiding something. And if they are hiding one thing—their failures—perhaps they are hiding other things. Showing only your successes erodes your credibility. Because everyone knows how challenging and even painful it is to reveal your failures, doing so and discussing how you have grown by overcoming them adds to your credibility. If you are willing to disclose something unpleasant, you must be communicating more transparently than if you did not.

My Harvard Business School section mate, Jim Whitehurst, former president of IBM, reflects on the benefits he has seen through his own public admissions of failure: "Who would you rather trust—the person who denies anything is amiss or the person who admits their error and then follows up with a plan to correct it? . . . I've found that leaders who show their vulnerability, and admit that they are human, foster greater engagement among their associates."[32]

One of the best examples I know of doing this is the Anti-Portfolio from Bessemer Venture Partners, the nation's oldest venture capital firm, which can trace its roots back to the Carnegie Steel empire. Bessemer's website proclaims that "this long and storied history has afforded our firm an unparalleled number of opportunities to completely screw up."[33] What follows on their site is a long list of familiar startup successes that Bessemer passed on when those startups were young and raising venture capital. My favorite is Google:

> A college friend of Bessemer partner, David Cowan, rented her garage to Sergey and Larry for their first year. In 1999 and 2000 she tried to introduce Cowan to "these two really smart Stanford students writing a search engine." Students? A new search engine? In the most important moment ever for Bessemer's anti-portfolio, Cowan asked her, "How can I get out of this house without going anywhere near your garage?"

Isn't it refreshing, humanizing to read such a transparent disclosure of the failure of one of the most successful venture capital firms? And doesn't reading about its failures give what Bessemer says about its successes and its ability to add value that much more credibility?

The night before their venture pitches, I encourage students to check out Bessemer's anti-portfolio to boost their confidence. The students tell me that, as nervous as they are, it's comforting to remember that even stellar venture capitalists with so many successes to their credit have failed many times, and that failure makes them more humble and more accessible. Many have told me that reading the anti-portfolio gave them the confidence they needed to do their pitch well.

I encourage you to check it out here: bvp.com/portfolio/antiportfolio[34]

Tim Herrera of *The New York Times* has a suggestion to increase the chances that you and your venture team will learn from your failures. Tim recommends creating and maintaining what he calls a failure résumé—an ongoing written record of your failures that you review and assess over time.[35] Rather than perseverating about and clutching the feelings associated with those failures, use this as an opportunity to assess why you and your venture team failed, and move forward in a different way.

Consider Aishetu Fatima Dozie, who has such an impressive professional track record that we might never imagine she has ever failed. Undergraduate degree from Cornell, MBA from Harvard, work on over $130 billion in transactions while at Goldman Sachs and Morgan Stanley, and now the CEO of a successful beauty brand called Bossy Cosmetics that targets working women. And yet, Aishetu reinforces the recommendation to reveal your failures: "record every failure and celebrate every win. I've tried to normalize getting rejected. I remember when I first started Bossy and I sent blind emails to tons and tons of VCs and NO ONE responded. I thought that meant that the business was doomed to failure. I now understand that failure is a very necessary part of the success journey. I keep a little note pad of every rejection and mistake. I go back and look every quarter when I write my quarterly investor update."[36]

 CAUTION: HUMAN ERROR

Our personal and organizational resistance to failure limits our ability to learn, iterate, and improve, and it reduces our ability to think big.

Unfair Competitive Advantage

As important as tolerance for failure may be, eventually we need to succeed. And to solve a consequential problem, we have to succeed over the long term on a big scale. To do so requires competitive advantage—even "unfair competitive advantage" that competition cannot replicate.

In his seminal research study, *Profiting from Technology Innovation*, economist David Teece analyzes different sources of this advantage. He distinguishes between **core assets** embedded in your venture's product or service itself and **complementary assets** that enhance the value of those core assets and help you to bring your product or service to market. Your core assets can provide competitive advantage if they are as Doug Hall would say "dramatically different"—think the Coca-Cola recipe, for example—and if through intellectual property protection like a patent, trademark, trade secret, or brand, you can defend against a competitor copying them. Your complementary assets can provide advantage, for example, through a proprietary manufacturing or distribution process— think Tesla's robot-enhanced manufacturing plant.

But how much advantage do these various assets provide? It turns out that some activities are much harder to replicate than others. Pankaj Ghemawat of the Stern School of Business at NYU has devoted much of his research career to analyzing variations in the endurance of different sources of competitive advantage. It's not surprising that competing on price is the least enduring. What might be surprising is that the lag before competition catches up with innovation—often the core asset in a startup's arsenal—is only two years. Advantages in complementary assets like manufacturing and distribution endure longer. Human resource–based advantages are the most difficult for competitors to replicate. I will have a lot more to say about this when I discuss the composition of venture teams in chapter 7 below.

In R&R, even Bob Reiss would admit that his core asset—the trivia game itself—was only subtly different from its main competitor and precursor, Trivial Pursuit. The game details were not different enough on their own to sustain a competitive advantage (let alone an unfair one) or to defend against future entrants to the gaming market. Instead, a valuable lesson from R&R is that, even in the face of limited product differentiation, the way Bob was able to leverage complementary assets—including advertising, manufacturing, distribution, and the composition of his team—was itself dramatically different.

In executing his trivia game venture, Bob had one part-time employee and outsourced all of the company's essential functions. Instead of investing significant resources to build and then defend his own brand, Bob leveraged through his partnership with *TV Guide* an established brand that 17 million subscribers would notice on toy retailer shelves. A factor-

RESPONSE LAGS	
Activity	Time To Replicate
Price	60 days
Advertising	1 year
Innovation	2 years
Manufacturing	3 years
Distribution	4 years
Human Resources	7 years

ing company, Heller, handled the credit checks and receivable collections. A previous collaborator, Alan Charles, designed the TV trivia game. A Wisconsin-based cheese manufacturer, Swiss Colony, picked, packed, and shipped the board game. Wait, a cheese company? What the heck does a cheese company have to do with a board game? Maybe nothing at first blush. Bob and Sam, however, were resourceful entrepreneurs, and they recognized a valuable complementary asset. They knew that if a cheese company could pick, pack, and ship a perishable dairy product, surely they could do so for a product made of cardboard and plastic. Bob orchestrated these functions and combined these complementary assets by outsourcing them all to experts who had already invested in their value and capacity that Bob's new venture could leverage on a variable-cost basis.

These strategic ways in which Bob combined complementary assets (marketing, branding, manufacturing, distribution, collections) and all of the talented people behind them with his core asset (the trivia game itself) were what gave his venture a competitive advantage.

Open Source Leverages Resources Beyond Your Venture's Control

I always knew true, long-term change cannot happen without involving the community.

—Kennedy Odede, *Find Me Unafraid: Love, Loss, and Hope in an African Slum*[37]

One of the Sustainability Models that has evolved since I began teaching in 2006 is open source—a model for developing software and now other things—that leverages contributions from the public developer community. If talent provides the most enduring competitive advantage, open source has opened the floodgates of Bob Reiss's outsourcing strategy. Like the Open Innovation Value Proposition approach, this Sustainability Model assumes that "the crowd" can make better and much more rapid progress than any single developer or team of internal developers. It allows anyone to use the evolving product for free as long as they share their contributions with the wider community.[38] Author and *New York Times* columnist Thomas Friedman in *Thank You for Being Late* describes how an open-source approach enabled the software startup, Hadoop, to scale quickly: "Since there is so much less friction on an open-source platform, and so many more minds working on it—compared with a proprietary system—it has expanded lightning fast."[39]

He also describes how established organizations can leverage this open-source Sustainability Model. Within six months of open-sourcing the development of its otherwise proprietary closed-source .NET platform for developing serious enterprise software for banks and insurance companies, Microsoft had more people working on .NET for free than they had had working on it inside the company.[40] In *See, Solve, Scale* terms, open source can accelerate a venture toward long-term impact at scale and do so by leveraging resources that the founding venture does not directly control.

One of the curious parts of open source is what motivates developers to participate and contribute in the first place. Open source does not provide financial compensation. If the motivation is not financial, what is it? Friedman argues that there is something wonderfully human about this open-source model and the community that is motivated to contribute. "At heart," he says, "it's driven by a deep human desire for recognition . . . It's amazing how much value you can create with the words 'Hey, what you added is really cool. Way to go!' Millions of hours of free labor are being unlocked by tapping into people's innate desires to innovate, share, and be recognized for it."[41] Open source reinforces the importance of *purpose* that I mention at the end of chapter 4: purpose is the intersection of goals that are both meaningful to you and important to others.

When they come to class each semester, Bob Johnston and Doug Bate share a related adage that they have seen have dramatic impact on the success of new ventures: *people support what they help to create.* They identify people whose support an initiative depends on, and they involve them in the process of creating that new initiative. Open source is a dramatic example of this dynamic. When people are engaged early and throughout the process, they have skin in the game, they have at least their pride and reputation on the line, and so they are much more likely to act like owners throughout the process. If what you are working on feels like "your baby," you are much more likely to take interest in its success. This is important for entrepreneurial initiatives in established organizations, where as we said earlier in the toy company example, the economic ties between employees and their projects are more tenuous than they are in a typical startup.

As open source has become a more mainstream Sustainability Model, it has become much more than a nice-to-have feel-good for employees, and has become even *critical* for recruitment. Software developers in particular know open-source approaches can feel rewarding and they are now an essential method for breakthrough innovation. While CEO of Red Hat, Jim Whitehurst helped lead the transition of open source from, in his words, "a kind of scary, cult-like thing, to the only way to do innovation in a whole bunch of categories." He reports, "I hear over and over again from our large customers, 'You have to help me convince my legal department that our developers need to be able to contribute to open-source projects, because if they can't, I can't hire them.'"[42]

As evidence of how mainstream open source has become, fast-forward to 2019, when IBM acquired Red Hat for $34 billion and Jim became IBM's president. As we look to the future for how we might structure our Sustainability Models to solve critical problems and have long-term impact at scale, Jim asks:

> Do we really think we're going to solve global warming with all those people patenting their little slivers? Can you have the layered and modular innovation that is going to be required? One of the powerful pieces of open source is its modularity and the iteration that happens. It's hard to have this modularity and iteration if every time you want to do something you've got to go get permission or get this license or pay this fee. . . . There's need for intellectual property protections. But I'd be more pragmatic around not defaulting to everything being closed. We should default to open and then be very crisp about what and why we want to close things. It's likely to lead to a better outcome.[43]

Brands Are Like Magic: They Reduce Searching Costs

One of the assets that all ventures should develop early is a strong brand—the relationship your customers have with your products. Brands seem to have magical powers. They create value in what would otherwise remain a commodity. They attract new customers who will even pay a premium to try your products. They help make those customers loyal to your products. Sure, the Duncan Hines baking mixes that I worked on at P&G had a slight product superiority, but it was the decades-old and continually refreshed brand that motivated families to try Duncan Hines products, to stick with the brand and refuse to buy a competitor's, and to ignore the same baking ingredients they already had in their pantries. It is the American Girl brand that causes children to *love* their American Girl Dolls and their parents to pay a hefty premium versus what other similar-looking dolls might cost. Many Stonyfield Yogurt eaters will walk out of the store without any yogurt before they would even consider buying a competitor's. And if they encounter a store that doesn't carry Stonyfield, they will lobby the store manager to order it. Trader Joe's supermarket shoppers drive miles out of their way to shop at a small store with a small selection of products, most of which are sold under the Trader Joe's brand. Brands are powerful, and every venture should invest in its brand to help it scale.

It turns out there is also a hardwired reason that brands work their magic. As Alec Beckett, Creative Partner at NAIL Communications, shared with me,

> In our neolithic past, the ability to make a quick recognition evolved as a life-saving shortcut. You are scavenging for food. You come across two berry bushes—one you recognize and know as safe and one you don't. You could stop and study the unknown berry. You could take a tiny taste and see if there is any potentially toxic bitterness. You could observe whether other animals are safely eating it. You could look for similarities to other safe berries you know. You could, but you can't waste time or risk exposure to predators.
>
> This is at the very heart of branding. Our brains desperately want shorthand signals that make decisions easy for us.
>
> This is why brands exist. A brand's job—first and foremost—is to reassure me that this isn't a poison berry.

What is not magic or hardwired is the care and effort it takes to build a brand. Many of the detailed strategies and tactics required to do so are beyond the scope of this book. But let me offer a few important guidelines. Too often, startup entrepreneurs pay lip service to the importance of their brand. At best they will think about the narrow definition of a brand as the label on the product or the tagline in an ad and not as all of the elements that contribute to the relationship the customer has with their product. If they do think about their brand, they think it is something they should focus on years down the line. So first, as you build your Sustainability Model, look for ways to build your brand from early on. You *will* have a brand; the only question is whether *you* will build it or will it be imposed on you. Be deliberate about it. It is so much easier and more efficient for you to build it and control it than to have to undo one you had not intended. If a brand is the relationship your customers have with your products, guide your customers to the relationship you want them to have. Even better, as I hinted in chapter 3, you can leverage the empathetic insights you gained through the Bottom-Up Research you did in step 1 even further, as empathy also forms the basis of successful branding campaigns.

Second, unlike other core and complementary assets that I mention above, a brand can enhance and differentiate all other assets. It can be both *core,* as the moist claim of Duncan Hines brownies brand promotes, and *complementary,* as in the Tesla-branded stores through which the company distributes and sells its electric cars. So look for ways to build your brand through all functions of your venture.

If, as Pankaj Ghemawat's research demonstrates, the most enduring competitive advantage is in our people, our team is an important part of our relationship with customers and therefore an important source of branding. When we think of Southwest Airlines flight attendants in their collared shirts and khaki shorts, for example, we think of them as the enthusiastic representatives of the Southwest brand, eager to please and even entertain. One of the main reasons consumers go out of their way to shop at Trader Joe's is the quirky employees who make shopping fun and who will do whatever it takes to make a customer happy. Loyal Apple users gush about the service Apple Store hipster techies provide. According to a PwC global survey, this kind of frontline customer service is one of the "key drivers that influence their brand loyalties. In fact, the price premium for quality [customer experience] among consumers worldwide is real—and it adds up to 16 percent on products and services."[44]

When talking about the importance of brands, I often begin by asking students what brands provide: "trust," "credibility," "reputation," "consistency," and "design" are some of the words they share. I then point out a random student with a MacBook and hypothesize that she is a nutrition nut who cares about what she eats. As they look back at me, confused, I point out the piece of fruit with a bite out of it on the front of her laptop. After a little banter, I ask why she would buy such a device that has that logo on it. What did that piece of fruit signal to her? Reliability, trust, confidence, design, cutting edge, cool . . . "All of that from a simple image of a piece of fruit?" I ask. "Oh, and do you use a mobile phone?," I follow.

"Yes, of course. I use an iPhone," she replies.

"And which device did you buy first?"

"The computer."

"When it came time to buy that iPhone, did you line up a full range of all the phone choices you had, and did you do in-depth scientific research to compare your choices?"

"No . . . of course not. I just bought the Apple one," she admits.

"Ah, so it was that piece of fruit after all that motivated you to choose another Apple device. But what if it had not been an Apple logo on the front of the computer or the phone. Let's say it was the same laptop and the same phone, but let's say it had a picture of a pineapple on the front. Would you have bought those devices?" I ask.

"Uh, of course not."

"So it is not a piece of fruit that gives you comfort and confidence. It's specifically an apple."

"Yes."

"How, then, can we describe the function that the Apple brand served in your decision-making process? What do brands do?" I ask. I ask the students to think about the decision-making process the student has just described. If they don't follow, I then share the definition of a brand that I learned from my favorite Harvard Business School professor, Richard Tedlow: "**Brands reduce searching costs.**"

But what do we do if we cannot afford the time it will take to build our own brand? We might do as Bob Reiss did, focusing on the second part of the definition of entrepreneurship, *without regard to the resources currently controlled*, and capitalizing on the resources others have built. With only eighteen months to exploit the TV trivia game opportunity, he had no time to build his own brand and instead leveraged *TV Guide*'s. I point to the red rectangle with white letters—the *TV Guide* logo—displayed all over the cardboard trivia game box that I bring to class on that first day. That simple logo is like magic. It transforms what otherwise would be Bob's Trivia Game to something that *TV Guide*'s 17 million subscribers will recognize and many of them will trust. That simple logo gives the retail buyers who will decide whether to put the game on the shelf the confidence that it will sell. It could be the same cardboard box full of the same plastic pieces and the same booklets of the same trivia questions. But that simple logo reduces searching costs for all the retail buyers and consumers who will recognize the *TV Guide* brand. In leveraging that established *TV Guide* brand, Bob is able to scale his venture far more quickly and efficiently than if he had had to invest resources in building his own brand.

Chinese Milk Whey

The first time I was invited to teach in China, it was at a university in Zhengzhou, which had been described to me as a small college town. "How many people live in Zhengzhou?" I asked.

"Four million."

"What's a large college town?" I wondered.

Considering it was my first trip to China, my generous host, Yi Xie, invited me also to visit Beijing. She made sure I saw all the major sites: the National Museum, the Forbidden City, the Great Wall. And then a couple of days before I was heading home, Yi told me that the next day we were going to try a local delicacy called Chinese milk whey. Her description made it sound like . . . plain yogurt. I was game, and she offered to take me to try the most famous milk whey. But it would require getting up early; she would pick me up at my hotel, and we would have to fight the traffic across town to the oldest section of Beijing and wait in a long line. She said that the shop that made this very famous Chinese milk whey made only a limited amount on that one day a week, and when they ran out they would not have more until the following week.

I confess that at first I wasn't that excited to get up early to eat yogurt. But then a strange thing happened. As the day wore on, I got anxious. What if the alarm didn't go off? What if the taxi was late picking me up? What if we ran into more traffic than we had expected? What if the line was so long that this famous Chinese milk whey sold out?

The next morning I got up on time, Yi drove by and picked me up, we drove across town, and when we arrived, sure enough we found this long line of people waiting.

My heart sank, but when we got to the front of the line I saw this.

I don't know any Mandarin, so I wasn't sure what this said or what Wen Yu Cheese meant or what this cute little blue cow represented, but I spooned out a taste of this very famous Chinese milk whey. Sure enough it was . . . basically plain yogurt.

Yet somehow I felt a strange sense of satisfaction. I had traveled all this way, I had visited the National Museum, the Forbidden City, and the Great Wall. Now I could return to Providence and say that I had tried this very famous Chinese milk whey. Then as we started to move on, we began walking down the road, and right next door I saw this. It looked like a store that no one had been in for generations. Because I could not read what kind of store it was, I asked Yi what they sold there. She said, "Oh, they sell Chinese milk whey."

"Wait a minute," I pushed back. "What was all the fuss? Why did I have to wake up early, fight the traffic, wait in a long line for Wen Yu Cheese Chinese milk whey if we could have just bought it here?"

Yi paused for a moment and said, "I don't know what you call this phenomenon, but no one wants this store's milk whey, they only want the blue cow one!"

I had to laugh. It was all about obsessive loyalty to a brand.

We have all experienced that kind of power that the blue cow of Wen Yu Cheese held over consumers who wouldn't have even walked just next door to buy the alternative plain yogurt. That blue cow, like the red *TV Guide* logo, and like Stonyfield's brand in our country, turned plain yogurt into something different, something that caused consumers to rush to that old section of Beijing to wait in line, excited to sample that brand of plain yogurt before it sold out for that week.

Honest Tea Brand

One of the companies we study in class is Honest Tea. Founded in 1998, it has built up a strong loyalty for its all-natural teas. It was cofounded by Barry Nalebuff—an economics professor and prolific entrepreneur at Yale School of Management—and one of his students, Seth Goldman. I like their story because Seth and Barry had no prior beverage experience. Like the Casper founders, they found and addressed a consumer need that they had experienced as consumers, and through their Bottom-Up Research, not as professionals. My students often mention its powerful brand when discussing its Value Proposition. At that point, I open a bottle of Honest Tea, pour out its contents into a clear glass, and ask, "Which is the product?"

You might conclude that it's the tea in the glass. After all, that tea is what consumers purchase to quench their thirst. You might talk about

the brand represented on the bottle that motivates consumers to pull the product off the shelf in the first place. Of course, the truth is somewhere in the middle. As all marketing boils down to trial and loyalty, you might note that it is the brand represented on the bottle that may motivate consumers to try Honest Tea, and it is both the tea, which delivers a long list of benefits, and the brand itself that keep loyal Honest Tea consumers continuing to purchase the product. The brand reduces their searching costs.

Consider how you can embed branding elements into your Sustainability Model from the very beginning. In transforming an otherwise commodity product or service into something that others cannot replicate, brands can even become the most valuable part of those models. Let's face it, without the *TV Guide* brand, Bob's trivia game would be just a box full of plastic and cardboard, my student's Apple MacBook would be just a combination of computer chips and wires, Honest Tea would be just brown colored water, and Wen Yu Cheese milk whey would be just plain yogurt. As you create a Sustainability Model, think through what dramatic difference in your Value Proposition you can defend and amplify through your brand.

Why My Friend Howie's Dog No Longer Thinks He's a Moron

My good friend Howie is an expert online marketer. He has advised many startups I have been a part of, and he is the author of the best-selling *Ad Words for Dummies*. One of the principles of Howie's marketing expertise relates to the word I introduced in step 1 of *See, Solve, Scale*—empathy. Putting yourself in someone else's shoes is the most important basis for a successful branding campaign because it helps you to understand your customers' priorities and needs. Once you know those, you can appeal to your customers in their language and on their terms. One of the most effective short pieces that Howie has ever written about the importance of empathy in brand building is about his dog, Layla. Rather than trying to paraphrase Howie's teaching, I invited him to share it with you.

> For the last ten months, my dog, Layla, has thought that I'm a clueless, blubbering moron. I say "stay" when I mean "come," I say "jump" when I mean "lay down," and I say "nibble playfully at my

hand" when I mean "walk next to my knee in a dignified manner."

But I just finished reading a remarkable book about dog training that has turned my communication style completely around. Now Layla understands most of what I say the first time, and has begun treating me with a good deal more respect.

Next month, I hope to learn how to say in Doglish, "Stop dragging me down the street just because that studly bichon frise is peeing in his front yard."

What Does This Have to Do with Marketing?

In the old days of dog training, things were simple. The process had three steps:

1. Tell the dog what to do.
2. Hit the dog (or yank on its leash, or yell at it) if it disobeyed.
3. Praise the dog for doing it right.

Three problems with this approach:

1. The dogs were terrified of us, and spent more energy avoiding beatings than trying to please us.
2. The dogs had no idea what we wanted, because we had no way to lead them to correct behavior.
3. The dogs often became adversarial and dangerous.

As human beings advanced, we figured out that there was an easier, more effective way. We learned it from dolphin and falcon trainers, who couldn't very well punish their animals. They could train only with rewards.

So now Operant Conditioners (the most common school is "clicker training") mold their animals' behavior by giving them treats for desired behaviors, and withholding treats for other behaviors. So I treat Layla every time she sits. Pretty soon she walks right up to me and sits, hoping for a treat. So now I say the word "sit" every time she sits, and I give her a treat. After a while, I only treat her for sitting when I say the word "sit." Now I've accomplished the task: I've taught her the meaning of an English word, and that she should obey it.

Teaching Layla English

But Layla sees no reason to listen to me. Like I said, she thinks I'm an idiot. Here's why:

I'm spending hours a day trying to teach English to a dog.

I don't want to brag, but I believe that I'm more intelligent, linguistically, than Layla. I have a bigger brain. I have whole circuits devoted to symbolic language. I don't spend my free time climbing into the dishwasher and licking the dishes.

So why am I knocking myself out teaching her English, a language in which "slow up" and "slow down" have the same meaning? In which "commence" means to start and to finish? In which "cleave" means to cut apart and stick together?

It's because I didn't realize I could learn her language. But *The Other End of the Leash* has taught me the basics.

Howie Learns Doglish

Here's the first giant revelation: humans are primates. We, and our cousins the chimps and gorillas, communicate very differently from dogs and other canids (that's the fancy word I learned—it means, "dogs and wolves"). So we naturally "speak" primate to each other, and we understand primate very well. But when we speak primate to dogs, they think we're nuts.

For example, primates show dominance by making lots of noise. (I think of a chimp in a Jane Goodall documentary who discovered how to bang on oil drums and quickly became alpha male.) Dogs show dominance by their silence—it's usually the nervous/frightened/longing dog who's doing all the barking and howling.

Another example—primates like face-to-face contact when greeting. Eye contact, kissing, shaking hands, hugging—these are all variations on how humans, gorillas, chimps, and bonobos greet one another. Dogs and wolves, on the other hand, greet and acknowledge each other in a more sideways fashion, sniffing and nuzzling.

One last example—showing affection. Primates use their arms to show affection—holding hands, hugging, walking arm in arm, putting their arms on each other's shoulders. Canids use their forepaws in much the same way, but with a very different message: dominance. Putting your arm around your dog signals to her that you have a higher ranking than her, and therefore priority access to important resources.

So now when I want Layla to sit, or stay, or come, I use my body like a dog would. I lean, I use eye contact, I vary my cadences. And here's the absolutely mind-blowing thing: she obeys, without any training. She understands me, because I'm finally speaking her language.

Are You Marketing in You-lish or They-lish?

When I start marketing a product, I naturally start by talking to myself. I write sales copy that appeals to my values. I argue the price/value question in ways that I find convincing. I use layouts and pictures that affect me.

Bad Howie.

Unless my market is very much like me (which rarely happens, believe me), I'm going to fail.

I'm speaking Gorilla-ish to Dogs again. To me, I'm saying "Buy my stuff," but they hear, "Run away! I'm a dork."

I'm not going to succeed in teaching my prospects Howie-lish. If I want to communicate with them, I have to learn their language.

How Do I Go About Learning Their Language?

First, I do research. I read what they read. If they're online, I visit their websites and newsgroups. I see how others are successfully marketing to them. I find out as much as I can about how much money they make, where they live, how old they are, how many kids in college, etc. Basic demographics and psychographics.

I interview some of them. I find out what's on their minds. I try to sell them on the product and capture all their objections.

Next, I go through some thought exercises. I imagine myself living their lives, having their problems, dreaming their dreams. The art of marketing, at its core, is empathy.

Finally, I start writing like I would talk to them, knowing everything I know. I may not be perfect, but at least I'm no longer trying to speak Gorilla to a Dog. And when they sense that I've made the effort to bridge the gap and understand them, my prospects often take a step toward me as well.

When market research is too costly or time-consuming or impractical, I fall back on quick and dirty trial and error. I make two offers, and count which one gets a better response. That's my control. I keep that one, chuck the loser, and create a new one. Again, I keep the winner and replace the loser.

What I'm really doing, of course, is training myself, rather than trying to train my market.

And that's why Layla no longer thinks I'm a moron.

Now it's time to convince my kids.

Lifetime Value/Customer Acquisition Costs

As brands reduce searching costs, they reduce how much you have to spend to acquire an incremental customer. Brands also increase customer loyalty and command a price premium for your products. All of these factors increase an important ratio: Lifetime Value (LTV) to Customer Acquisition Costs (CAC). This compares how much value your venture derives from a customer for as long as they remain your customer with how much it costs to acquire that customer. As my former Specialized Systems and Software partner, venture capitalist Troy Henikoff, says, "if those 'unit economics' are profitable, you can repeat that process of acquiring profitable customers many times to become a profitable venture."[45]

These measures popped up and started to become popular when the data that eCommerce businesses generated made calculating them trivial. Even though it may be more challenging, all types of ventures should calculate these measures and analyze this LTV/CAC ratio. Although it varies a bit depending on the type of venture, a rule of thumb is that LTV should be at least three times the CAC. Today it is a requirement to understand this concept and to quote your LTV/CAC ratio to any prospective investor. A few years ago, my students who did so would impress the venture capitalists to whom they presented their class plans. Today, those same investors expect it.

Let me caution you about mistakes entrepreneurs make when calculating LTV/CAC. The most common one both Troy and I see is when entrepreneurs use lifetime *sales* when calculating Lifetime Value instead of a measure of product profitability called lifetime *contribution*. Sales do not equal value. You need to subtract the direct costs associated with generating those sales, such as the cost of manufacturing and delivering the product or service. Contribution is similar to gross profit, which is sales minus costs of goods sold at the company level. If your product or service does not have a positive contribution, no matter how many you sell or how inexpensively you acquire customers, you do not have a venture that is worth scaling.

A related second mistake is not remembering the adage that I shared in the ProfitLogic discussion above that a dollar today is worth more than a dollar tomorrow. That matters here because even if you do use profit to account for the value an incremental customer is generating, that value projected years down the line is not worth the same as the value generated today. An accurate account will "discount" future values back to today.

A third common mistake is using a "blended" or average customer acquisition cost. "Blended" is a big red flag because the venture may have attracted some of its initial customers for free, like from organic Google searches or word of mouth, which is not sustainable for scaling further. What matters is not the blended average costs to acquire initial customers, but what the next incremental customer will cost to acquire. Why? Because acquiring new customers may be one of the reasons you are proposing to raise additional resources. Why LTV/CAC matters is not because it tells us something about our history. What matters is how it guides our future intentions to scale for the long term.

Fourth, a blended Lifetime Value obscures the value of acquiring a customer by the "channel" or specific marketing approach. Here's a good example that Troy shared about one of his portfolio companies, EatStreet, a successful app for ordering food online. After Troy joined its board, EatStreet raised the "blended" red flag, proud of its average ratio of $50 LTV to $20 CAC (not quite three times, but close). After shuddering at the use of a blended average, Troy dug in deeper to discover something interesting. He examined one of EatStreet's biggest marketing promotions that was acquiring new customers by issuing a $10 pizza coupon when you signed up. Analyzing EatStreet's Lifetime Value by marketing channel helped its founders to discover that most of these new customers were college students who kept signing up with new emails just to get the $10 coupon. They did not stay past that first promotion and were therefore never profitable. Rather than $50, the Lifetime Value of these particular customers was $0!

So what did Troy advise EatStreet to do? Stop that promotion and fire these unprofitable customers. That's right. Even though this slowed down EatStreet's customer growth, it increased its profitability. Today, EatStreet is growing, it is profitable, and it is poised for an attractive exit because of it. Had they not understood LTV/CAC and Lifetime Value by channel, they could still be burning cash.[46] Arming yourself with this granular level of Lifetime Value analysis also enables you to reward your best customers with incentives to remain loyal to your products, increasing their Lifetime Value further.

Regardless of how you use this kind of Customer Acquisition and Lifetime Value data, the key for your purposes in Creating a Sustainability Model is how it emphasizes the word *Sustainability*. It's one thing to acquire customers who will buy something. Acquiring ones who will do so at a profit over the arc of their projected customer lifetimes is what enables you to scale your venture for the long term.

Is Shurgard a Sexy Venture?

Sometimes the extent of a venture's surface appeal can obscure how attractive it is. It may score high on the competitive metrics we just discussed in the last few sections—unfair competitive advantage, a valuable brand, and attractive Lifetime Value compared to its Customer Acquisition Costs, all of which enable high impact—and yet, it may still seem unattractive. Why is that and why is it dangerous to judge based on attractiveness? In the Managing the Growing Venture module of my courses, we study a self-storage facility business called Shurgard that is looking to expand to Europe in the late 1990s. At that time, Shurgard is twenty-five years old, has 980 employees, has 348 managed properties in twenty states, has dominated its industry in the United States, and has $159 million in revenue.[47] My students react to this company with muted enthusiasm. To my twentysomething students who are thirsting to start the next Casper, Premama, or RUNA, storage isn't sexy. I can always sense that, and at some point I pause and pose the provocative question: "Is this a sexy business?"

At first the students chuckle and are a bit taken aback, and then we start to dig in to the company's Value Proposition and Sustainability Model—the features and benefits it delivers to its tenants to address their unmet needs, how the company makes money, its cost structure, its balance sheet, how it funds its growth, and the key success factors that drive the business, among other details. A pretty impressive, if not sexy, pattern emerges: the company has tens of thousands of delighted tenants, 72 percent store-level profit margins; 80 percent occupancy (breakeven is 35 percent); low labor needs; a powerful and effective brand; low payment risk (tenants prepay and Shurgard holds a tenant's goods for security). Shurgard is what's called a Real Estate Investment Trust (REIT). That means that it is a public company whose stock trades on the stock exchange, and it can continue to fuel its growth by continuing to raise money through the public markets; and on and on. So is Shurgard, which on the surface builds and maintains pretty boring cinder block storage units, sexy? In the eyes of an entrepreneurial beholder, the answer for you may be, heck yeah!

I include this anecdote to remind you to avoid the trap of seeking surface sexiness. In fact, non-sexy sectors may offer more opportunities because the sexy-obsessed ignore them. So as long as it hits the four Ikigai criteria, look past the surface and apply the criteria you now know are essentials for a successful entrepreneurial venture—a Value Proposition that addresses a validated unmet need and a Sustainability Model that thinks big and has long-term impact at scale. Now that's sexy!

Doing Well by Doing Good

Do well by doing good.

—Benjamin Franklin

Never doubt that a small group of thoughtful, committed citizens can change the world. Indeed, it is the only thing that ever has.

—Margaret Mead

Aravind Eye Hospitals

Aravind Eye Hospitals[48] is a chain of eye hospitals in India whose founder, Dr. Venkataswamy, had a mission to cure blindness. What is most striking about Aravind is how profitable it is: 51 percent net profit margin, meaning that it still has half of its revenue after deducting all of its expenses! I have never seen another venture with a 51 percent net margin. A very robust net margin is 15 percent and in rare circumstances (like Apple and Google) around 20 percent. In addition to the most ambitious and meaningful Value Proposition of the organizations we study in class—to cure blindness—Aravind is the most profitable. It is the best example I know of Ben Franklin's adage to do well by doing good.

Toreva

The first time Gwen Mugodi visited me at our Center for Entrepreneurship, she told me she wasn't sure she belonged. She questioned whether a woman from Zimbabwe, and a student of Africana Studies and Literary Arts who wanted to improve the literacy rates in her country, would find potential collaborators at our center. She opened my eyes to the fact that even in this age when so many companies espouse a social agenda, many people still view entrepreneurship as synonymous with for-profit business. She was open to talking about it, and I explained how a process focused on solving consequential problems was as, if not more than, appropriate for people trying to fulfill basic human needs as for someone trying to anticipate the next board game craze.

Gwen joined our center's eight-week summer Breakthrough Lab accelerator program that provides funding, training, and mentorship for Brown and RISD students developing high-impact ventures. During that 2018 summer, she developed and launched her startup, Toreva, a nonprofit publisher that produces engaging storybooks that represent a diversity of African cultures, languages, and peoples. The unmet need that Gwen and her partner, Kelechukwu Udozorh, identified was a dearth of children's books written in African languages. That meant that many children in Gwen's country of Zimbabwe and other African countries never learned how to read. Gwen and Kelechukwu used Bottom-Up Research to find and validate that need and developed a solid Value Proposition to address it on a small scale.

But of course, doing good does not make you immune to the need to develop a Sustainability Model. While their first run of books found an avid readership, Gwen and Kelechukwu had not yet figured out Toreva's Sustainability Model. They faced significant challenges, including some that are particular to the context of their market. "When we started out, we had worked out that the cost of a book at US$12 was easily within reach for most parents as that was equivalent to ZWL$12. Because of the depreciation of the Zimbabwean dollar," Gwen noted, "that amount is now equivalent to $1,380 Zimbabwean dollars, but people's incomes haven't gone up to match. A teacher, for example, earns about ZWL$18,000. So most of our customers of late are within a certain income level, meaning we have fewer children who can access our books than we would like."

When I probed further about how Toreva would iterate in response to these challenges, Gwen went on to say,

> Obviously, our Sustainability Model has to change, and we've been trying to iron out the kinks. One idea we are pursuing now even more seriously because of the COVID-19 pandemic is how we can make use of animated videos with captions to help teach children how to read, to bring in income, while still meeting our core desire of making our stories accessible to all children.

———

As I have indicated a few times, I teach entrepreneurship as a methodology, not an ideology. As we have seen, this methodology is relevant in contexts ranging from Seeds of Peace fellowships to Don Operario's public health initiatives, from Chris Moore and Diane Lipscombe's brain research to RUNA's fair trade farmer engagement and energy drink startup. Just like I would resist labeling brain scientists Chris Moore and Diane Lipscombe's application of our process "neuro entrepreneurship," I resist labeling Aravind or Toreva as a special kind of entrepreneurship.

This broad application of entrepreneurship blends the many students interested in what some think of as "social entrepreneurship" into the mainstream of our center's students tackling a wide range of unmet needs. We do not treat "social" entrepreneurs as different from students tackling environmental challenges or linguistic challenges or culinary challenges or technical challenges or any others. They are all aspiring entrepreneurs, and they all come together at our center to tackle all of those challenges using the Entrepreneurial Process.

Dr. Venkataswamy of Aravind and Gwen of Toreva are good examples of entrepreneurs who are solving problems in their own home communities. Often, in contrast, students in my courses are tempted by what Courtney Martin calls "the reductive seduction of other people's problems." "If you're young, privileged, and interested in creating a life of meaning, of course you'd be attracted to solving problems that seem urgent and readily solvable."[49] One reason that Martin cautions well-intending problem solvers about this is the tendency that they have not done enough Bottom-Up Research to understand the complexity of these problems and are naive to think that they are easy to solve. Well-trodden paths to far-flung locations are littered with simple solutions that don't work. A shorthand way of describing this phenomenon is the white savior complex. The other caution is what I might call the "entrepreneur drain" of young talent that could be solving problems in their own backyards, whose complexity they can observe firsthand. Seeds of Peace Fellow Micah Hendler and Patrick Moynihan of the Haitian Project avoided these problems by becoming important and long-term members of the Israeli/Palestinian and Haitian communities they serve.

For-Profit or Nonprofit?

The Sustainability Model tools in this third step of *See, Solve, Scale* can empower for-profit businesses, nonprofit charities, grant-funded research, tax-funded government agencies, other entities, and even hybrids of all of these. In all of them you can do well by doing good. So how should you choose?

In 2019, Brian Moynihan (Patrick's brother), CEO of Bank of America who serves on our center's Advisory Council, framed this macro view of how for-profit Sustainability Models are necessary for solving the world's most pressing problems. "All the charity in the world is not enough to come close to making the progress we have to make on the sustainable development goals or on environmental [or other goals]," he said. "[There is] $800 billion a year in charity in the world, [and] we need maybe $5–$6 trillion a year. All the endowments and foundations, and they are wonderful people doing wonderful things, you could empty them all tomorrow and [that] still won't do it. The entire U.S. budget, $4 trillion, still can't do it. It takes the private sector to drive the change."[50]

If you are trying to decide between a for-profit and nonprofit model, consider the structural constraints that limit the scalable impact of a nonprofit and that favor for-profit ventures. Many of these constraints reflect the spending limitations donors place on things like salaries and branding. As a nonprofit, you will not be able to take the types of risk and tolerate failure in the ways that I discuss above. You may not have the same time horizons that achieving scale requires. And you will not have the same investment structures available.

Dan Pallotta, in his book *Uncharitable: How Restraints on Nonprofits Undermine Their Potential* [51] and his TED Talk "The Way We Think about Charity Is Dead Wrong," details five things that tend to limit nonprofits' ability to achieve long-term big scale. All five reveal friction that limits the ways that nonprofits answer that fundamental question of How. How are we going to follow through on the small-scale Value Proposition we developed to address the unmet needs we found and validated? How are we going to do so in ways that will build a sustainable venture and create long-term impact on a large scale?

This third step of *See, Solve, Scale* is arming you with tools that you can deploy when looking to scale. Sources of funding for nonprofits hold the entrepreneurs leading them to different standards, making it difficult for them to use these same tools. This comes from a movement to make nonprofits deliver more bang for the buck. That might sound sensible, but it has had unintended consequences. As Dan puts it:

In a nonprofit, because donors scrutinize overhead percentages,

- You can't use money to lure talent away from the for-profit sector.
- You can't advertise on anywhere near the scale the for-profit sector does to attract new customers.
- You can't take the kinds of risks in pursuit of those customers that the for-profit sector takes. In the humanitarian sector, risk is viewed not only as a flaw, but as unethical, immoral, sinful—criminal even. It's a near-religious belief that organizations must not risk donor funds intended for charitable purposes on some new endeavor that might lose money.[52]
- You don't have the same amount of time to find large-scale solutions as the for-profit sector allows.
- You don't have a stock market with which to fund any of this, even if you could do it in the first place.

Dan argues that these restrictions put the nonprofit sector at an extreme disadvantage. To illustrate the effects of what he calls "this separate rule book," he shares the following sobering statistic about how these rules have restricted nonprofits in language we would use in *See, Solve, Scale*, thinking big and getting big:

> From 1970 to 2009, the number of nonprofits that really grew, that crossed the $50 million annual revenue barrier, is 144. In the same time, the number of for-profits that crossed it is 46,136. So we're dealing with social problems that are massive in scale, and our organizations can't generate any scale.[53]

As we just saw in the examples of Chinese milk whey and Honest Tea, a critical approach to building a Sustainability Model that can have impact at scale is to develop and leverage the power of brands. Yet when we evaluate the efficiency and potential of problem solvers who designate their Sustainability Models as nonprofit, we tie their branding arms behind their backs, and we burden them and their potential supporters with unnecessary searching costs. As Dan observes:

This weekend the main sections of the *New York Times* and the *Daily News* contained big ads for Hummer, T-Mobile, AT&T, Macy's, Bloomingdales, and a host of electronics and furniture retailers . . . No ads on any of these pages for Darfur, ending AIDS, or curing breast cancer—indeed no ads for any 501(c)3. This is not an anomalous day. Gigantic consumer brands advertise. Gigantic causes don't . . . It's a testament to the dearth of advertising in the [nonprofit] sector that the I.R.S. Form 990 [which reports financial data about nonprofits] doesn't even have a specific line item for reporting it.

And why is this?

Donors consider paid advertising wasteful. "It's OK if you can get advertising donated, but I don't want my donations spent to buy advertising." (Imagine if we told Coca-Cola it could advertise, but only if it could get the ads donated—ads that would run at 2 in the morning.) The donor prejudice is that advertising spending steals from "the cause," so charities are loath to do it, for fear of donor reprisal. Meanwhile, Coca-Cola, which understands the power of advertising, is spending to indoctrinate us for life.

Dan and I are aligned in our desire to empower all problem solvers with the same entrepreneurship tools. Brands are an essential and accepted tool for building a Sustainability Model for, say, Chinese milk whey or Honest Tea. Yet overhead scrutinizers might deprive Penta—a 501(c)3 nonprofit that a former Brown student of mine, Trang Duong, launched to address the shortage of lower limb prosthetics in Vietnam—of those same powerful tools. If P&G uses advertising as well as any company ever has to turn commodities into brands that drive trial and loyalty and accrue long-term value, why would we prevent nonprofit problem solvers from deploying the same branding toolkit? Dan summarizes his sentiment well in his *Harvard Business Review* piece, "Why Nonprofits Should Invest More in Advertising":

The best way to create a world that works for everyone is to start doing the same thing Apple did to create a world in which everyone wants [its tech products]: start building demand for the idea on a massive scale. If the *New York Times* every morning were full of ads for ending AIDS, eradicating poverty, and curing cancer, those causes might just stand a chance against Bloomingdale's and Netflix. And make no mistake about it—that's who the competition is.[54]

I suppose we could overcome this friction by persuading our nonprofit supporters to treat us like for-profit ventures. True. Or we might form a for-profit entity in the first place. Either way, my main point here is as you look to scale, be aware of these forces that constrain the nonprofit Sustainability Model.

CHAPTER 7

STEP 3
SCALE: CREATE A SUSTAINABILITY MODEL—GROWING YOUR TEAM

As you scale your venture, your most important resource will be the additional team members you attract. In any problem-solving context—from a classic startup to an established corporation or nonprofit and even a research lab—entrepreneurship is a team sport. Alone, you are one person with one set of experiences, perspectives, and skills. Your team fills in the parts of the big picture that you or your initial founding team doesn't cover. Among the thousands of startup teams that Noam Wasserman, author of *The Founder's Dilemmas*, studied, only 16 percent were solo.[1] And David Beisel, Partner at NextView Ventures, reports that fewer than 5 percent of all the startups in which NextView invests began with a sole founder.[2] In scientific and corporate contexts, too, "teams increasingly dominate the frontier at which new creativity is taking place, and they're increasingly creating high-impact products."[3]

What may be surprising is that team formation and composition are so important that 65 percent of startups fail because of people tensions and team problems.[4] And who is on your team is so critical that a common adage among venture investors is "I'd rather invest in an 'A' team with a 'B' idea than a 'B' team with an 'A' idea."[5]

But what makes an A team? Because it is such a critical part of entrepreneurial success, I want you to know what contributes to a successful entrepreneurship team. I also want to warn you about a few common mistakes to avoid.

Teams whose members come from different backgrounds, contribute different skills, embrace different points of view, and draw on these differences develop breakthrough solutions. Alas, entrepreneurs tend not to form diverse teams. In fact, that is one of those unconscious biases that we need to become conscious of and overcome. To help you avoid making that same mistake, I will share strategies for how you can push through what seems to be a common resistance to doing so. I will also share characteristics of what I call the Team Composition Sweet Spot, the ideal composition of a successful entrepreneurship team. In the twenty-first century this ideal composition includes a balance of both human and digital resources. And finally, I will help you see that benefiting from the addition of new team members requires more than checking a diversity box. It requires looking beyond what all members have in common to leveraging the full extent of what every member brings to the team.

Diverse Venture Teams Are More Successful

The best possible time to start being mindful about diversity is time to equal zero, when you're just starting; starting a new company; starting a new team; starting a new project. The next best time is now.[6]
—Dharmesh Shah, HubSpot cofounder

Creative Abrasion

Not all teams are created equal, and it turns out that diverse teams enjoy more entrepreneurial success. That should not surprise us as diversity is a benefit in many contexts. We can look to biodiversity in nature as a compelling analog for the benefits of diversity in organizations, as "greater diversity leads to greater productivity in plant communities, greater nutrient retention in ecosystems and greater ecosystem stability."[7] The same is true in economies, as my Brown colleague, Oded Galor, and Quamrul Ashraf of Williams College argue that, "the interplay between cultural assimilation and cultural diffusion have played a significant role in giving rise to differential patterns of economic development across the globe."[8] As urban studies theorist Richard Florida interprets Galor's work: "Diversity spurs economic development and homogeneity slows it down."[9]

In entrepreneurship, it is important to avoid what Harvard Business

School professor Dorothy Leonard and Professor Walter Swap of Tufts University call a "chorus of monotones" of team members who are alike in training and attitude. Instead, managers should select as heterogeneous a group as possible, representing different experiences, thinking styles, cultures, and attitudes.[10,11]

Why is that? What exactly is the virtue of a diverse team? In short, it is based on the benefit of seeing the world differently. Complementary ingredients improve the taste of the "creative soup." *Creative abrasion* is my favorite way of describing what we are looking for from diverse teams. Coined by Jerry Hirshberg, founder and president of Nissan Design International,[12] Harvard Business School professor Linda Hill et al. define creative abrasion as "the ability to generate ideas through discourse and debate."[13]

I drive my family crazy with evidence of *See, Solve, Scale* everywhere I look, in some cases in unexpected places. In the movie, *Bohemian Rhapsody*, for example, Freddie Mercury of the band Queen recognizes this indispensable value of diversity when he apologizes to the rest of the band for having left them to strike out on his own. "I went to Munich, I hired a bunch of guys, I told them exactly what I wanted them to do, and the problem was . . . they did it. No push back from Roger, none of your rewrites, Brian, none of your funny looks, John. I need you. And you need me."[14] That is an example of the virtue of creative abrasion that I can relate to, and perhaps you can, too.

Linking back to my comments about the benefits of liberal arts, I often sense a lack of confidence in my own liberal arts students because they wonder what they, as say a history or philosophy concentrator, might offer a startup team. And then I have them read *Range: Why Generalists Triumph in a Specialized World*, in which David Epstein describes the benefits of incorporating diverse points of view, and especially those from people who don't feel like they are trained to do anything of specific value. Citing evidence from Northwestern sociologist Brian Uzzi, Epstein notes that successful teams tend to have members from different backgrounds. You may recall that this was my own experience as a history concentrator on the team of Clearview Software that we sold to Apple. In Uzzi's research, teams with more far-flung members, from different institutions, were more likely to be successful, . . . and teams that included members based in different countries had an advantage as well.[15]

If you are working in the corporate world, you will appreciate this diversity insight from Stephen Dunmore, CEO of North America Schools at Sodexo. He shared with the Harvard Business School alumni community what he describes as the most unexpected lesson he learned at HBS when he recounted the different strategies students used to form study groups. "The top performers came from the eclectic groups—those with both business-minded students and those coming from the arts, law, medicine and the military. These were students who respected each other's different backgrounds and ideas. They were the ones finding the creative solutions and innovative ways forward."[16] That lesson stuck with Stephen and throughout his career has influenced how he has managed groups looking to solve problems and develop new opportunities. "My company has won many awards for Diversity and Inclusion and many of us consider it Sodexo's greatest strength." he asserts. "Yes, it's the right thing to do, but it also drives creativity and innovation in developing customer solutions that are critical to our growth and competitiveness."

Diverse Personality Types and Working Styles

There's zero correlation between being the best talker and having the best ideas.[17]

—Susan Cain

As I mentioned in the Introduction there is no one personality type that tends to succeed in entrepreneurship. Not left-brain dominant or right-brain dominant. Not creative or analytical. Not any one Myers–Briggs personality type. That includes what for many is a surprise and for some a relief: there is no evidence that extroverts tend to succeed in entrepreneurship more than introverts. I emphasize this because the myth that there is such a personality type blocks many would-be entrepreneurs. I love seeing the relief on the faces of many of my introverted students when I hand them a copy of Susan Cain's *Quiet: The Power of Introverts in a World That Can't Stop Talking*. I also love sharing her conclusion that their preferred style of working through problems alone often helps introverts to contribute more to the overall creative objective of their team than if they forced themselves to adopt the approaches that extroverts prefer. Although entrepreneurship tends to be a team sport, the most successful startups create space for different work styles, and that includes alone, apart from the rest of the team.[18]

Cain refers to the research of psychologist Anders Ericsson who has studied how elite performers acquired their expertise. Describing what he calls "deliberate practice," Ericsson concludes that the key is not how much time they devote to developing and honing their skills but the fact that they do so in solitude. As Cain writes, "Deliberate practice is best conducted alone for several reasons. It takes intense concentration, and other people can be distracting." Citing a range of elite performers including Charles Darwin, Steve Wozniak, and Madeleine L'Engle (author of *A Wrinkle in Time*), Cain explains how all of them benefited from their ability to work in solitude.[19] Again, that often surprises many aspiring entrepreneurs who think that if successful solutions come from teams, all of the "in the trenches" work within the team needs to be done as a group.

If you're an extrovert, I hope it will expand your range of who you'd consider a valuable recruit to your team. And if you are an introvert, I hope this insight will raise your level of entrepreneurial confidence and encourage you to diversify your team by including extroverts.

Collisions Combine Different Skill Sets and Points of View

It is in Apple's DNA that technology alone is not enough—it's technology married with liberal arts, married with the humanities, that yields us the results that make our heart sing.

—Steve Jobs[20]

Brown is of course not the only university that emphasizes liberal arts. There are also plenty of other universities that have an open curriculum. In my teaching at other institutions around the world, however, I have learned that Brown does distinguish itself in its interdisciplinary academic culture. On many other campuses, it would be rare or even unheard of for a professor in the sciences to reach out even to another in a related scientific field, let alone to someone in the social sciences or humanities. At Brown, it would be odd if that did *not* happen. Researchers carrying their "chocolate" are always looking for those carrying their "peanut butter" knowing that the combination will taste even better. The great thing about our Center for Entrepreneurship is that we are not tied to a specific academic department. Instead, we are a connector, a hub that encourages collaborations. In doing so, I have witnessed and been part of many such collaborations that have demonstrated to me how powerful the combination of ideas from different perspectives can be in solving challenging problems.

There are lots of historical precedents for this collision phenomenon, and even precedents for how physical spaces can improve the odds of their happening. In *Where Good Ideas Come From*, Steven Johnson talks about how big ideas come from the collision of "smaller hunches." The history student in me likes Steven's reference to how Enlightenment coffeehouses and Parisian salons were fertile ground for the kinds of collisions that resulted in intellectual, political, economic, social, scientific breakthroughs. The entrepreneur in me loves his adage that "chance favors the connected mind."[21]

A more modern example of the same dynamic was at work in the mid-1970s Silicon Valley–based Homebrew Computer Club, the diverse membership of which launched the modern computer industry. It encapsulated what Walter Isaacson calls the "fusion between the counterculture and technology. It would become to the personal computer era something akin to what the Turk's Head coffeehouse was to the age of Dr. Johnson, a place where ideas were exchanged and disseminated."[22]

Like twenty-first-century Parisian salons, liberal arts schools in general, and Brown's open liberal arts curriculum in particular, encourage this kind of interdisciplinary collaboration. Our Center for Entrepreneurship provides a space where we encourage "accidental collisions." It brings students and faculty from different disciplines out of their academic silos. We encourage them to join forces as diverse teams to find and validate a wide range of unmet needs, to combine complementary points of view and skill sets to meet those needs, and to craft Sustainability Models that leverage insights from across disciplines. We are so intentional about this dynamic that I suppose we ought to call them "deliberate collisions."

One of our student ventures, EmboNet, for example, is developing a double-layered, pocketed mesh designed to capture and remove embolic debris from the blood of a cardiac bypass surgical patient, reducing stroke risk and cerebral injury. The most exciting thing for me about this winning student team and perhaps unexpected for many—even for the founders themselves—is that it involved a biomedical engineer teaming up with two medical students and a Rhode Island School of Design Textile graduate.

But living in a constant state of collisions can be counterproductive. Let me share another cautionary note from Susan Cain, this one about how many tend to design their workspaces and about what they imply or even enforce in terms of expectations about workstyles. Some 70 percent of Americans, Susan reports, now inhabit open-plan offices, in which no one has "a room of one's own." These "open-plan offices make workers hostile, insecure and distracted. They're also more likely to suffer from high blood pressure, stress, the flu and exhaustion. And people whose work is interrupted make 50 percent more mistakes and take twice as long to finish it."[23] Yikes!

In a seminal study about the effect of workspace on productivity known as the Coding War Games, Tom DeMarco and Timothy Lister compared the work of several hundred software coders at close to one hundred companies. What distinguished programmers at the top-performing companies wasn't greater experience or better pay. It was how much privacy, personal workspace, and freedom from interruption they enjoyed.[24] Here is how DeMarco and Lister put it in "Programmer Performance and the Effects of the Workplace":

> We concluded that the two groups work in significantly different environments. The top performers are in fairly generous space that manages to protect them from at least some distractions . . . The space is relatively pleasant and . . . people have relatively long periods of interrupt-free work. The bottom 25% work in tiny cubicles . . . The phones ring until answered and cannot be diverted . . . People are forced to work in short periods of time between interrupts.[25]

Cain's account of Apple's earliest days is instructive for how we might envision the right balance between leveraging the value of a diverse team while respecting the differences in workstyles and work environments the team members prefer: "The story of Apple's origin speaks to the power of collaboration. Mr. Wozniak would never have started Apple without Mr. Jobs. But it's also a story of solo spirit. If you look at how Mr. Wozniak got the work done—the sheer hard work of creating something from nothing—he did it alone. Late at night, all by himself."[26]

Digital Diversity

The Terminator's an infiltration unit. Part man, part machine. Underneath, it's a hyperalloy combat chassis, microprocessor-controlled, fully armored. Very tough ... But outside, it's living human tissue. Flesh, skin, hair ... blood. Grown for the cyborgs.[27]

—*The Terminator*

In encouraging you to form diverse teams, I am using diversity in a more expansive way than how diversity is defined in academic research and often in organizations that are recognizing its value. As leaders in those fields study and define it, I, too, encourage you to recruit cofounders and other members who bring gender, racial, and ethnic diversity to your team. As I have demonstrated, diverse venture teams also benefit from different skill sets and points of view. And soon I will share more detailed advice regarding how to recruit more diverse teams, common mistakes to avoid when you set out to do so, and even how diversity can backfire. Before we get there, I want to challenge you to expand your perspective of diversity even further by introducing a concept I call Digital Diversity, which includes computer and robotic members in your venture teams. Sometimes these digital additions have replaced human team members (e.g., robots in factories). Sometimes they work alongside, complement, and interact with human members as in the case of "cobots" (collaborative robots). Some cobots even become appended to a human to help nurses lift patients out of their beds.[28] Artificial intelligence (AI) is a software-based addition to many teams already, and it is gaining traction quickly.

None of us can predict what advances in artificial intelligence and robotics will bring, but as an entrepreneur, you at least need to be aware of these evolving trends. An optimistic view identifies an unprecedented degree of suprahuman diversity in which computers complement otherwise all-human teams. Dr. John Kelly, senior vice president of Cognitive Solutions at IBM Research and Solutions Portfolio, heralds this collaborative approach in *Smart Machines: IBM's Watson and the Era of Cognitive*

Computing: "By working in concert, humans and cognitive systems have the potential to dramatically improve and accelerate outcomes that matter to us and make life on earth more sustainable. This alliance of human and machine offers the promise of progress on a massive scale."

Former World Chess Champion Garry Kasparov demonstrated the benefit of this human/computer diversity in freestyle tournaments in which the most successful players combine their prowess and computer assistance. "Teams of human plus machine dominated even the strongest computers," Kasparov relates. "Human strategic guidance combined with the tactical acuity of a computer was overwhelming."[29] Citing other examples in finance, government regulation, and medical diagnostics, Kelly argues that the true potential of this human/computer diversity will be "realized by combining the data analytics and statistical reasoning of machines with uniquely human qualities, such as self-directed goals, common sense and ethical values."[30]

Even in the world of design, Carl Bass, former CEO of Autodesk, sees this evolving diversity as he acknowledges that we are moving toward a "collaboration of man and machine, because, with the computer's help, the designer is now able to understand the whole range of any system beyond what any human mind can comprehend on its own."[31]

Digital diversity is already improving surgical outcomes by pairing machines with surgeons. Across different fields of surgery, over five thousand daVinci Surgical Systems are in operating rooms, being used in one million surgeries every year. Dr. Ben Davies, for example, a professor of urology at the University of Pittsburgh School of Medicine, has been using daVinci Surgical Systems for the six to seven prostatectomies he's been doing every week for the past decade. Before daVinci Surgical Systems, when he operated on his own without robotic collaboration, this very invasive open procedure would be a challenge because the prostate gland is surrounded by sensitive parts of the body that need to be delicately dissected. Poor technique can result in a lot of blood loss. With the assistance of daVinci Surgical Systems, the doctor operates the precise controls while watching a feed from a camera set inside the patient. Blood loss is minuscule, Davies says.[32] This trend continues to grow, as Medtronic, one of the world's medical-device leaders, and Verb Surgical (a Johnson & Johnson and Google joint venture), are soon expected to enter the surgery robot market.

My former student (and fellow history major) Daniel Breyer is now an investor in cutting-edge technology ventures. Based on his experience, he reminds me that AI has the potential to unlock more creativity and autonomy. In the best of circumstances it can free us from repetitive tasks and provide more strategic agency.

There are some data to support this. In a research study by Oracle and Future Workplace, employees felt that robots are better at maintaining work schedules (34 percent), providing unbiased information (26 percent), problem-solving (29 percent), and managing a budget (26 percent). Supporting our hybrid diversity approach, workers said that while in general they trust robots more than managers, the top three tasks that managers can do better than robots are: understanding their feelings (45 percent), coaching them (33 percent), and creating a work culture (29 percent).[33]

At the same time, Daniel agrees that none of us should be naive enough to think that this leveraging of digital diversity will yield only positive results any more than leveraging any other kind of diverse team will. Artificial intelligence is already having significant impact on the present of work, and will have a profound impact on the future of work—and not all for the good. We need to be cautious and remember that "unchecked, unregulated and, at times, unwanted AI systems can amplify racism, sexism, ableism, and other forms of discrimination."[34] While I hope that you will deploy AI to develop solutions at scale that will repair the world, I know that any breakthrough methodology has the potential of being used otherwise. My point in identifying this evolving human/computer form of diversity is to help you think about new ways to form diverse teams as a source of entrepreneurial advantage. It is up to you how to deploy it. Remember, *See, Solve, Scale* is a methodology, not an ideology.

Family and Friends Founding Teams Are Less Stable

As I promised earlier, I want to share important caveats about team formation mistakes to avoid. The challenge with these is that they happen when we follow our intuition. One of them is that although it can feel natural to form a team with family or friends, doing so leads to teams that are less diverse and therefore less successful. Our intuition, our comfort, and even our fears and risk aversion can cause us to flock together with birds of a feather. We tend, therefore, to add team members who look and behave like we ourselves do. Again, that is hazardous because it leads to undiverse teams and lower success rates.

In Noam Wasserman's data set, for example, 40 percent of the founding teams included at least one set of cofounders who were "founding with friends," and 17.3 percent who were "founding with family." The problem with this trend is that, as you can imagine, family and friends tend to come from similar or even identical backgrounds. They often behave like each other, and, therefore, they may not form the types of diverse teams Linda Hill et al. prove are more successful. They are the example of a "chorus of monotones" mentioned above. What's more, as you can also imagine, friends and family members may tend to act in ways that protect those prior relationships and may not act in the best interests of the venture.

Beyond this homogeneity hazard, Wasserman's data demonstrate that cofounders who have prior social relationships are much less stable. Once they become professional relationships, these prior relationships are more likely to dissolve, and they do so far sooner than the relationships of cofounders who had prior professional relationships. Here is the real surprise: they also dissolve far sooner even than those who had no prior relationship.[35] In other words, you are more likely to be successful starting a venture with someone you do not know than you are with a friend or family member!

Other Homogeneous Teams Are Also Less Stable

Beyond family and friends, "people of the same gender or race and people of similar geographic origins, educational backgrounds, and functional experience are disproportionately likely to found companies together."[36] Part of that is a reflection of general societal tendencies. The idea that birds of a feather flock together is true. We tend to socialize, for example, and interact with others who look, pray, eat, and behave like ourselves. It is faster to form a team from a pool of potential cofounders whom we already know. It should not surprise us, therefore, that founding venture teams, without any special effort to do otherwise, tend to be homogeneous and do not benefit from the diversity we discuss above.

At the same time, we need to acknowledge that part of this tendency is a reflection of conscious sexism and racism. And an important and insidious part is that, even if it is a result of unconscious bias, this "cycle of sameness"[37] is part of what contributes to the deplorably low numbers of women and people of color in startups. As a white American male, I am certain that I have benefited from privilege throughout my career. I am, therefore, not qualified to speak for the women and people of color whom these tendencies have disadvantaged. I also don't want the subtitle of this book (*How Anyone Can Turn an Unsolved Problem into a Breakthrough Success*) to sound like it ignores the persistent barriers that women and people of color continue to face.[38] From my teaching around the world, I know that this statement is true. Anyone *can* in the sense that anyone can learn *See, Solve, Scale*. The field on which entrepreneurs from different backgrounds seek to apply it, however, is not level. For this part of step 3, I hope it is not naive of me to think that sharing the proven disadvantages of teams that lack diversity will make at least some founders more conscious of their bias and will motivate some of us to form more diverse teams. This is one diversity factor that as venture founders we have the power to control.

———

If you are working in a corporate environment, you may be interested to learn that in addition to being burdened by their abundant resources, corporate boards have a second blind spot. Or to put it in our language, on Seeing: Finding and Validating Unmet Needs. In their *Harvard Business Review* article, "Innovation Should Be a Top Priority for Boards. So Why Isn't It?" two Harvard researchers, J. Yo-Jud Cheng and Boris Groysberg, report on their survey of five thousand board members from around the world. They find that "innovation does not rank as a top strategic challenge for the majority of boards . . . [and] the widespread lack of board-level engagement in innovation processes could be a major blind spot and a potential liability."[39] That blind spot does not let them see! Why is that? Groysberg blames a lack of diversity for impeding a board's ability to be innovative. The backgrounds of board members "are often very homogeneous, and this is not really positioning boards to think outside of the box," Groysberg says. Recent research has backed that up, says Cheng. "So many directors are recruited through social networks and informal channels," she says. "Directors tend to recruit people similar to themselves, and our survey results suggest that many boards are not proactively evaluating potential gaps in their knowledge or addressing their shortcomings."[40]

CAUTION: HUMAN ERROR

More than half of venture teams are formed with friends and family, though research shows that those teams are less likely to succeed. Founding venture teams, without any special effort to do otherwise, tend to be homogeneous, and do not benefit from the diversity we discuss above.

Teams of Past Coworkers Are More Enduring

What about the performance of teams whose founders have already worked together? Here, too, Wasserman's data set is instructive, as he concludes that those ventures grow faster and are less likely to dissolve than those whose founders previously knew each other socially or were related to each other. To illustrate, he contrasts companies whose founders were close friends before founding the venture and whose friendship got in the way, with Ockham Technologies, whose founders had already worked together and managed various challenging issues, including equity splits.[41] I describe Ockham in more detail when I discuss team equity splits later.

When I reviewed the above conclusions from Wasserman's data regarding three cohorts—1) Previous collaborators 2) Teams who know each other as friends or family members 3) Strangers—it seemed reasonable that teams that included previous coworkers performed the best. What surprised me was that relative strangers performed better than the teams of friends or family. These are the averages that emerge from the data and do not mean that you should never form a team with a friend or family member. But knowing these trends will help you avoid simply going with the flow and doing what feels natural, because natural is not always right.

———

To overcome the natural homophily of entrepreneurial ventures, where over half of all startup teams are founded among friends and family,[42] I require all venture teams in my courses to maximize team diversity. I discourage friends from forming groups together, I encourage those who may have worked on another successful project together to form teams, and then I nudge together students who don't know each other. This effort has proven fruitful, as the most diverse teams—with gender and racial diversity, and whose members come from different backgrounds, study different academic disciplines, and have very different skills—have produced the most breakthrough Value Propositions to address the most significant unmet needs.

Every semester, several students from the Rhode Island School of Design join my class. RISD is one of the best design schools in the world, and its students often contribute different expertise and experience and a different way of looking at the world from my Brown students. In the Fanium example that I mentioned earlier, Alicia Lew, a talented RISD Industrial Design student, pitched a Brown math concentrator, Grant Gurtin, on a concept that she had been kicking around that was inspired by the success of the Farmville game app: What if we capitalized on the craze for collecting sports memorabilia and created a virtual sports memorabilia platform? Along with a team of three others (one studying development studies, one studying environmental studies and architecture, and one studying cognitive neural science and economics), they completed the business plan and at the end of the semester presented it to a venture capitalist. Grant and Alicia have both contributed as mentors through the years to subsequent teams in the course. As Grant notes regarding the way that their different skills complemented each other, "Working with Alicia elevated me as an entrepreneur and enhanced my creative skills. Prior to Danny's class I had never been exposed to someone with Alicia's deep ability and experience in product design. Her ability to visualize the product, combined with my analytical skills, enabled us to create a vision for a business far bigger than either of us could have as individuals." After the course ended, Grant recruited a diverse and talented team to launch Fanium, the first all mobile fantasy football game, which they ultimately sold to CBS Sports.

Looking back at his class experience and to the additional ventures he has started, Grant continues to emphasize the value of diversity:

> When forming a team, I always ensure that we have a diverse set of experiences, gender, age, skills, and background. Diversity is often discussed as only race or gender, but I like to think about it as bringing as many points of view to the table

as possible. I took the largest step in my career when, after the Fanium acquisition, I started work at CBS Sports and was put in a position to manage a far more diverse team, all of whose members were older than me. At first we clashed, but over time our different points of view made our products far better than they would have been otherwise.

Now also a frequent early-stage venture investor, Grant continues to look for the value of team diversity: "When investing, I always ask for the team formation story to determine what unique skills each person brings to the table. It is much more valuable to have three people who own three different domains, than three people with a similar toolbox."

The Team Composition Sweet Spot and the Strength of Weak Ties

If the collisions of diverse teams create the kind of *creative abrasion* that leads to breakthrough solutions, I want to share what I call the "sweet spot" or ideal composition of a diverse entrepreneurship team.

Research from Northwestern sociologist Brian Uzzi identifies the "sweet spot" for diverse team composition that leads to the kinds of scientific and creative breakthroughs that have the biggest impact. Uzzi's insight combines what we have already learned from Wasserman's three cohorts—1) Previous collaborators 2) Teams who know each other as friends or family members 3) Strangers—and Uzzi takes Wasserman's insights an important step further. He concludes that the most effective teams combine cohorts 1 and 3. They have some team members who have already succeeded together as well as a sprinkling of new members who both have less domain experience than the others and have not already worked with the other team members.

You may recall that, in the various entrepreneurial startups I have been part of, I have never been the domain expert. I was not one of the tech-savvy software developers at Clearview or Specialized Systems, nor a publishing expert at Getaways. Like Luke and Neil at Casper who were able to benefit from their scarcity of knowledge resources, I was able to ask the *Columbo* questions. I didn't know any better when I asked my Specialized Systems partners why we were not looking to install our systems at much larger clients; that naive question helped shift our team's focus to the much more lucrative Fortune 1000. When we were launching Getaways, I didn't know any better when I suggested to my colleagues who had publishing experience that we launch a multi-platform product, not just in print but also online. The sweet spot was a combination of industry experts and someone like me, whose lack of meaningful domain experience brought a different viewpoint to the team.

Just knowing about this sweet spot, however, is not enough. It may even beg the question of how we find venture teammates who we may not even know. These days, we might look to our online networks like Facebook or LinkedIn. Those networks on all of our devices provide quick, easy, and unprecedented access to lots of prospective team candidates. Here is the problem with this approach: the recommendation algorithms of Facebook and LinkedIn favor members with whom we already have what we might call "strong ties." Facebook's recommendation engine suggests would-be friends who are already connected a degree away as mutual friends. Linked-In does this, too, limiting those to whom we can "link in" to only second or third degree members of our current network.

Even if we do not know them, these "strong ties" are likely to have many of the same characteristics as our immediate contacts whom we do know, with whom we have worked before, and who may even have the same likes, dislikes, and areas of expertise as we do. Relying on Facebook or LinkedIn, therefore, puts us in the homophily trap that Wasserman warned us about. It is not the only strategy we should employ if we want to ensure a diverse team that includes new ideas, skills, perspectives, and approaches.

Instead, when we are looking to find and recruit a few team members with whom we have not already worked, who are not our friends or family, and as Uzzi suggests whom we do not even know, let me recommend what Stanford sociology professor Mark Granovetter calls "the strength of weak ties." In his seminal 1973 research article, Granovetter demonstrates that the best way to land a new job, access new information, or collaborate on a new idea is not through our close connections, but through our more distant acquaintances.[43] Granovetter characterizes developing weak ties as engaging in diffuse social networks, which leads to new connections,

perspectives, and unforeseen opportunities. In language you will recognize as similar to Wasserman's, here is how Malcolm Gladwell draws
on and reinforces Granovetter's original research in a *New Yorker* article
called "Six Degrees of Lois Weisberg":

> Weak ties tend to be more important than strong ties. Your
> friends, after all, occupy the same world that you do. They work
> with you, or live near you, and go to the same churches, schools,
> or parties. How much, then, do they know that you don't know?
> Mere acquaintances, on the other hand, are much more likely
> to know something that you don't.[44]

When looking to add diversity of all kinds to your team, the key to
achieving the Uzzi sweet spot is not to rely on what modern networking
platforms have trained us to do. Instead, we need to look beyond our "mutual friends" and our third-degree connections and leverage the strength
of our weak ties.

I suspect Noam Wasserman, Brian Uzzi, Linda Hill, Dorothy Leonard,
and maybe you, too, may like the way Gladwell reinforces this critical insight into effective venture team composition: "The most important people
in your life are, in certain critical realms, the people who aren't closest to
you, and the more people you know who aren't close to you, the stronger
your position becomes."[45]

It occurs to me that in writing this book, I have benefited from these
Uzzi sweet-spot forces. Even though my name is on the front cover, this
has by no means been a solo endeavor. I have benefited in many significant
ways from both close and distant collaborators, and I know the teaching
in this book is more effective because it has been a collaborative effort. The
content of the book reflects the perspectives of contributors from around
the globe, from Slovenia and Egypt to Zimbabwe and Israel to Rhode
Island and everywhere in between, and from experts in a wide range of
fields. Some are experienced entrepreneurs, while others have brought
new perspectives and different domain expertise (e.g., design, legal, political, writing) to this team. I have had previous successes with most of these
collaborators. And in line with Uzzi and Granovetter's seminal research, a
few of our team members (my agent and my editors, for example) are new
to our team, and even new to the field of entrepreneurship. As a proxy for

readers who might not recognize the jargon I am so used to using, they help make concepts more accessible. Their path to this team leveraged ties in my network that were weak, not strong.

When you are considering who is going to join you in your pursuit of an entrepreneurial opportunity, remember that team-based ventures tend to be more successful than solo ones, that diverse teams are more successful than homogenous ones, and that the "sweet spot" is a collaboration of both prior collaborators and new members.

⚠ CAUTION: HUMAN ERROR

To find and recruit team members, you may be tempted to mine your network of close contacts, yet you are better off tapping your weak ties more than your strong ones.

Diversity Without Inclusion Will Backfire

As necessary as diversity in venture teams is, it is not sufficient if you want your team to achieve entrepreneurial breakthroughs. This is because members of any team tend to default to focusing on areas of common expertise, where their skills and knowledge overlap. In the virtual memorabilia example above in which the math concentrator, Grant, teamed up with the RISD designer, Alicia, imagine if they had capitalized only on the skill areas where the two of them overlapped. I suppose that might have been in areas like numerically based design details, ignoring the wealth of skills each brought to the venture where they did not overlap.

It may surprise you to hear that if diverse teams do not draw on, leverage, or celebrate the differences of their team members, they perform *worse, not better* than homogeneous teams. As Frances Frei and Anne Morriss point out in "Begin With Trust," "diverse teams, by definition, have less common information readily available to them to use in collective decision-making."[46] That is why we hear a lot these days about one of diversity's counterparts—inclusion. The key to your team benefiting from its diversity is to make sure that you establish a dynamic of trust in which all team members feel comfortable sharing the full extent of their authentic experience and point of view.

This simple graphic from Frei and Morriss depicts the limitations of homogenous teams and the great promise (and potential pitfalls) of diverse teams, depending on whether they are inclusive. If the diverse team depicted on the left draws on only the knowledge and skills where the three members overlap in the middle, that team will benefit less from that shared knowledge than even the homogeneous team in the middle where the knowledge and skills overlap of its members is greater. Inclusive teams like the one depicted on the right draw on the knowledge and skills that its diverse members bring to the table.

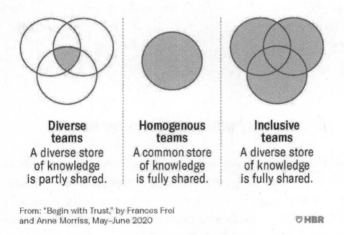

Diverse teams
A diverse store of knowledge is partly shared.

Homogenous teams
A common store of knowledge is fully shared.

Inclusive teams
A diverse store of knowledge is fully shared.

From: "Begin with Trust," by Frances Frei and Anne Morriss, May–June 2020   ☉HBR

Right in the first part of the title of their *Harvard Business Review* article, three directors of the NeuroLeadership Institute acknowledge what some of us might be feeling: "Diverse Teams Feel Less Comfortable." It's true. At first diverse teams can feel less comfortable than the "cozy" familiarity of homogenous teams. It's the second part of the title that we need to remember: "And That's Why They Perform Better." Pushing through that discomfort, embracing team diversity, and empowering everyone on the team to be authentic will yield better results.

Here is a quick example that illustrates what I mean. In a 2012 experiment, teams of three were asked to create a business plan for a theater. Diverse teams came up with better ideas than homogeneous teams—but only if they had been instructed to try to include the perspectives of their teammates. They had to push through their initial discomfort and embrace the differences of their team in order to benefit from them.[47]

⚠ CAUTION: HUMAN ERROR

Even in diverse teams, many focus on what they share in common, rather than leveraging the full range of diverse expertise and insight available.

When I first started teaching at Brown, we did not talk about diversity and inclusion as much as we do today (shame on us), and I had not been exposed to the research I cited earlier. It was my male and white privilege and unconscious bias that permitted me not even to notice when, in my early classes, most of my students looked like me. Because entrepreneurship appealed to so many different types of students across campus, I wanted to understand why fewer students of color and fewer women students took my course. To learn more, I met with a couple of experts at Brown who help faculty and staff learn more about diversity and inclusion issues.

The key issue this training helped me to understand was that many of the students of color and women students who were interested enough to attend class on the first day, did not return. In following up with some of them and especially being open with some of my alumni who are people of color and women, I learned an important inclusion lesson. The students who did not return did not feel overt hostility. Nonetheless, I had been sending subtle signals that this course was not for them. Bob Reiss, who I gushed about in that R&R case, is a white man. And I did not show the diverse group of other entrepreneurs we would be studying throughout the semester. Worse, because most of the students on that first day were white men, the few students of color and women looked around and concluded this course must not be for them. Some said even if they knew intellectually that was not the case, it was hard for them to push beyond that discomfort and stay.

The key insight was that I had to be deliberate about including them. And so I did two things that at first I worried would appear like window dressing. It turns out that they both have made women and students of color feel more welcome and included. I asked some of the women alumni and students of color alumni to share their thoughts about the impact the course had had on their professional and entrepreneurial trajectories. And I showed pictures of alumni that included these diverse alumni and their testimonials in slides at the very start of the first class, even as students were filing in (easier still as I taught over Zoom during the COVID-19 pandemic). I also compiled and showed a montage of pictures of the diverse entrepreneurs we would be studying throughout the rest of the semester. I made a point of being clear that because diversity was so central to entrepreneurial success, I had selected a diverse set of entrepreneurs for them to study. Neither approach hit anyone over the head, but both conveyed clearly at the very beginning of the first day of class that I welcomed a wide diversity of students to the course, that as this book states anyone can be an entrepreneur, and indeed that diversity would be the most important characteristic we would use when we formed class venture teams.

Since I began being more deliberate about inviting both diversity and inclusion, I have seen a significant increase in the numbers of diverse students enrolling in and sticking with the class.

Create a Dynamic, Not Static, Ownership Split

I can tell that a founder is inexperienced right away by how they navigate equity splits. It is by far the biggest red flag I see with new founders.
         —Daniel Breyer, venture capitalist

Few issues facing founding teams provoke as much anxiety as how to split the ownership of a new venture. Founders worry that they won't get a fair deal or won't be fair to their cofounders. They worry that because they don't have a crystal ball to predict what they and others will contribute over time, they don't know how to make a fair long-term split. They worry about what will happen if they or one of the founders decides to leave the venture. They worry that they are not versed in some "secret science" that will guide them how to make these ownership splits precise. For good reason, they worry that messing this up will turn off financial investors, both because the split will be untenable and because the investors will see these founders as unsophisticated. Most of all, they worry that even broaching these concerns might imply disloyalty to their cofounders or to the venture itself. After all, how would it look if, while you were making wedding plans, you broached the topic of divorce? One of the most common ways I see founders manage these anxieties is to ignore them. They procrastinate. They delay. That makes things worse as founders' perceptions of contribution and deserved ownership become more entrenched. That makes negotiating fair and objective splits even harder.

Before I illustrate this dynamic with a few examples, let me share what I advise is an indication of whether you've gotten this right. The most important outcome is that you achieve what I call "feel-good" splits. "Feel-good" means that you feel that the splits reasonably account for the value that you and your partners are contributing. Some of the factors that Noam Wasserman would advise you to consider include time, opportunity cost, past contributions, future contributions, and even fire in the belly. "Feel-good" splits will motivate you and your team to work hard to make the venture successful. If you were envisioning some kind of equity split science guiding you to make an airtight permanent split up front, this might surprise you. Well, let me break it to you. Splitting ownership equity is more art than science. Getting this right is less a reflection of whether the nominal percentage splits are ideal. Once you acknowledge that you cannot know up front all that will transpire over time, you need to bake into your agreement how your split might change once you learn more about who contributes what over time.

R&R's Feel-Good Equity Split

R&R, mentioned earlier, provides a good example of what I mean by a feel-good split. In that case, Bob Reiss recognized the trivia game opportunity in his travels to Canada and decided to apply his previous experience and engage his network of industry contacts to start a gaming venture in the United States. His cofounder and former collaborator from other ventures, Sam Kaplan, invested $50,000 and shared valuable supply-chain relationships, including with the company that would manufacture the game. Because the faddish nature of the gaming industry left only eighteen months to exploit this opportunity, Reiss and Kaplan could not afford to waste time negotiating the split. Because of the trust they had developed from their prior collaborations, they settled on a split that felt good and that would motivate both of them to work hard. They split the equity ownership fifty-fifty. Does this strike you as fair?

Some of my students, when asked this question, argue that Bob should have owned more: after all it was his idea that leveraged his years of experience and ability to recognize patterns in the way that games tended to migrate from Canada to the US. Others say that Kaplan should have owned more, given that he was the sole investor whose value-added contributions of relevant industry relationships enabled the venture to succeed. Most of the class tends to feel good about the even split given that Reiss and Kaplan each contributed what felt "spiritually" like comparable value. Students also recognize Noam Wasserman's insights about prior collaborators having a better chance of succeeding in a subsequent venture. And recognizing the futility of squandering months of a short product life cycle over a couple more percentage points, most see the wisdom in an entrepreneurship adage that we will discuss in greater detail below: it is better to own a smaller percentage of a bigger pie than a bigger percentage of a smaller one.

It is of course dangerous to extrapolate on the basis of one data point and conclude that equal-equity splits are always best. Each circumstance is different and demands a nuanced approach, and I never want to hear anyone say "Warshay advocates 50 percent/50 percent splits," because as you will soon see, sometimes I do and sometimes I don't.

More than the nominal percentage split, what I care about and what you should too is whether an initial split is written in stone or whether it responds to inevitable changes that no one can anticipate up front when you first commit to the split. One of the shocking insights that emerged from Noam Wasserman's data is that 73 percent of startups split equity within a month of founding, and in most cases those splits are permanent. In fact, while it is a good example of a feel-good split, the R&R split between Reiss and Kaplan is flawed, not because of its nominal 50 percent / 50 percent split, but because the split is static. To illustrate the harm this can cause, we'll look at two more examples—Zipcar and Ockham Technologies—that deal with equity split issues.

The Stupid Zipcar Handshake

In Zipcar, the two cofounders, Robin Chase and Antje Danielson, shake on splitting the company 50 percent/50 percent before ever working together, at the outset of the venture development process, and their agreement does not allow for any future factors to change that split. Chase quits her day job to work full time on Zipcar, while Danielson keeps her job, works on Zipcar only part time, and then stops working on it entirely. Without having any provision in their equity split agreement to accommodate Danielson's significant shift, Chase was stuck with their equal split. In a talk at Harvard Business School, Chase acknowledged her regret over not having a more dynamic agreement that would have adjusted in response to Danielson's change in plans. "We shook across the table 50/50 and I thought 'great!' That was a really stupid handshake because who knows what skill sets and what milestones and what achievements are going to be valuable as you move ahead. That first handshake caused a huge amount of angst over the next year and a half."[48]

Life happens. Founders get sick, they have children who demand changes in work/life balances, they get bored, they get excited about an alternative professional path. No one should judge these inevitable influences that will change the dynamic of founder commitments that no one could anticipate when the venture was getting started. At the same time, knowing that the circumstances surrounding the initial founding will change, it does not make sense to write an initial equity split in stone the way Chase and Danielson did.

Ockham's Dynamic Split

Ockham Technologies tells a different equity split story. Former colleagues Jim, Mike, and Ken team up to start a software company that addresses a sales force management need they perceived while working together at a consulting firm. One of the surprising details of this venture is that none of these founders has any programming experience. Their business insights into customer needs were what created value. With outsourced coding talent, they are able to sell IBM on the value of their

sales management software, and only months into the startup, they land
a million-dollar contract.

The key insight from Ockham for where we are in the process is that
the three founders create an initial unequal-equity split based on how
much money each invests in their initial $150,000 capital raise: Jim invests
$75,000 and has 50 percent, Mike invests $45,000 and has 30 percent, and
Ken, who is working only part-time on the venture, invests $30,000 and
has 20 percent. But their agreement is not set in stone. Rather than sticking with these early equity splits, their agreement indicates how the split
might change at the end of their first year of operation. Like Danielson
of Zipcar, Ken has not committed to working full-time on Ockham yet.
Part of this dynamic split, therefore, motivates Ken to become a full-time
founder and motivates Jim and Mike to continue to stay involved. Here is
an excerpt from their Shareholders Agreement as depicted in the Ockham
HBS case study:

1. 2.1 <u>Purchase Right of Founding Shareholders</u>.
   b. In the event any Founding Shareholder (a "Terminating Share-
      holder") ceases to perform services for the Company on or before
      April 19, 2000 [one year after the initial split] . . . , the remaining
      Founding Shareholders shall have the pro rata right to purchase
      some or all of the Shares held by such Terminating Shareholder . . .
   c. In the event Ken Burrows is not a full-time employee of the Com-
      pany by April 19, 2000, the other Founding Shareholders shall
      have the right . . . to purchase fifty percent (50%) of the Shares
      owned by Burrows . . .
4. 2.2 <u>Purchase Price Paid by Founding Shareholder(s).</u> The purchase price to be paid by the Founding Shareholder(s) for Shares
   purchased pursuant to Section 2.1(a) from a terminated Founding
   Shareholder shall be the price originally paid for such Shares by
   the terminating Shareholder.[49]

If Jim and Mike are still working at Ockham even part-time, they are
entitled to retain all of their equity, and the others would be able to purchase their shares only if they are not working at all. If Ken is not working
for Ockham at all, he, too, would have to surrender all of his equity, and
only in his case, if he is not working full-time, he would have to surrender

up to 50 percent of his equity. Note, too, that the price for surrendered equity is the original purchase price, which can be punitive if the company has made significant progress.

This solution to the Zipcar-type problems of a static split might have included other factors. The agreement looks out only one year, so what happens if and when things change beyond April 19, 2000? It uses that date as some kind of magical point in time to assess commitment. What about during the year leading up to that date? It uses a binary measure of full-time employment in Ken's case and part-time in Jim and Mike's as the sole measure of commitment and contribution which may miss other measures of value contributed. Nevertheless, in my experience, even a less-than-perfect attempt to adjust an original split based on new information learned over time can cure a lot of ills imposed by a static split. If Chase and Danielson, for example, had baked something like this into their agreement, it would have saved Chase a huge amount of heartache and preserved a significant amount of equity that Danielson retained even after leaving the company.

While I realize that it might feel comfortable to have the equity allocation "settled" with an initial permanent split, the market standard in the new venture world is to avoid static splits. The most common and often easiest way to bake in dynamism to an equity split is through vesting based on how long you have worked at the company—earning your equity over a period of time, rather than owning it outright at the outset. A typical vesting schedule is four years with a one-year cliff, which means that you do not retain any of your equity unless you remain at the company for at least a year. The above Ockham agreement is a form of this kind of cliff with April 19, 2000, as the one-year cliff date. In a typical agreement, at the one-year mark, you own 25 percent of your equity, at the two-year mark an additional 25 percent, at the three-year mark an additional 25 percent, and at the four-year mark you will own outright 100 percent of your promised equity. This time-based vesting mechanism alone, in which you outright own your equity only over time, helps to ensure that no one will walk away with equity that he or she did not earn.

Outside investors will compel you to include vesting provisions on the equity of all employees, including the original founders. It can come as a shock when a venture capitalist interested in investing tells you that you need to rewind and vest the equity in your company that you thought you already owned outright. But imagine an investor's point of view. What does he or she care about? Investors want to keep the equity in the hands of those whom the equity will motivate to stay and work hard. Although Zipcar recovered from Chase and Danielson's "really stupid handshake," it caused a huge amount of angst for Chase. And who knows how many investors their static split turned off. Unfortunately, many ventures that do not at least vest even their founder's equity are dead on arrival when they look to raise outside funding. As my former Brown student, venture capitalist Daniel Breyer, says: "It is by far the biggest red flag I see with new founders." Creating a static split makes it much harder to raise capital from outside investors. Creating a dynamic split from the start signals to investors that you are savvy founders.

Beyond vesting based on time, you can get as creative as you want, and just as Jim, Mike, and Ken at Ockham did, you can weave in other details like the terms of repurchase. At a minimum, I recommend creating a dynamic equity split through which you earn your equity ownership rather than the Zipcar-like static split that locks in how much you and your partners own, regardless of who does or does not remain involved in and committed to the venture.

I hear back from students who wish they had taken in the lessons of this discussion. Either they were not paying attention, or they had believed the nature of their partnership was different from that of the Zipcar founders and would never change.

Now their partner or partners had left or otherwise changed their commitments to the venture. They were stuck trying to negotiate out of this conflict, and there was no motivation for their partners to do so. Sometimes I am enlisted to help them untangle the situation. Trust me, you do not want to find yourself in that situation. It is hard to negotiate after it becomes a problem. The best time is at the outset when no one knows which side of a negotiation you or your partners may be on, when you have no idea yet who is leaving and who is staying. Everyone at the outset is motivated to create a fair dynamic agreement for everyone else.

You might think of this scenario like a prenuptial agreement. On one level it's a downer to anticipate divorce before you even walk down the aisle. But as humans, we change. You or your partner might have a problem in your personal lives, you might experience a health problem, you might suffer a personal tragedy, or you might just lose interest. One of you is likely to change your commitment to the venture. Gary Keller, founder of the largest real estate company in the world, labels this not an agreement, but a "disagreement" because "the only time you're going to read it is when you disagree."[50] At a minimum, vest your shares on the basis of time. That alone will save you painful headaches down the line.

This is a tough conversation, because as I say above, it envisions a time when the best-laid plans of founders may change and broaching this might imply disloyalty. In fact, it is so difficult that I recommend you do not try to do it without help. Ask a trusted adviser, mentor, or teacher to help you facilitate this discussion. Ask them to hold your collective feet to the fire and make sure that you follow through and talk this issue out, that you create a dynamic agreement. The small amount of discomfort you might feel up front about having this conversation and working out such an agreement will save you far more heartache later.

David Beisel of NextView Ventures has some excellent advice for how to manage this difficult conversation. He advises decoupling the part about the criteria you will use to determine the splits from the specific amounts of equity that each will receive. I like that advice because it frames the discussion in terms of earning equity, and it helps the founders step back, be more objective, and think about what is a fair approach for all of them.

Ideas Are Worthless

All the great ideas and visions in the world are worthless if they can't be implemented . . .

—Colin Powell

As you think through equity split criteria, and as I indicate above, some of the factors you could consider include time, opportunity cost, past contributions, future contributions, and even fire in the belly or how motivated someone is. Often, who thought of the idea is something that founding teams try to value. Let me break it to you: ideas alone are worthless. I have thoughts about new ideas in the shower and while walking to campus every day, and no one is prepared to pay me a dime for them. Nor should they. Maybe all of my ideas are bad ideas. Even if I think up some good ones, the three steps of *See, Solve, Scale* are about converting an idea into an opportunity. Before you begin to do so, ideas in isolation—without **Seeing** to find and validate the unmet need, **Solving** by developing a Value Proposition, and **Scaling** by creating a Sustainability Model—are worth nothing.

One of the reasons that ideas are worthless is that if you are thinking of something, you can assume that at least one other person has already thought of it. The early eighteenth-century mathematicians Newton and Leibniz each developed the idea of calculus, at roughly the same time. How could that possibly be? For all of human history no one had thought of a mathematical framework for measuring incremental change, and then two people came up with the idea at the same time? Yes. It was time for someone to think up calculus, and two people—if not many more who we do not even know of—thought of it.

You have probably heard of Charles Darwin and know that he is credited for having crafted the concept of natural selection as the basis for evolution. What you may not know is that Alfred Russel Wallace thought of the same idea at the same time, and some claim that others did so before Darwin. Just thinking of the idea of natural selection was in itself not valuable. Publishing accessible articles about it, popularizing it, applying it—in *See, Solve, Scale* terms, converting the idea into an opportunity by developing a Value Proposition and Sustainability Model—are the basis for why every middle school science student knows the name Darwin and not Wallace.

At this stage where you are forming teams and assessing the value of equity based on who brings various things to the table, be careful about assigning much value to the idea itself. As David Beisel of NextView Ventures puts it: "In general, successful startups are based on execution and not merely on an idea, so I personally attribute a small portion of the split to this factor."[51]

CHAPTER 8

STEP 3
SCALE: CREATE A SUSTAINABILITY MODEL
—RAISING FINANCIAL RESOURCES

As I began to think through this next chapter about raising financial resources, I paused, as I realized how varied the details are about how to provide those resources in different disciplines and different contexts. Grant funding in academic contexts has its own rules and idiosyncrasies. Nonprofits raise financial resources in other ways. Angel funding and venture capital, typical in high-growth technology ventures, have still different rules of the game. There are many other places accessible even via a simple Google search where you can dive in to access these details. Instead of duplicating them here, I will distill fundamental principles that apply to any entrepreneurial funding process and share those.

Founder's Dilemma

Noam Wasserman identified the fundamental dilemma that surfaces when entrepreneurs have to choose between continuing to control their venture and raising resources to help them scale. In short, to be rich or to remain queen or king. I argue that if you are not willing to cede at least some control to allow your venture to grow to the point that it will have long-term impact at scale, you are limiting its sustainability, and therefore you are not practicing entrepreneurship. Perhaps there are ways both to avoid bringing in investors and other partners, and to preserve control while still maximizing your venture's ability to grow. If so, I encourage you to pursue them. In my experience (and in Wasserman's), you need to choose between those two objectives.

This dilemma applies to other contexts, too. For example, when a re-searcher decides to apply for a grant, say from the National Institutes of Health (NIH), she has to be willing to cede some control over the course of her research. Part of the deal in applying for and then accepting NIH and other similar funding is that you accept their terms for how you con-duct yourself as an investigator, you agree to abide by ethical standards of research, you agree to publish the results of your research, and you accept many other terms. No one is forcing you as a researcher to accept NIH funding, but when you bring NIH in as a research partner and you accept its funding, you are no longer the exclusive queen of your research study. Most researchers would be overjoyed to accept that trade-off as they know that NIH funding and endorsements are critical for the kind of impact they are hoping their research will have.

One way we might view the open-source Sustainability Model mentioned above is as an extreme example of the Founder's Dilemma. In exchange for the contributions of many new developers who will help you move quickly to have long-term impact at scale, you agree to cede control over how the prod-uct gets developed and over who has the right to use your product. Imagine doing so even in the research context mentioned just above. Imagine ceding not only some control to NIH, but ceding control to the full, diverse com-munity of relevant researchers who collectively can contribute much more to the research and development process than you and your limited number of contributors ever could. We covered a version of that earlier in the lung cancer open innovation Topcoder.com contest. In short, imagine pursu-ing your research objective without regard to the resources you currently control—that is, as an entrepreneur. We also saw this Founder's Dilemma when Scott Friend realized that he did not have the right prior experience when the company needed to pivot its Sustainability Model to licensed soft-ware. Again, I will not preach about how much or how little control you ought to yield. As you create a long-term Sustainability Model, however, you ought at least to be knowledgeable about and weigh these various options.

Exit

Once you have opted for the "think big"/impact at scale/maximize re-turn approach that requires resources and support from outside investors, you will need to think about how you will exit your venture to allow your investors to recoup their initial investment plus a return. "But this is my baby. How can I bear to part with it?" Yes, that is a reasonable sentiment, and I would be surprised if any enthusiastic entrepreneur did not feel that. That, however, is one of the trade-offs inherent in the Founder's Dilemma. If you are looking to attract financial and other resources from outside investors as a vehicle for fueling your venture's growth, you need to provide a way for those investors to earn a return on their investment and to get their money out. In a for-profit startup, the primary way is through a merger or an acquisition (M&A); a rare way is through an initial public offering (IPO). In the case of grant or other funding, similar concepts apply in that whoever is stepping up to help support your venture will expect it to come to some form of conclusion. Having the mental discipline to realize that you do not have forever to succeed and that you will need to wrap it up in some form of conclusion like an exit is another example of the benefit of scarce resources. In this case, time is the scarce resource that disciplines our minds and focuses our actions toward achieving our objectives.

A Smaller Piece of a Larger Pie

Another way of considering the trade-off between having ultimate control and achieving long-term impact at scale, and an important corollary to thinking big, is that as you grow your venture and bring in investors, you will end up owning a smaller percentage of it. That is a more exact way of saying you will have less control. That is not something I am imposing on you here, if you are more interested in the being queen or king side of the Founder's Dilemma ledger. But it is a critical concept that you need to get used to if you want to be an entrepreneur and achieve impact at scale over the long term. Most savvy entrepreneurs who care about the personal benefit (e.g., getting rich) and the "having big impact" side of the Founder's Dilemma realize that it is not their percentage ownership that matters. It is the value of that ownership. When at exit you liquidate your piece, if you care about optimizing its value, who cares what percentage it represents? What you care about is how much it is worth. Put it this way, when you buy a share of IBM, what do you care about—the percentage of the company it represents? Of course not. You will never even try to figure that out. All you care about is that you buy low and sell high. I realize that there are many other details you will consider when you start and run a new venture. Just don't let yourself get wrapped around the "my percentage" axle.

Raise Time, Not Money

When raising financial resources, think in terms of months, not dollars. A good rule of thumb for an early-stage venture, for example, is to raise between twelve and eighteen months of what entrepreneurs call "additional runway." This additional runway should get your venture to the next fundable milestone. This is not a random point in time, but an inflection point at which you will have achieved something specific. That could be a technical milestone on your developmental path. Or on the business side, that could be a revenue-based milestone like your first paying customer. If all you do is envision more cash in your coffers, you are missing the point of staged financing—a concept covered in detail below. Envision that those additional financial resources buy you more time in which to achieve something valuable. Bill Sahlman from Harvard Business School expresses this mindset using the reverse of the old adage that time is money: in entrepreneurship, money is time.

Debt, Equity, and "Dequity"

There are many ways to structure raising financial resources, and I will discuss three of them briefly here. There are loads of resources online if you feel like learning more nuanced detail. Debt means a loan that is more short term since you have to pay it back. Equity means an investor buys part of your company and becomes your long-term partner. And a hybrid of the two (dequity?), which I will explain below, is a common funding mechanism for an early-stage venture.

When you raise money through debt, you borrow money, you promise to pay it back with interest in a defined period of time, and you pledge something valuable for collateral. For the lender, the risk is not being repaid. The benefit to them is the interest paid on the debt. In other words, debt limits the return for the lender to the interest on the debt, and collateral limits the lender's downside. That relationship tends to be time-limited. In debt language, there is a "term" that defines by when the debt has to be repaid. You might think of it as if you are renting money. Just like in renting an apartment, you expect to do so short term, you pay rent in the form of interest, and you pledge a form of security deposit called collateral.

When you raise money through equity, you do so by selling a portion of your venture, and in this case the risk/reward profile is reversed. You are not obligated to pay the investment back, but there is also no limit to the upside the investor can enjoy if the venture succeeds. Here, there is no "term" to define the length of the relationship. It is critical to remember that equity investors become your partner with many legal rights that determine how and to what extent they can call the shots that previously had been only yours to call. The Equity Term Sheet Concepts section later in this chapter covers these rights in more detail.

Convertible debt is a hybrid of debt and equity. It is a loan that the investor can opt to convert to equity in a future round of equity investment. And why has it been such a popular investment structure for early-stage financing? One reason is that it finesses the challenge of having to declare a valuation that an equity investment would require, which is often difficult to determine in early stages. Convertible debt allows you to wait until a future round of investing when a subsequent investor with experience and with more information will make valuing the venture easier. Documenting convertible debt is also easy and inexpensive. If you Google "convertible debt documents," you will find hundreds of examples of the few pages of standard documentation you can download. Equity, on the other hand, is complicated and expensive to document.

There are a couple of nuances to convertible debt that vary depending on the specific deal: a discount and a cap. To reward the convertible debt investors who are investing earlier and are therefore taking more risk, when they convert their debt into equity, they get a discount of typically 20 percent on the price of that equity. They also are able to convert their loan into equity at a predetermined maximum valuation (the "cap"), even if this valuation is lower than the market value at the time of conversion.

Imagine that we invested in a high-flying early-stage startup via convertible debt. We punt on setting a valuation and hold an option to convert our debt into equity at the next round of equity investment. Then, before we convert to equity, the startup takes off and its valuation goes through the roof. Even a 20 percent discount will not compensate us for the extra risk we took by investing earlier when the company was worth much less. To entice us to make that convertible debt investment today, therefore, we set a cap on valuation for when we decide later to convert. If, for example, we set a valuation cap of $6 million and the actual market valuation for the next equity round is $10 million, we convert our debt to equity as if the valuation were $6 million, plus we get our 20 percent discount. All the new investors in this round invest at the full $10 million valuation and they do not get the discount. Both of those sweeteners—a discount and a valuation cap—motivate us to invest earlier.

In reality, in convertible debt, the feature that would entitle the lender to receive their loan back in the case of default is a fiction. Because whatever collateral the company pledges could be worthless if the company goes under, it does not function in all the ways debt would in reality, even though it is structured as debt. In this way, convertible debt differs from a standard bank loan.

To avoid that fiction, a more transparent and direct way of structuring such a deal is what is called a Simple Agreement for Future Equity (SAFE). SAFEs were invented by the popular venture accelerator, Y Combinator, as a mechanism for structuring this early-stage investment without what they determined was unnecessary complexity and "wink, wink" fiction of convertible debt. You can read more detail about SAFEs and download SAFE documents on Y Combinator's website,[1] but for now think of a SAFE as a simpler version of convertible debt. And think of both as popular, simple and inexpensive vehicles for getting financial resources into an early-stage venture.

How E Ink Staged Its Financing to Mirror Its Venture Development

Why do entrepreneurs raise resources in stages? After all, in big companies, government, and nonprofits, proposals often seek full project funding and funding sources award them on a binary basis: they receive all of it or none of it. It has to do with how investors stage their investments to mirror the milestones of the venture's development. Doing so mitigates the risk investors take because they have limited information about how the future will unfold. Doing so also ensures discipline and drive in the management team. Because staging benefits both investors and founders, it ends up also aligning the interests of both.

We can see those benefits of staged investment play out in the E Ink venture and understand those benefits in detail. Twelve years before the creation of the Amazon Kindle, E Ink's "electronic ink" technology envisioned powering something called radio paper that would look, feel, and function like actual paper. Its inventor, Joe Jacobson, a physicist at the MIT Media Lab, identified the underlying need on a day when he brought the wrong book to the beach. His Value Proposition envisioned an electronic version that would allow him on the spot to choose a different book.[2] We all know that is what tablets now enable us to do, and as it happens, E Ink's technology is at the heart of the Kindle.

One of the primary themes of E Ink is a concept called a *critical path*, which describes the incremental steps that the company's development team takes to evolve its technology from a crude large-area display for large retail environments to a flat-panel display intended for consumers and ultimately envisioning radio paper. Each step demonstrates additional technological mastery, each step increases the likelihood that the company will reach its ultimate objective, and each step reveals additional information and reduces the risk associated with continuing along this path. Critical path is an essential concept in product development and a key part of creating a Sustainability Model with large and long-term impact. E Ink's large-area display demonstrates that on any level, the electronic ink technology will work, even on this large and crude scale that is nowhere near what it would need to be for the company's long-term goal of radio paper. If it does not work on this scale, there is no reason to continue to the next milestone—flat-panel displays—which would demonstrate a higher display resolution and more efficient power usage. Again, if E Ink cannot achieve these advances, there would be no reason to continue to the next milestone—Radio Paper—which would require among other advances, a flexible panel that feels and behaves more like paper. Those three product advances, in other words, are not random choices or even choices that have sales or other business appeal. They reflect the underlying developmental critical path.

In parallel, investors (venture capitalists in this case) see each step along this critical path as an experiment that will prove or disprove the company's ability to achieve these technological breakthroughs. On the basis of what each experiment proves, investors have an option to continue to fund the company or not. If not, they can try to harvest what has been developed to this point, or they can abandon. In poker terms, as additional cards are dealt revealing additional information, the players can choose to bet more or fold.

Consider these two scenarios. In one, we offer to invest the full $170 million that E Ink would need to develop radio paper over the next ten years. In the other, we invest in stages: $20 million to fund the first stage of the critical path: large area displays; then, only if the first stage experiment succeeds, we can opt to invest an additional $50 million to fund the next stage: flat-panel displays; and then, only if this second stage experiment succeeds, we can opt to invest an additional $100 million to fund the next stage: radio paper.

Imagine if we invested all $170 million up front and told Joe Jacobson and his team that we would see them in ten years. While there are always exceptions, people facing a shorter window and a need to prove progress are going to be much more motivated to work as hard as possible. This is another good example of the benefit of scarce resources. The scarcity of financial resources and also of time imposes discipline on the E Ink team to perform, or they will run out of money and not be able to attract more financing. That discipline benefits both the investor and the entrepreneur.

The staged approach also allocates reasonable amounts of equity to investors while preserving enough in founders to continue to motivate them to work hard. You measure how much an investor will own and how much is left for the existing shareholders through a simple calculation called pre- and post-money valuations. The pre-money valuation is the value of the venture before a new investment. Post-money valuation is the value after the new investment: pre-money valuation + new investment = post-money valuation. The percentage ownership the new investment represents = new investment/post-money valuation. And the percentage ownership of other shareholders = pre-money valuation/post-money valuation. At an early stage, an investor might look to own roughly 30 percent, leaving 70 percent to continue to motivate the founding team.

In the early days of E Ink, let's imagine the pre-money valuation was $1 million. If we invested all $170 million up front, that would mean the post-money valuation is $171 million, we new investors would own $170 million/$171 million or 99.4 percent of the company and that would leave only .6 percent for Joe and his team. Even if an investor were willing to make that $170 million bet without gaining additional information along the way, such a deal would leave only an infinitesimal amount of the company for the E Ink team. No founder would do that deal. And no investors would do that deal, either, because they want the team to continue to own a significant part of the company so it will be highly motivated to perform. With each successive stage of investment, if the team has succeeded in the previous stage, the value of the company will increase. That means that the percentage of the company the founders need to sell to investors will decrease and therefore the percentage they can retain for themselves will be much greater. In short, this staged approach aligns the interests of the investors who provide additional resources to the entrepreneurial team.

Large companies and other established organizations tend not to stage their investments in internal projects. Knight Ridder, for example, did not stage its investment approach to joining the internet. When Tony saw new entrepreneurial entrants like Google and Yahoo! eroding his most profitable advertising products, he went from being blasé about this new medium to seeing it as an existential threat: "If we don't get this right, we put the entire franchise at risk,"[3] he thought. In that panic, what does a large company do? It commits large resources in big bets, not incremental ones, to fight off the threat.

Earlier, before Knight Ridder begins to feel the pressure from its web-based competitors, Bob Ingle feels the freedom to fail fast and fail cheap, to run hundreds of inexpensive experiments, and to iterate with nobody even paying much attention. As we discussed earlier, this scarcity enabled Bob to get the newspaper online. In this next part, when Knight Ridder was feeling the heat of new competition, we see the opposite behavior. Tony and the senior leadership team expended significant resources to defend their turf, to sustain their fortress. They went from depriving Bob of resources to spending over $70 million in three years. That is an approach equivalent to giving the E Ink team the full amount it would need to develop radio paper. Or said another way, because Knight Ridder tried to solve its problem *with regard* to the resources currently controlled, its approach was not entrepreneurship. Staged financing is a Sustainability Model resourcing structure that disciplines us to behave as an entrepreneur.

What Makes an Investor a Good Fit?

We need to be discriminating in who we ask to become our venture's financial partner *because they will be our partner.* There are two important characteristics to look for in an investor: they will add value beyond the money they invest, and you will enjoy having them as a partner. As we discussed in the Growing Your Team section, a good partner makes us better—by sharing complementary areas of expertise, perspectives, and relationships. As in any realm of life, a bad partner can undermine our sense of purpose, distract us from our objective, and sap our enthusiasm. It is important that you want to spend time with this new partner because you will be spending a lot of time with them. It is a heady experience to have someone share and validate your passion for your enterprise, whatever it is. But that is not enough.

Value-added investors contribute value way beyond their capital. When Bob Reiss attracted his old friend and former partner, Sam Kaplan, to join him in the trivia game venture, it was clear that Kaplan fit that description. If you described Kaplan's role, you might rattle off a long list of things that Kaplan could contribute, like his connections, knowledge of printing, office space . . . and eventually you might say, "Oh, and he also wrote a check for $50,000." I love it when these insights unfold in that order, because that is the right priority when accounting for the value of what Kaplan contributes. Yes, he provides the financial capital, but his other contributions were far more valuable.

I remember learning firsthand these two characteristics of good investor fit when, as a newly minted venture capitalist, I made my first significant investment in an online vitamin startup called Greentree. In addition to our money, our firm, which specialized in consumer health products, could offer both relevant expertise and valuable connections. We were a value-added investor whose industry expertise and relationships meant more to Greentree than our capital. We weren't the biggest investor, and another larger firm was going to "lead the deal." That lead would negotiate the terms of the deal, do the investor due diligence, and invest a significant portion, if not the lion's share, of the deal.

The other characteristic—that we will enjoy partnering with the investor—became even clearer when one day Greentree's cofounder, Eric, spent a few hours with a prospective lead at a San Francisco Giants baseball game. After the game, Eric told me he had a hard time spending even those few hours with this prospective investor. He was abrasive and un-pleasant, and he didn't share Eric's interest in the vitamin industry. As much as we had hoped it would work out, I asked Eric if he found him hard to take at a baseball game, what was it going to be like in the trenches, at board meetings, and in other situations when the stress level rose? That became my baseball game investor litmus test. My Harvard Business School classmate Mike Troiano puts it this way: "Remember a typical VC relationship lasts longer than a typical marriage. It's important we both be excited about working together during the courtship, because it's rarely going to get more starry-eyed as reality intrudes on the romance."[4]

When Bill Stone—a Harvard Law grad, expert in venture capital financing and cofounder of an innovative law practice called Outside GC—teaches a class for my course, he asks the students to identify the most important term in a long and detailed venture capital term sheet. We spend over an hour diving in to esoteric concepts like anti-dilution protection, preferred stock, board composition, and dividends, all of which we will cover below. As the ending bell rings, Bill points to the most important term: the name of the venture capital firm at the top of the term sheet Cheatum Fund IV. In all the years having Bill come to teach this session, only one student has identified the name "Cheatum" as the most important part of the term sheet or even expressed concern over such a name. Yet, just as I advised Eric from Greentree, the partnership you create with your investors can make all the difference between a successful and unsuccessful outcome.

Investors of any type will do a ton of diligence on you. Don't you owe it to yourself to return the favor? Ask other companies in their portfolio what they are like as partners. Do they dive in to assist and earn the label of value-added investor? Be sure to speak with portfolio companies that did not succeed. Did the investor stand by them and try to add value even when the chips were down? Here is a piece of valuable advice from Rob Go, a partner and cofounder at NextView Ventures. When doing diligence on an investor, Rob advises digging in a little deeper than looking at an investor's current portfolio that you find online, "to see if there are com-panies that the VC has invested in that have since disappeared from their online profiles. Companies fall off a VC's profile when they fail or when something has gone wrong, and these are the founders you may want to speak to at some point in the process."[5]

If investors are going to be your partner, make sure you consider what that partnership will be like, and be sure to consider more than just their money when you evaluate with which investor you will want to partner.

Focus First on Finding a Lead Investor

At every stage of investment, there are two types of potential investors: leads, who have the ability to negotiate the terms of the deal with you, do the investor due diligence, and invest a significant portion, if not the lion's share, of the capital; and followers, who accept the terms and write a check. Even if they will add value and you will enjoy working with them, not all investors are capable of or interested in being a credible lead investor. Credible means that they have a good track record for making successful investments, and they know what the role of lead investor requires of them. Inexperienced entrepreneurs often make the mistake of assuming all potential investors are capable of leading, and waste time in the process. There is no reason to meet with or court followers until you have secured a credible lead. Once you have secured that lead, others will follow. If, for example, you are looking to fund a medically related humanitarian venture, the commitment of a lead funder like the Gates Foundation will more likely solidify the interest of other less known benefactors than the other way around. How do you know who is capable of or interested in leading? Ask them if they are. It is a reasonable and sophisticated question, and both leads and followers will appreciate your forthrightness.

Equity Term Sheet Concepts

Equity Term Sheets outline the deal that an investor is proposing to you in a few pages. They allow you to confirm that you are on the same page with the investor, so that you can digest and negotiate before you move to the much more detailed and complex legal documents that will formally record the deal. Because definitions of all the various terms in such a term sheet are only a Google search away, I will not cover them here. I will mention a few to illustrate how they tend to fall into two essential categories: control of the company and return to the investor.

Control

Preferred Stock: It is important to understand two different types of stock. The first is common stock, which is what founders and employees own, and which grants the holders a percentage ownership in the company, a proportional right to any dividends and liquidation proceeds, and a proportional voting right to elect the board of directors. Bill Stone of OutsideGC would call common stock "vanilla." Preferred stock is "Rocky Road" with many different flavored toppings. That is, preferred stock conveys all the same rights as common plus a long list of other rights: some that grant additional control in areas such as board representation and some that affect the potential financial return of their investment, such as dividends and priority in dividing the proceeds in an acquisition.

Voting Rights: Outside investors have a legal right to participate in shareholder votes.

Board: Investors also almost always hold seats on the board of directors.

Restrictions and Limitations: In addition to the above, investors also retain the right to restrict the behavior of the company with respect to a long list of important issues. This may surprise you if you think that control means owning > 50 percent of the company. That is not true. You could sell one share of preferred stock and give up control over a long list of important issues. Again in the spirit of the Founder's Dilemma, while not good or bad in the abstract, restrictions and limitations are things you need to consider when you decide to bring in new investors. To give you an appreciation for the detail, range, and extent of these limitations, here is that section right from a sample term sheet that Bill Stone shares with the students:

> So long as any shares of Series B Preferred Stock remain outstanding, the Company shall not, without the vote or written consent of at least a majority of the then outstanding Series B Preferred shareholders, take any action that would: (i) alter or change the rights, preferences or privileges of any series of Preferred Stock, (ii) authorize or issue any equity security senior to or on a parity with any series of Preferred Stock with respect to dividend rights, voting rights, redemption rights or liquidation preferences, (iii) amend or waive any provision of the

Company's Articles of Incorporation or By-laws in a manner that would alter or change the rights, preferences or privileges of any Preferred Stock, (iv) increase or decrease the authorized number of shares of Common or Preferred Stock, (v) result in the redemption or repurchase of any shares of Common Stock (other than pursuant to equity incentive agreements with service providers giving the Company the right to repurchase shares upon the termination of services), (vi) result in any merger, consolidation, or other corporate reorganization, or any transaction or series of transactions in which in excess of 50 percent of the Company's voting power is transferred or in which all or substantially all of the assets of the Company are sold, (vii) increase or decrease the authorized size of the Company's Board of Directors, except with the approval of the Board, including the Preferred Directors, (viii) result in the payment or declaration of any dividend on any shares of Common or Preferred Stock, (ix) issuance of debt in excess of $200,000, (x) result in a change in the Company's line of business; or (xi) creates or commits the Company to enter into a joint venture, licensing agreement, or exclusive marketing or other distribution agreement with respect to the Company's products, other than in the ordinary course of business.

CEO Search: One of the most surprising terms in a different section of this term sheet is the one that discusses the search for a new CEO. What more explicit illustration of the Founder's Dilemma might we imagine? Right in the term sheet of the deal, the investors are telling the founder that he or she will be replaced as CEO!

Return

Dividends: One of the ways that preferred equity investors lock in a financial return is through dividends—an annual amount of cash equal to a fixed percentage of the original investment, in the 8 percent range. Because investors are looking for *huge* returns, upward of ten times their investment, no investor is excited about 8 percent. But this keeps the company honest about their responsibility to deliver investors a return. One of the subtleties of dividends is that they come in two forms: cumulative and noncumulative. Noncumulative means that if they are not paid in any given year, they do not carry forward and accumulate. Cumulative dividends carry forward and accumulate, and even more, they compound. What looks like an innocuous 8 percent dividend over several years can build up to something much more significant.

Liquidation Preference: An even more significant way that preferred stock provides returns to investors is by providing a preference in how the spoils are divided upon liquidation. Liquidation, as Bill Stone clarifies, applies not only to the downside scenario when things go south and you have to sell off the assets of the venture. Liquidation can be great news when a venture is acquired or in the rarer case when it goes public. No matter the specific scenario, a liquidation preference allows the investors to take their investment back before anyone else—you as the founder, for example—gets theirs. In some cases, investors receive a multiple of their investment—2x, 3x, I've seen as high as 4x—back before anyone else. In these cases, investors have a choice: to receive their preferred return or to convert to common stock and share in the proceeds pro rata like any of the other shareholders. In other cases when the investment is characterized as "participating," investors get more than one bite of the apple: they first get their preferred return through their liquidation preference or even a multiple of liquidation preference, and then they also convert to common stock and share in the remaining proceeds pro rata.

Anti-dilution: Preferred investors get downside price protection. This means that if the venture ever sells stock in a future round of financing at a lower price, the anti-dilution provision kicks in and reprices these shares at that future lower price. How much the new financing affects the value of the earlier investors' stock depends on how the anti-dilution provision is written.

The Raising Financial Resources Dance

Raising financial resources can sometimes feel like a dance in which both partners are expected to know their steps. If either one tries to vary them too much, they will throw off the other and the dance itself.

As you have seen when finding and validating unmet needs and when developing a Value Proposition, there is a lot of room for getting creative. When you raise financial resources, because of the power imbalance between the founders and those with the resources, inexperienced entrepreneurs should err on the side of convention.

Remember the RUNA Ecuadorian energy drink venture? No team in my class has been more creative than RUNA in creating a range of Value Propositions to address both environmental and consumer needs. But when they began raising money, they sketched out some unconventional approaches that I thought might spook investors. I encouraged them to abide by what was tried and true. Reflecting the power imbalance I mention, RUNA needed the funding more than the investors needed RUNA. They agreed and did as good a job as any startup I have seen raising all of their original funding through successive rounds of convertible debt. When they later raised a formal equity round from venture capitalists, that early funding converted into equity.

How Honest Tea Broke the Rules

To study music, we must learn the rules. To create music, we must break them.

.—Nadia Boulanger, composer, conductor, and teacher

Damn the rules.

—John Coltrane, jazz musician

Just like in many fields, once you have experienced following the rules, there are times when it can be appropriate to break them. Think in terms of a musician who, after spending years mastering classical music, begins to improvise as a jazz musician. Some veteran entrepreneurs who have experience raising capital in conventional ways get creative and figure out ways to vary financing terms.

Consider the creative funding approaches of the founders of Honest Tea[6]—the venture I covered in the branding section earlier. At first blush, their approach seems conventional. When they launched the beverage company in 1998, Barry Nalebuff and Seth Goldman invested a total of

$300,000 of their own money, which they used to develop and refine their first tea products and secure Honest Tea's first distribution agreements. A little while later, to cover additional costs, they supplemented that initial infusion with $217,500 more from friends and family. In late 1998, they raised another round, this time from an unexpected source: enthusiastic and loyal Honest Tea customers who liked the products so much they approached the company about investing. Barry and Seth received commitments from these customers for $1.2 million.

A typical equity deal will set a valuation and an explicit share price so that investors know with certainty what share of the company they are getting for their money. Figuring out that valuation and share price involves a negotiation that begins with the investor proposing a valuation. The back-and-forth that follows revolves around how confident both sides are in their projections. Optimistic founders argue that they will hit their projections and will do as well as they say they will. Investors poke holes in those projections, arguing, for example, that the sales ramp is too optimistic. The investors have to take a leap of faith and trust the founders as they come to a resolution and arrive at a valuation and implied share price.

Barry and Seth tried a different approach, saying, "Don't trust us." Let's not set a firm ownership split based on what we imagine the future will hold, on what our projections predict, or on how we think the game will turn out. Let's instead wait to confirm ownership percentages until we see how things turn out, and only then, in retrospect, determine them. Why did Barry and Seth structure their deal that way? Well first, doing so finessed the awkward dance of having to set a valuation based on limited, anticipated information about the future that neither the founders nor the investors could predict. So why try? Similar to the way we said convertible debt punts on valuation, Barry and Seth structured their deal to do so as well. We don't need a crystal ball to predict the future. Let's arrive at the future first and then rather than projections, let's use the new information about what happened to confirm who owns what.

Second, and this is game theory in action, their approach demonstrates that Barry and Seth have so much confidence in their product that they are willing to take on more risk than a conventional investment structure would require of them. Through this approach, they are putting their ownership on the line. If they do not hit their projections, they surrender more of their company ownership. And if they exceed them, they surrender less.

In this case, investors do not have to trust that Barry and Seth will need to perform as promised. Barry and Seth have built in unconventional downside to not performing and upside to overachieving; and that dynamic will discipline and motivate them to perform more so than the typical valuation approach.

Do you see any potential downside to this approach? After all, why is this the exception and not the rule? How might this approach misalign the incentives of the investors with those of Barry and Seth? Can you imagine how that might happen? At least in the short term, opportunistic investors can capture more ownership if the company misses its projections. That is unlikely as the investors and founders alike all have much more to gain by pushing for long-term success than by trying to engineer near-term failure. In short, that is a dangerous game to play. It is tough enough in any early-stage venture to push in one direction and aim for success. It's ever so much tougher to pull for a short while in one direction and plan on turning on a dime in the other.

I have been reluctant to complicate my own investments with the kind of "pay for performance" terms that Barry and Seth baked into their deal. And investors are reluctant to misalign interests.

Nevertheless, after you have mastered and considered dancing to classical steps, in some circumstances, you might at least explore creative alternatives like Barry and Seth did. Even RUNA's founders, once they raised early funding through conventional convertible debt, varied their approach by creating a foundation in Ecuador that raised government grants. Sometimes those creative twists can bridge differences and get a deal done. Besides, all of the deal terms that we now consider conventional were at one point creative breakthroughs. Perhaps an approach you invent will one day become the norm.

Noodles and Franchising

Franchising illustrates several of the underlying entrepreneurship principles that we have covered throughout this book. It is a Sustainability Model that enables the franchisor to grow without regard to the resources it currently controls. It leverages financial resources of franchisees who as entrepreneurs invest their own money into each franchise. In turn, the franchisees leverage the resources of the franchisor, which has spent years finding and validating unmet needs, creating a Value Proposition, standardized operational systems, a strict company culture, and a recognized brand. Franchising is also another excellent example of the Geographic Follower entrepreneurship strategy that Bob Reiss followed to translate Trivial Pursuit's Canadian success to the US market.

Noodles & Company[7] is a fast casual restaurant chain that offers convenient, tasty, and affordable noodle dishes that draw on Asian, Mediterranean, and American cuisines. Its founder, Aaron Kennedy, a Pepsi marketing veteran, leaves his job after he does some Bottom-Up Research that reveals a restaurant market white space between fast food and sit-down and after he experiences an authentic noodles diner in New York City. In 1995, he develops an initial Value Proposition that draws on the dining value and authentic cuisine of that diner. And after a rocky start with his first three locations, he hones a Noodles & Company model that is worthy of expansion. By 2001, fueled by investments from wealthy individuals, Noodles & Company had grown to twenty-seven locations in several states and plans to expand to three hundred stores by 2006. As Aaron and his team look to scale over the long term, the key question they face is how. The key question facing Noodles & Company is whether to continue to grow through company owned units or to franchise.

When I introduce Noodles & Company to my students at Brown, I ask how many of the students wrote their college admissions essays describing how they had envisioned owning a restaurant franchise after they graduated. Few if any hands are raised. But franchising is an effective form of scaling that can be lucrative and efficient for both the franchisor and franchisee. One of the most striking entrepreneurial details of Noodles & Company's experience contrasts the financial resources that Noodles & Company requires to continue to grow through company-owned units ($80 million) versus what it requires to grow through franchising ($25 million)![8] And similar to Bob Reiss's outsourcing, which provided financial incentives to his partners, the franchising model would engage franchisees who have personal incentive to grow their businesses. As Geographic Followers, Noodles & Company franchisees who know their local markets better than the Noodles & Company franchisor identify appealing geographic locations to open new units. As entrepreneurs who invest their own money, Noodles & Company franchisees capitalize on resources they didn't invent and don't control: the fast casual restaurant concept, menu and recipes, standardized operational systems, company culture that produced an employee loyalty rate of two times the industry average, and the Noodles & Company restaurant brand. While there are some potential hazards of the franchising model such as entrusting the valuable brand Noodles & Company and its culture to franchisees who Aaron and his team do not control, these synergies clarify why franchising is a common Sustainability Model that many ventures deploy. For your purposes, if you are like most of my Brown students who would never have imagined it, I want it at least to be on your list of models to achieve scale over the long term.

Crowdfunding

Crowdfunding is a recent phenomenon that has proved an important resource for early-stage ventures. Similar to Open Source, which recruits members of the crowd to your team, and Open Innovation, which taps creative solutions from the crowd, crowdfunding taps its financial resources. Jon Margolick, a student in my first class back in 2006, proposed an online private company investment platform. He was enthusiastic about this idea, and like many entrepreneurial visionaries, he was proposing something a little before its time, as the regulatory environment was not ready for what he had conceived. Although still early, the regulatory environment has begun to catch up to Jon, and it is now possible to raise funds by selling equity through online platforms. At the start of our class on venture capital, we begin by having the students list the various sources of funding. Crowdfunding was not even on the list for the first few years. This past year, it was the first source that students listed.

The most common form of crowdfunding is through established platforms like Kickstarter or Indiegogo which provide an alternative to raising equity capital. Instead of selling shares of your venture, you sell early versions of your product or at least preorders. Raising money this way has significant advantages as well as some drawbacks. Advantages include how quickly you can raise funds compared to more conventional forms of funding. The early revenue you generate is "non-dilutive" compared to selling equity, as it does not decrease your ownership percentage. Like "walking around money," this early revenue adds credibility when you do want to raise investor money. Like users of a minimally viable product, these early customers can provide valuable feedback. The cash flow is attractive because customers pay in advance (remember the adage that a dollar today is worth more than a dollar tomorrow). And remember the loyal Honest Tea customers who invested in the company? These early customers can become loyal "investors" and continue to promote, evangelize, and support your venture over the long term. This is also a resource that established organizations can leverage when they are launching a new product.

To give you a sense of how mainstream and successful crowdfunding has become, consider the following stats:

- The global crowdfunding market size is expected to reach $114 billion by 2021 and continue to grow annually by 16 percent between 2020 and 2025.
- Successful crowdfunding campaigns raise an average of $33,430.
- Forty percent of crowdfunding investments are focused on business and entrepreneurship, while 20 percent focus on social causes.
- Kickstarter has helped orchestrate more than 185,400 successfully funded projects.
- GoFundMe, which is a platform for charitable causes, has raised more than $9 billion from 120+ million donations worldwide.[9]

Crowdfunding does have a few drawbacks. The application and qualification process for the big-name platforms is rigorous, time-consuming, and competitive. You should not count on being accepted. Once you are accepted, you have to generate your own marketing interest, which requires time, money, and expertise. On some platforms, if you do not hit a funding target threshold, you do not get to keep what has been pledged to that point. That kind of failure can tarnish your venture's reputation.[10]

As critical and fundamental as thinking big is, *How* is the word to remember more than any other from this chapter. Once you are thinking big, *How* is the basis of a Sustainability Model, and it is often where entrepreneurs of all kinds get tripped up. Even if they have found and identified a strong and enduring unmet need, they might focus on the wrong part of the value chain, as RUNA almost did. Despite overcoming hurdles that would have stymied most of us, even in scaling Pussyhat virally, Jayna might have focused only on the sustainability of this one project and missed the potential of her community of craftivists to scale other social and political movements. As Gwen from Toreva admits, she and her partner Kelechukwu have to iron out their Sustainability Model kinks if they want to have the long-term impact at the degree of scale they envision. Casper, which created monumental scale in short order, has lost much of its market value since it went public, as branding alone has not sustained a sufficient long-term competitive advantage.

Deciding when to build your own capacity and when to outsource, what kind of entity to form, and how to benefit from open-source resources; projecting how much it will cost to acquire a customer and building your brand to lower those costs; applying the standard rules of the raising financial resources "dance" and knowing when to improvise; failing your way to success—these are all ways you are now able to answer the question, "How are you going to deliver on the promise you articulated in your Value Proposition?" Most of all, you now know how your Value Proposition will address the problem you found and validated by having long-term impact at scale.

PART 3

Pitching

The single biggest problem in communication is the illusion that it has taken place.

—George Bernard Shaw

I grew up in Shaker Heights, Ohio—a suburb of Cleveland known for its commitment to public education. The city's motto, which most of us took for granted, was, "A community is known by the schools it keeps." Once, when the school system began to explore opening a magnet science school, some of the early planners approached my father, a chemical engineer at NASA, for his advice on what subjects to emphasize. His response, "Writing," took them by surprise. "No, sorry, you may not have heard us—this will be a science magnet school," the school officials clarified. "Yes, I know," my father replied. "Writing is the most important skill scientists can master, because no matter how much chemistry, physics, or biology students learn, if they cannot communicate what they have learned or discovered, none of that will matter." My father recounted that story dozens of times in my early years because he wanted me to understand that priority, too.

Effective written communication will allow you to pitch your venture in a way that clearly conveys your application of the three elements of *See, Solve, Scale*: what problem you have identified, how you are solving it, and how you plan to scale that solution over the long term. This is an area where a little bit of extra effort can allow you to separate yourself from the pack, because standard approaches lead many entrepreneurs to miss the mark.

CHAPTER 9

THREE RELATED PITCH DOCUMENTS

Entrepreneurs spend a great deal of time thinking about how to communicate—or in entrepreneurship lingo, to pitch—what they have discovered, formulated, and are proposing to do. These days, many entrepreneurs rely on pitch decks—a collection of beautiful slides that try to tell a story about their venture and how they intend to scale. And while they have visual appeal, pitch decks in many cases include too much information to pique someone's interest, but less information than is needed to solidify that interest.

In some cases entrepreneurs email pitch decks to potential investors or collaborators in the hope of spurring interest in their venture. But often, there isn't enough detail on the slides for the story to tell itself. In other cases, they use a pitch deck as the name suggests to "pitch" their idea in person, and in those cases, the slides have too much detail. The investors and others trying to absorb the pitch have trouble concentrating on both what is being said and what they are reading. In short, in these multiple contexts, pitch decks are too often "neither fish nor fowl."

Worse, pitch decks miss the polar ends of the communication process: the first parts of the courting stage, when you want something far less detailed to pique the interest of an investor or other collaborator; and the later stages that you hope you reach when an interested party wants much more detail than just what you initially shared. What do I propose instead? I recommend having three documents that serve different and related purposes: an Executive Summary, a longer-form Sustainability Plan, and a ten-slide presentation.

Executive Summary That Is Both Concise and Comprehensive

The first document you should create is a one-page Executive Summary that is both concise and comprehensive. *Concise*, in that it should be short—one page—to be respectful of the recipient's time; and *comprehensive*, in that it should in short form address all of the key elements of your plan. Although that may sound contradictory and a challenging balance to strike, we all can learn a lot from Mark Twain's addendum to a letter to a friend: "I didn't have time to write a short letter, so I wrote a long one instead." You might think of an Executive Summary as you would a résumé. In a job search, a résumé is not going to get you hired, but you hope in the initial stages it will get you noticed. Its purpose is to pique someone's interest in you to the point that they want to know more—perhaps in a meeting or interview, or through asking you for more detailed information.

While short, an Executive Summary should nevertheless be comprehensive. Again like a résumé, it should in abbreviated form contain all of the major themes on which you would expect to elaborate in a future discussion or in a future longer-form document. It requires anticipating the themes the reader would want to understand in order to assess whether it would be worth asking for more detail. Because, as you know, *See, Solve, Scale* applies to a wide range of problem types, the exact themes and content elements on each Executive Summary will vary. You begin by identifying the key elements in your pitch. In the case of Casper, this might have included how broken the mattress sales and distribution process was, the elements of the Casper solution, the Casper team, year-five sales projections, the customer acquisition strategy (perhaps including the lifetime value/cost of customer acquisition ratio), how much money they were seeking to raise, and eventual exit strategies.

In this one-page form, it can be easier to spot and rectify gaps, flaws, and redundancies than in a longer document. All the pieces of your puzzle are right in front of you.

For years, Bill Sahlman of Harvard Business School taught an effective framework for identifying the key concepts: People, Opportunity, Context and Deals (POCD). In his *Some Thoughts on Business Plans* that my students read for the very first day of my class, Sahlman emphasizes that the key to understanding a venture is based on fit, "which is defined as the degree to which [these four concepts] together influence the potential for success."[1] Students use POCD to evaluate and analyze ventures that we discuss in class, and then they apply this model to their own ventures. When they communicate their ventures, they do not outline these four concepts per se, but rather as broad categories under which more granular key concepts can be grouped.

Investor Guy Kawasaki's *Art of the Executive Summary* offers a complementary way of communicating that more granular progression of nine key concepts that will enable you to grab your reader's interest from the start and pitch enough detail about your venture that they will want to learn more.[2] Although you will vary the details, make sure you hit all these essential concepts, and while you might find these helpful reminders, do not use these headings or sections as-is in your summary.

The Grab: Right up front, grab the attention of the readers so that they will be interested enough to read further. Lead with a concise and compelling statement of your anticipated scaled solution to a big problem. It should be direct and specific (Imperfect fights food waste by sourcing ugly produce from farms and delivering it to customers' doors for about 30 percent less than grocery store prices), not abstract and conceptual (Imperfect's mission is to fight food waste). If you have recognizable team members, advisers, investors, strategic partners, or customers already on board, make sure to mention them here. Don't make investors wait six paragraphs to discover that you have impressive cofounders and advisers— they may never get that far. In the summary for its Series B investment, Imperfect would say right up front that Starbucks founder Howard Schultz's venture capital firm, Maveron, had already invested $14 million.

The Problem: Use your Bottom-Up Research to illustrate that you have firsthand, direct evidence of the strong and enduring unmet need you are planning to address. And better than telling it, show the pain your prospective customers are experiencing: the revenues they are forgoing, the unnecessary costs they are enduring, the friction in their process that is slowing them down, the narrow distribution or market reach they are suffering, the inefficiencies they are experiencing, or however you would identify and illustrate their pain. Don't confuse your statement of the problem with the size of the opportunity (see below). In Imperfect's case, the team could cite the Bottom-Up Research gathered while watching the apples being sorted that revealed the problem of 40 percent of fresh produce going to waste.

The Solution: Remember the three Value Proposition Questions: What are you offering? To whom? And most important, why will they care? Use familiar terms, and avoid acronyms. You might also clarify where you fit in the value chain or distribution channels—whom you work with in the ecosystem of your sector, and why they will be eager to work with you. If you have customers and revenues, make it clear. If not, clarify when you will. Imperfect would explain its direct sourcing of ugly produce from farmers who would otherwise be throwing it away, and its direct-to-consumer distribution for 30 percent less than grocery store prices. The Why here would also include the quantifiable environmental benefits, including one billion pounds of saved and sold food by 2030 and more than 20,000 tons of avoided carbon emissions by not having to produce, transport, and landfill that food. In Imperfect's case, it could even translate these environmental benefits into more relatable language: the equivalent to taking 2,800 cars off the road.[3]

The Opportunity: Spend a few more sentences quoting Top-Down Research to illustrate the basic market segmentation, size, growth, and dynamics—how many people or companies, how many dollars, how fast the growth, and what is driving the segment. You will be better off targeting a meaningful percentage of a well-defined, growing market than claiming a microscopic percentage of a huge, mature market. Remember to clarify your *addressable* market. So for example, don't claim you are addressing the $24 billion widget market, when you are addressing the $85 million market for specialized arc-widgets used in the emerging self-driving car sector. Make sure to source your research.

Imperfect could include the validating quote that I cited in the Introduction to pique the readers' interest in the size of problem that Ben and his team were looking to solve. As the Natural Resources Defense Council puts it, "if the United States went grocery shopping, we would leave the store with five bags, drop two in the parking lot, and leave them there. Seems crazy, but we do it every day."[4] And they would size the aggregate opportunity by indicating not just what percentage is wasted, but how many billions of pounds that equates to, and how many billions of dollars.

Your Competitive Advantage: No matter what you might think, you have competition. At a minimum, you compete with the current way of doing business. Most likely, there is a near competitor or a direct competitor that is about to emerge. Understand what your real, sustainable competitive advantage is, and state it. Remember, Bill Stone would encourage you to strive not only for a competitive advantage but for one that is so dramatically different that an investor would call it "unfair." A patent, which gives you a government-granted monopoly, a contract that locks in a proprietary supply of a scarce resource, a switching cost that makes it cost-prohibitive for your current customers to defect to a competitor—all of these are "unfair" and far more durable than a simple competitive advantage. Do not try to convince investors that your only competitive asset is your "first mover advantage." Here is where you need to articulate your unique benefits and advantages. You should be able to make this point in one or two sentences.

Imperfect would describe its "direct from the farm" model of sourcing its produce and its direct-to-consumer distribution. These supply and distribution differentiators add credibility to Imperfect's claim that they can sell their produce for 30 percent less than mainstream retail.

Sustainability Model: How are you going to generate revenues, and from whom? Why is your model leverageable and scalable? Why will it be capital efficient? What are the critical metrics on which you will be evaluated—customers, licenses, units, revenues, margin? Whatever the case, what impressive levels will you reach over the next few years? Imperfect would emphasize its attractive cost structure and profit margins of its direct sourcing and direct-to-consumer revenue model. Just as Luke Sherwin described the cash-flow virtues of Casper collecting the cash payments from its mattress customers well before it had to pay its suppliers, Imperfect could refer to similar capital efficiency benefits from its cash-flow model.

The Team: Why is your team qualified to succeed? Don't just abbreviate each founder's résumé; explain why the background of each team member matters. If you can, state the names of recognizable past employers and expect the reader to ask for a reference at any you mention. To substantiate the Imperfect team, Ben and his cofounders could cite advisers who were adding value through their impressive experience and the prior $14 million investment from Howard Schultz's venture capital firm, Maveron.

The Promise: When you are pitching to investors, your fundamental promise is that you are going to deliver huge returns. The only way you can do that is if you can achieve a level of success that far exceeds the capital required to do that. Your Summary Financial Projections should show that and be credible. You should show five years of revenues, expenses, losses/profits, cash, and number of employees. It might also make sense to show a key driver, such as the number of customers or units shipped. Imperfect would project year-five revenue of $100 million, positive profit margins, and millions of pounds of food saved to substantiate its environmental impact.

The Ask: Include how much funding you are raising, which is how much you need in order to reach the next major milestone. Indicate your estimate of when and how much you will be raising in future rounds, and your current expectation of when and how you will exit. For its Series B round, Imperfect would indicate that it is raising $30 million toward an eventual exit through an initial public offering or acquisition.

I am a stickler about one detail in any of your communication documents. Be sure to write your paragraph headings in your Executive Summary as conclusions that could stand on their own and that tell the story of the paragraph, rather than as generic placeholders (e.g., rather than "Exit," conclude something like "Recent Point of Care Device Acquisitions Validate Lucrative Exit Strategy"). Doing so will signal to readers what they should be gaining from the rest of the detail in that paragraph and doing so will connect the dots for them. Don't risk that the readers will conclude something different. Test the overall logic and flow by reading the paragraph headings together to see whether they alone can tell your story. Here is an example of the Executive Summary headings in last semester's Brown course from a team called Melior that solves retailer's disposable inventory problems and provides a platform for fast-fashion brands to eliminate textile waste.

84 percent of clothing ends up in landfills each year, and Melior's solution addresses both the fast-fashion retailer and Millennial/Gen Z consumer sources of the problem.

Consumers are looking for sustainable options that don't exist, retailers are faced with a logistical nightmare of offloading unsold inventory, and fashion waste is piling up.

Melior is capitalizing on consumer attitudes towards sustainability and retailers' methods of managing large inventories.

Our three-phase marketing strategy, focused on social media, will help us obtain customers and maintain organic growth. Our target market is Gen

Z and millennial fast-fashion consumers who want sustainable options.

Melior's business model is driven by secondhand apparel sales to a rapidly growing demographic and declining expenses supported by capital commitments towards operational improvement.

Melior's team has experience ranging from successfully founding sustainable startups, venture capital, finance, tech, and marketing, and our advisers have vast experience in fashion, reverse logistics, and start-up companies.

By dedicating the proposed investment of $3 million toward improving our logistical solution provided to retailers, we project to achieve $112 million in year-five revenues and an exit via IPO or acquisition.

Just like having a résumé, having handy a one-page Executive Summary will give you confidence that you can communicate with someone who expresses interest. Not having one will cause you to avoid putting yourself in a position where you can request a first meeting. Many of my alumni consider this valuable advice for communicating anything in any context. In the liberal arts tradition, this entrepreneurial skill is something that can benefit you in many different types of roles, not just in the traditional, classic startup business roles.

Sustainability Plan That Follows the Outline of the Executive Summary

You've written a brilliant Executive Summary and received requests for more information. Now you'll need your second tool, a fleshed out Sustainability Plan that follows the same logical flow and topics in more detail. If you have crafted an effective Executive Summary, the Sustainability Plan should write itself. The summary can function as an outline for the plan, even to the point that the paragraph headings that you have crafted can be carried over to section headings in the plan. A Sustainability Plan will help you detail the issues that your concise summary, or even a pitch deck, can only hint at. If you have piqued the interest of collaborators and investors, they will ask you for the type of detail that you will have available in this plan. If they do not, they are not serious. And if all you have available for them is a pitch deck, neither are you.

Ten Slides That Follow the Same Logical Flow

If your fleshed-out plan works in solidifying interest, the next step will be investor meetings. For these, you will need a third communication tool, created to scaffold a discussion with an investor—a group of ten slides once again following the logical flow and using the same headings as the earlier documents. Take a look at Guy Kawasaki's advice for an effective set of pitch slides as another quick guide.[5] These mirror the structure that Kawasaki shared in his Executive Summary guidance. Once a collaborator or investor expresses interest, use these slides to structure, frame, and scaffold an in-person discussion. Use them to illustrate, reinforce, and punctuate the key points you want to share. Be sure to make your headings conclusions—the same ones that you used for paragraph headings in the Executive Summary that carried through to the section headings in your Sustainability Plan. Note: Do not send your slides in advance of the meeting—that's what the first two documents were for.

Bill Stone of OutsideGC has some excellent advice based on the many investor presentations he's seen. "Slides should have very few words. They can be pictures depicting the problem or showing the solution. They can be screenshots of an app; a prototype sketch or photo; they can be a single number or word to emphasize during a live pitch. Because the Executive Summary and Sustainability Plan are available, no one needs a slide deck with a bunch of words." To put a fine point on this, marketing expert Seth Godin's rule of thumb is fewer than six words on any slide![6]

Because repetition is a valuable and effective rhetorical device, sharing your plan in these three different formats helps to communicate and reinforce the logic of what you are presenting. You have become an expert in what problem you are looking to solve and in how you intend to solve it. Show some empathy for your readers or listeners, and realize that it might take a few repetitions for them to understand the potential of what you are proposing. Because different sensory approaches will have different appeal, a succinct one-page text-based story will engage in some cases, and in others the graphics of your slides may carry the day. Remember, the key is to perfect your message first in short form in the Executive Summary, and only then to flesh out the Sustainability Plan and the ten slides.

One of the nuances of what Guy Kawasaki shares is his 10/20/30 rule: ten slides, twenty minutes, and thirty-point font. The thirty-point font rule is one that my twenty-year-old students never knew was important and my fifty-seven-year-old eyes appreciate!

Grant Gurtin, the founder of Fanium, whom we covered earlier, advises startups to follow Kawasaki's method. "Having had success as a founder, and now an active investor, I'm often asked about fundraising. The first thing I always do is walk startups through Guy Kawasaki's 10/20/30 method. It is incredible to me how often entrepreneurs of all ages/experience think 'more is more' when providing materials to potential investors. Investors are pitched thousands of opportunities, so the more concisely one can state why their venture presents a significant opportunity to make money and that the team can execute on it, the higher the probability of a successful outcome."

CHAPTER 10

PITCHING MISTAKES TO AVOID

Having seen common mistakes crop up in my roles as entrepreneur, investor, and teacher, I have created a cumulative list entitled *Pitching Mistakes to Avoid* that I update regularly. Reading this is a bit like having the answers to the test. Your plan will not be perfect. Just don't make these same mistakes—make new ones!

Take notes on feedback

One of the most egregious communication mistakes to avoid that presenting teams make is that, in the heat of the moment, they fail to take notes on feedback from the people they're pitching. That is a surefire way to alienate your audience and lose the value of feedback, often from those with much more experience than you.

Remember the ask

Whatever the purpose of your communication, remember to be clear about what you are asking of the recipient. It is amazing how many pitches do not state what the pitch is for. If you are pitching to an investor, you do need to indicate how much capital you are seeking. If you are submitting a grant application, be clear about what you are requesting. If you are trying to attract a member to your team, be explicit about whom you are asking to do what.

Raise, do not ask or hope for

This is a minor wording choice, but one that signals that you are sophisticated. You are *raising* $x million, not asking or hoping for.

Don't expect to get married on a first date

Shark Tank is *not* realistic. Except on TV, investors will of course not write you a check on the spot, grantors will not award the grant on the spot, and potential teammates will not join the team on the spot. What are you looking for them to do? You are looking to pique their interest enough to take a next step toward all of these things, and that next step is another meeting to talk about the plan in more detail or perhaps some due diligence on their part. In short, do not expect a marriage on a first date, expect another date.

Explain your numbers

Appending unexplained financial projections or other numbers in the back of the plan with no explanation is not effective. What matters are the logic and sophistication behind the numbers to illustrate the logic and sophistication of your thinking. You should not leave it up to the readers to figure that out for themselves. Anyone to whom you are pitching reads hundreds of plans and receives hundreds of pitches, and you need to lead them by the hand to what you want them to focus on. Otherwise, you risk their drawing conclusions and making inferences you had not intended. Instead of showing an impressive bump in revenues at an unexplained inflection point, for example, make sure to annotate with the cause of the sales increase.

Reference the biggest number

Too often plans reference a profit number as a measure of how big a venture will be. Investors measure the size of a company in terms of revenues ("It's a $175 million company" means it is doing $175 million in revenue), so do not confuse them by using any other measure. That is not to say that profit and other measures are not relevant. They are, but when using shorthand to indicate size and that you are thinking big, use the biggest number you can, which is the top-line (revenues in a business, the equivalent elsewhere), not the bottom-line (profits or net income).

Include details to make your plans real

"Make it real" has become a mantra in my courses. The more real you can make your plan the better. One way to do this is to draw from specific Bottom-Up Research examples. Instead of describing a hypothetical contract manufacturer you might use to make your product, for example, interview a few specific manufacturers and share the details of your conversations. Instead of describing your hypothetical intention to sell your products to Whole Foods, talk to a Whole Foods buyer or at least a local store manager and include the results in your plan. Can you make even a raw prototype along the lines of a minimally viable product? Going the extra step to include these types of real details often takes little extra time and effort. Doing so makes a significant difference in whether a reader or investor will consider your plan.

Do not forget that POCD starts with P

Remember, in Bill Sahlman's People, Opportunity, Context, Deal model, the most important area is the people. Young and inexperienced teams should supplement with experienced advisers. Doing so is not as challenging as it may look if you are sincere and professional about building those relationships. And doing so is one of the most important ways of making your plan real.

Most student teams develop at least a couple of these relationships over the course of a single semester, and these add enormous credibility during their venture capital presentations. Note that you should not refer to them as a *board* of advisers or as your advisory *board* since *board* implies things that you may not intend (e.g., fiduciary responsibility, permanence). Be sure to ask these advisers for permission to include them in the team section of your plan. There's nothing worse than when an investor follows up with one of them only to discover that they did not even realize they were such an adviser. And make sure not to list advisers like window dressing: clarify what each one has already contributed and will continue to contribute moving forward (e.g., credibility, access to other people, specific business or technical expertise). In your Executive Summary, Sustainability Plan, and presentations, to benefit from the credibility your team adds, include the team section close to the beginning. Remember that even more than an A idea, an A team is what investors will look for first.

Too little validation of problem/solution

There is no excuse for failing to conduct sufficient Bottom-Up Research. And too many plans do not discuss their research in enough detail. It is one thing for your team to assume that customers will like their product. And while research will not be decisive, it can often make the difference between someone taking you seriously and not.

Sprinkle, don't dump

Rather than dumping your research into one section, be strategic and sprinkle it throughout your Sustainability Plan and presentations. You almost cannot overdo it. One way to approach this is, every time you make a statement, back it up with research evidence (top-down and bottom-up).

Cash flow positive too soon

Many plans project break even and positive cash flow too soon. Most startups need to remain in the negative/investment phase much longer than you might expect. Often the size and success of a company is proportional to how much the company invests early on. Far from being concerned about your uses of cash in the early days of your venture, investors are more impressed with your understanding that it may take time and meaningful investment in R&D and marketing to develop and launch a significant venture.

Not enough "Why"

In general, plans do not have enough "Why." Answering the implied question on many topics demonstrates sophistication and thinking in your plan. For example, plans often claim that it is a good thing that this venture will be first, but nothing about why that is. It is sometimes not an advantage to be first, so more than saying so, you need to discuss why that is. Other examples include outsourcing or franchising. Why you decided to (or not to) tells a lot about your mastery of your plan. Indicating merely that you are or are not outsourcing does not convey mastery. Remember the Simon Sinek emphasis on Why over What.

The marketing budget is arbitrary and too small

Here, too, is a good example of not answering the implied Why questions. Why did you determine to spend this amount on marketing? Why is it adequate to penetrate the market to the extent you say you will? A common error on this topic is that the marketing budget stays flat as sales are projected to ramp. These two items are cause-and-effect (or why else would you spend money on marketing in the first place?). A good way to approach this topic is to find out what percentage of sales comparable ventures in your industry spend on marketing. You could do a lot worse than to project to spend at least similar percentages and more since you are going to be catching up. Doing that (e.g., "because Microsoft does it") would be a good example of at least the minimal type of thinking and sophistication you should communicate. Even better would be to devise a marketing strategy that outthinks the competition.

The balance sheet does not balance

Enough said.

Being too precise can make you look silly

Writing an early-stage Sustainability Plan is about setting a general course, not about precision. Quoting financial projection in cents, which I sometimes see, for example, is just silly.

Hair is not on fire

Too many plans suggest there is a "need" for their product or service and too often that is not the case. As I wrote earlier, someone whose hair is on fire needs a bucket of water. But too few plans describe the urgent scenario of selling buckets of water to people with burning hair. Be careful about overstating the need and, better yet, use Bottom-Up Research to search harder for these "burning" needs to address in the first place.

Revenues per employee are off

One of the tells that there is something wrong with your projections is a calculation of how much revenue the company is generating per employee. In round numbers, a manufacturing company should expect to generate $100,000 per employee and a software company might double that ($200,000 per employee). Now you might wonder: how the heck are you supposed to know that? The answer, like the amount you should spend on marketing, should follow norms for your industry, and those are available by examining how much your prospective competitors are spending. Through some quick online research, you can find out in a matter of minutes.

You do not indicate where you are in the process

Be sure to include a time line chart (and a graphical time line is easier to read than a table) that lists milestones hit and ones yet to be hit that you will use the reader's resources to hit. Make sure that you do not make today the first spot on the time line. Note the valuable achievements you have already accomplished before you got to this point of raising money.

No use of funds

Again, perhaps hard to believe, but too few plans outline the use of funds or other resources being raised. If you expect readers to take an interest in participating or contributing, be sure to tell them what you plan to do with those resources.

Claims are not sourced

Another one of those credibility things is being sure to source the claims in your plan, especially from your Top-Down and Bottom-Up Research. Too often, plans include unsubstantiated claims of things like market size, demand for a product, and other critical assumptions. If a plan lacks a source, the reader might as well assume your uncle told you.

Plans include valuation and ownership percentage details

It is very bad form to include these or other "term-sheet" details in your pitch. One of our venture capital guests gasped when one of our class teams presented their valuation assumptions in a detailed slide and said that when that happens in real life, she stops listening. It is the kiss of death to your credibility. As she said, the only answer you should give to the question of valuation is "we will let the market determine our valuation." That does not mean that you should not think through what you might expect your valuation to be. You should do a sanity check of your projections as an impetus to change them if they do not look sane. In short, you need to know whether the ownership and valuation numbers can work. But I will say it again: DO NOT INCLUDE THEM IN YOUR PITCH OR IN YOUR PLAN.

Do not waste the valuable real estate on your title page or first slide

Put a validating quote on the title page of your Sustainability Plan and first slide of your presentation to pique the interest of the investor and set a positive tone. This can be from someone credible you encountered in doing your Bottom-Up Research, or even someone you do not know from your Top-Down Research. Sometimes that slide will be up there for several minutes, so why waste it? Here is an example of such a quote on the cover page of a medical device company with which I am involved that will help diabetics prevent the onset of debilitating foot ulcers: "I marvel that society would pay a surgeon a large sum to remove a patient's leg but nothing to save it."—George Bernard Shaw

Always be closing

This famous line from *Glengarry Glen Ross* applies to Sustainability Plans. If you do not put contact information in your plan, how can anyone think you are serious about wanting them to contact you? Put it on the front cover to make it easy to find.

Tell 'em what you are going to tell 'em, tell 'em, and tell 'em what you told 'em

This old adage is a helpful guide for the overall structure of your presentation. Leverage the two serial position effects of primacy and recency (what you say first and last will be remembered most). Up front, insert a brief executive summary slide that outlines the three primary things you want the listeners to remember. (They will not remember more anyway.) In the end, circle back to emphasize these three points again with an ending summary slide.

Tell the punch line first, and then the joke

Because anyone listening will decide within the first thirty seconds of your presentation (if not sooner) whether they are interested, be sure to cut to the chase and share your long-term vision right away (e.g., we are building a 150-store $175 million herring national retail chain in a $3 billion market growing at 17 percent). And then circle back to flesh out the details. Too many presenters start with where they are today (e.g., "We are selling fish out of our basement"), and build to their long-term vision. By that time, you will have lost the listener, so be sure to start with the punchline.

Too many marketing tactical details

While the marketing plans tend to be the weakest sections of many plans, the solution is not to pile on lots of tactical details (e.g., what size ad in *Sports Illustrated* you plan to purchase in month 17). The reader is instead looking for the logic behind your thinking about how to acquire customers. There is a balance to strike here and you may need to be clear about some marketing and sales tactics, but not at the expense of being clear about the overall model. With that in mind, be explicit about customer acquisition versus lifetime value of that customer. If you cannot demonstrate that the lifetime value exceeds the cost of acquisition, you do not have a business. Remember, a good rule of thumb is that Lifetime Value should be at least three times Cost of Acquisition.

The 1 percent mistake

Many venture teams default to an argument that if they can penetrate just 1 percent of a huge market they will have an enormous business. I empathize with the tendency to do so: the logic goes that, if we can build a big business by penetrating only 1 percent of a huge market, imagine what we will look like if we are not quite as conservative. I cringe every time I hear that for several reasons. First, this 1 percent claim is like sticking your finger in the air to check the wind—1 percent is arbitrary and investors and others evaluating your opportunity will be looking for a Bottom-Up Research basis to these kinds of projections. Second, if you are proposing a breakthrough solution to a real problem that you have found and validated, why would only 1 percent of a market embrace it? And third, 1 percent of a market is not sustainable. No one will expect you to have a crystal ball, but think through the logic of whatever numbers you are proposing, and make sure they are Bottom-Up Research based and sustainable, not arbitrary.

No distinction between entry and expansion

It is not realistic to expect that your eventual growth strategies (including all elements of the plan, especially products and marketing) will be the same as those that launch the company. Too often, plans project growth over time based on the same initial entry strategy. Instead, you should distinguish between the characteristics of your entry and expansion strategies (e.g., What different resources will you need? What different markets will you look to penetrate? What different products or services will you launch?). As Harvard Business School professor Thales Teixeira puts it in "Turning One Thousand Customers into One Million," "Going from 1,000 to 1 million can be a fast ride—but only if companies are willing to shift their tactics to try something new. The strategies that incentivize early users to join are fundamentally different from those required to scale up."[1] By now, I hope you will notice that this concept is fundamental to the three steps in *See, Solve, Scale*. Developing a Sustainability Model is a different step that requires different skills, resources, and strategies from the step of developing a Value Proposition. When you communicate these steps, make sure you do so recognizing their distinctive differences.

Bake the cake before you frost it

This point expresses the above Lifetime Value/Customer Acquisition Cost concern with different emphasis: extraneous details obscure the fundamental economic model. Venture capitalists who have listened to our semester presentations have mentioned that the basic way the venture works, and makes money, is too often not clear. Before you pack the plan or presentation with too much executional detail of any kind, make sure you are crystal clear about the economic model. One example that VCs have raised in class to help clarify this point is a retail plan. While it is critical to think big, before you start to explain details about how you intend to build out 150 locations, make sure the economics of the first pilot location are compelling enough to warrant expansion. Too often, plans rush past these critical details about their entry plan. In a presentation, you might even pause and ask the listeners whether these granular economics are clear before moving on to expansion. This, too, should seem familiar by now. Said another way, make sure you clarify the Value Proposition before you try to explain the Sustainability Model.

Do not mix kasha with borscht

Okay, so that is how my grandmother Sadie would have said it. In this context, I mean do not try to make qualitative data look quantitative by including things like percentages (e.g., 75 percent of those to whom we spoke said they love our product). Bottom-Up Research that is the hallmark of this process relies on *qualitative,* not quantitative methods. Leverage those qualitative insights by quoting and "sprinkling" anecdotes that can have more impact than something sounding more quantitative.

Barriers to entry—you say that like it's a bad thing

Too often, plans and pitches use the phrase barriers to entry (BTE) incorrectly, citing them as what they have to overcome in order to enter a market. Those make barriers sound like a bad thing. On the contrary, barriers are obstacles you need to establish in order to prevent your eventual competitors from entering the market, and are therefore a good thing—indeed essential—to sustaining a successful business. A powerful barrier to entry is switching costs—ways in which you make it costly for your customers to switch to a competitor. Phone companies make these switching costs explicit when they charge you to break your contract. More creative are implicit costs such as Google Photos where you can store your photos and purchase copies. Once users have stored and organized all of their photos on Google Photos, there is an implied cost to switching to a different photo storage site. Be sure to think through what barriers you can establish in the wake of the market penetration you project. Do not rely on the obvious ones that cost significant investment dollars like patents. And be sure to use the correct meaning of the phrase, referring to the barriers that you *intend* to establish, not to the ones you need to overcome to enter the market.

Not all risks are created equal

Most plans I read have a section that details the risks that the venture will face. Not having such a section is a mistake in itself. Make sure also to address how you will overcome those risks. Even better is to group them into subcategories (e.g., operational, competitive, regulatory, financial), so that there is some logic to which ones you list where. To win the gold medal for this risks section, do what one team did in my Brown Spring 2020 class. They rated every risk on two measures: Likelihood and Impact. Doing that helps the investor understand how likely you think each risk is to occur and, if it does, how much impact it will have on your venture.

Do not promise the wrong kind of financial returns

Venture capital investors in particular do not want a venture to promise cash dividends. They are looking for capital gains by growing the biggest entity possible, and therefore want you to reinvest your profits into the venture rather than dividending them out to shareholders. The problem with projecting significant dividends is looking naive—it is better to understand what your investor prospects are looking for and project giving it to them.

Pigs get fat, hogs get slaughtered

If you are pitching a venture that has suppliers and different contributors throughout a distribution network, make sure that everyone throughout that value chain makes money—your suppliers, you, your distributors, retailers, etc. Too often plans promise high margins in their own financials, but inadequate margins for all of the others on whom the company will depend. It is critical that you provide enough incentive for everyone up and down the value chain, or you will not be able to motivate these key players to participate. Because it is sometimes difficult even for those writing the plan to see this need, I recommend you illustrate who is making what at each stage of the chain in one concise and clear chart. Be sure to benchmark each stage against standards in your particular industry to confirm that what you are proposing makes sense.

Order and stitching matter

Remember that all of your communication should illustrate a logical argument, and as such, the order of sections in the plan matters. Too often, the individual sections of plans read well, but the order or stitching is flawed. In some cases, that is because different people are writing different sections. An example is when financials do not relate to the other sections and are dumped into the plan—often too early and out of context. Stitching means the transitions from one section to another that help guide the reader through your argument.

Do not sell an aspirin before you conclude there's a headache

Or, be sure to demonstrate the pain before you propose a pain reliever. Entrepreneurs are by nature excited about their proposed solution—about their Value Proposition—and they should be. Proposing pain relief before you demonstrate the pain, however, is a plan for a solution in search of a problem. As another example of order, be sure to draw on your Top-Down and Bottom-Up Research to clarify and illustrate what problem you are solving before you propose the solution or describe the product.

Too many Cs in the C-Suite

Avoid fancy titles for everyone on your early team. Too many early-stage plans include them, and that makes the team look naive, grandiose, and top-heavy. Most startups have no need for a CEO, COO, CFO, CTO, and CMO. It is also likely that as you grow you will want to hire for some of those positions, and occupying them now may signal that you will be resistant to doing so when the time is right. Instead of assigning titles, you can describe the functional area of focus (e.g., marketing, finance, engineering). The one exception about which you should be clear is the CEO (or equivalent).

Co-CEO = No CEO

Regardless of what you call the position, you should be clear about which one person is the head of the team. This is sometimes tricky, but investors and other contributors expect that the buck will stop with one person—not a team of several. They will be looking for you to have figured this out before you approach them, not in the discussion with them. Sometimes teams try to squirm out of this decision by assigning the title co-CEO to more than one member of the team. Although this works in rare circumstances, investors want to see one person in charge. And in practice, co-CEO does mean no CEO.

Skin, but not muscle and bone in the game

Although I understand the potential "skin-in-the-game" appeal intended by taking no salaries, it is not reasonable to do so for longer than the pure startup phase. Once you have raised money, it is expected that you will be paying yourselves something, even if not market-based rates. If you do not, investors may worry how long you will be able to stick it out, and taking no salaries also does not reflect an accurate cost basis of what the venture needs separate from the participation of the founders.

When you want money, ask for advice

Bill Stone of OutsideGC reminds me that no one expects you to be an expert in everything, especially right at the start. So don't be afraid to ask questions and don't think you need all the answers. Asking an investor for advice about something she may know will communicate a lot of things: (a) you know the investor's background; (b) you value input and advice from others; (c) you don't pretend to know what you don't know; and (d) you know how to ask thoughtful questions. Asking for advice will also build good rapport and can lay the foundation for financial support in the future.

I hope sharing these most common mistakes will help you avoid them. You can access the current list and additional relevant content at dannywarshay.com.

CHAPTER 11

PERSUASIVE COMMUNICATION

Barbara Tannenbaum, a rock star professor at Brown, teaches one of the most popular and life-changing courses on campus: *Persuasive Communication*. I experienced the impact of that course (taught by a colleague of Barbara's named Nancy Dunbar) and cannot imagine now speaking so frequently in public without having taken it.

Back in the spring of 2006 when I taught my first Brown course, students delivered a practice pitch in advance of their longer pitch to venture capitalists. That was a good thing, because those pitches were terrible—not because of the content, which followed the format described above, but because the students did not know how to present. I panicked, realizing that in a matter of days those students were going to present their venture plans to venture capitalist friends of mine, and I did not want the students or me to be embarrassed. I went to see Barbara and asked whether she could help. She offered for one of her star Ph.D. students, Paige McGinley (now director of Graduate Studies for Theater and Performance Studies at Washington University in St. Louis), to lead a one-class session of Persuasive Communication, and it worked like magic. The pitches to VCs were fantastic—again not because the content changed much, but because they had learned and applied the fundamentals of doing a formal presentation.

Most of us are not born with the skill of persuasive communication. Worse, as many of you know, the fear of public speaking is acute and widespread. To be a successful entrepreneur, you have to overcome this fear and inexperience to master and apply the skill of pitching. The good news is that, just as with other critical elements of *See, Solve, Scale*, you can learn how to pitch well, too.

If the idea of Paige fitting in a semester's worth of Persuasive Communication guidance into one class session was a bit of a magic trick, even more is trying to do so here in a few written paragraphs, but at very least I can offer the fundamentals.

- All speaking is public speaking, as 90 percent of what you communicate is not in the content, but in how you look and how you sound
- Effective communication is goal-oriented and audience-centered
- Focusing yourself on what the audience cares about helps you achieve this effective communication

You Cannot Not Communicate, Because All Speaking Is Public Speaking

The bedrock of Barbara's approach is that we are always communicating, whether or not we are conscious of doing so. She loves starting every workshop and every course with the double negative that "we cannot not communicate." We can allow that communication to happen on autopilot, or we can do our best to control it. Barbara and her Ph.D. students focus most of their semester course and most of our one-session workshop on helping you do so.

Their first suggestion, which sounds simple and often is not easy to do, is to be organized. Make two to four main points (I recommend three), and repeat them two to four times (again, I recommend three: tell 'em what you are going to tell 'em, tell 'em, and then tell 'em what you told 'em). Stating what you want your audience to remember at the very beginning and then again at the end leverages two phenomena called the primacy and recency effects. We have the highest recall for what is stated first and then what is stated last, as we covered earlier.

Goal-Oriented/Audience-Centered

Leveraging Aristotle, Barbara advises that, before you do any type of communication, ask yourself, "What is my goal and with whom am I communicating?" and adjust yourself accordingly. Remember that we can change only one of these variables: our goal, not our audience. In our Value Proposition terms, you might think of the goal as the features of our presentation.

WIIFM

One way Barbara teaches us to be audience-centered is to remember this acronym, which stands for **W**hat's **In It For Me** (the audience). Doing so answers the question of why the audience should listen. It helps us convey the message and content that we are intending to communicate. It helps us persuade our audience to take the action we are intending for them to take. If our goal reflects the features of our presentation, think of WIIFM as the benefits. As Barbara says, "Your WIIFM can't come early enough or often enough." Don't assume that investors have a reason to listen to you. In the face of thousands of other investment opportunities, you need to give them a reason to listen to *you*, and you need to do so early and often.

Directing our focus to our audience helps us to stop obsessing about our own nervous state during our presentation. In my experience with students, this last point is a biggie. Many tend to be so anxious about their presentations that they focus too much on themselves and on just getting through it. Shifting your focus instead to your audience will help you to feel less anxious and help you to modify your technique based on how your audience is reacting.

Credibility

One of the strongest sources of persuasion is credibility. If WIIFM tells the audience members why they should listen, credibility tells them further why they should listen to *you*. As even the etymology of the word indicates (my high school Latin teacher, Dr. Strater, would have been happy that I am sharing that *credo* means "I believe"), credibility helps your audience to believe you. It is critical that you gain that credibility up front so that your audience believes what you say throughout the rest of your presentation. Too often, teams miss that opportunity by sharing the background of the team at the end rather than at the beginning. If teams include advisers and others with impressive backgrounds and experience, move that topic earlier in your presentation and earn that credibility right at the start. Remember also what I suggest about using that valuable real estate of the cover page or very first slide that your audience will be staring at while you are getting set up to present.

Build Common Ground When There Is a Hard Sell/ Opposition /Tension

One valuable source of credibility is establishing common ground with your audience. Present in terms of "we," not "I" or "you." Anytime you are tempted to say "I" or "you" see if you can change it to "we." When you are making a hard sell, when there will be opposition or even tension, it is helpful, even critical, to identify areas where you and your audience agree.

What: Extrinsic Credibility

Much of your credibility—the part that we call extrinsic—is *what* you have built over your lifetime. *What* you have studied, *what* you have learned through experience, and all of *what* you bring to your presentation and to your venture that will prove valuable. All of those should give you confidence as you present and all of those can work in your favor with your audience. It works best if you can establish extrinsic credibility even before you arrive. Work in those parts of your pedigree and background through prior communication and before you speak. If possible, have someone else brag about you in an introduction. I always share Barbara Tannenbaum's impressive background, experience, and recent teaching and consulting engagements when I introduce her so that by the time she begins to present, the class is impressed and views her as extrinsically credible.

How: Intrinsic Credibility: 60/30/10

If sources of extrinsic credibility precede your presentation, you can earn intrinsic credibility through the confidence you project during your presentation. To help you remember sources of this form of believability, let me share three numbers that I learned from Barbara that you will never forget: 60, 30, and 10. Any guesses about what these are? Well you might notice that they add up to 100. Percentages? Yes. Based on the research of psychologist Albert Mehrabian, who studied the importance of nonverbal communication in the 1970s, these percentages represent the relative impact of three different components of any presentation.[1, 2]

Because most students at a university assume that the lion's share of impact must come from the content they have spent weeks researching, developing, and honing, that must be the 60, right? Wrong. The 30? Wrong again. Even though we often spend all of our time and focus almost all of our effort on the content of our message, research shows that the content or the **what** represents only 10 percent of the impact of the presentation. That leaves 60 percent of the impact coming from "visual" or how we look. And 30 percent of the impact of our presentation comes from "vocal" or how we sound. That 90 percent represents **how** we present. The good news is that you can influence and even control visual impact and vocal impact and use them to project confidence and be more believable. Here are a few suggestions about how you can do so.

Visual

Barbara and her Ph.D. students advise us to "take up space" when we present. They remind us that it is the candidate who takes up space most effectively who wins election campaigns. Sometimes that is the taller candidate, but often it is the candidate who does things to appear that he or she is taking up more space:

- Keep your feet hip distance apart
- Square your shoulders
- Don't let your arms close you off by folding them in front of you or in what Barbara likes to call the "fig leaf pose"
- Distribute your weight evenly between your feet
- Move around a bit off of your "home" by building in deliberate and meaningful movement. Just because a lectern is there does not mean you have to stand behind it. I, for example, try never to use one, and instead I move closer to the audience, which helps build rapport with them.

- If you have trouble knowing where to put your arms and hands, try this simple trick: raise them above your head and let them drop at your sides. That is their home.
- To avoid looking and feeling robotic, gesture off this "home"
- Have a visual "home" for your gaze—a neutral site, not at a clock that will be giving you information, not at the ceiling or floor, but right above the heads of the audience
- Over the course of your presentation, continue to make eye contact with everyone in the audience. This engages the audience to feel that you are not just presenting, but that you are presenting to them in particular.
- Avoid hip shifting, fidgeting with jewelry (don't wear it) or keys or change or hair (put it back) or pen (don't hold it) or pockets (don't wear clothing with pockets, or pin them shut)
- Avoid holding your head at a tilt, which biologically submits or communicates subjection by showing the jugular vein and also shows low confidence
- Use a stiff note card that does not shake rather than a piece of paper
- Throw focus to whoever is speaking
- Stretch/do yoga/run beforehand to calm down and get rid of nervous energy

Vocal

- Speak at a volume at which you can be heard; at a pitch you can sustain your full presentation; and with natural variation in tone
- Writing a document has the advantage of emphasizing through italicizing, bolding, underlining. In speaking, use pitch/speed/volume.
- Habits to Avoid:
    * Nonverbal fluencies: ums, likes, OKs
    * Upspeak, which is inflecting up at the end of the sentence (say "dammit" in your mind to make the sentence declarative rather than a question)

* Tag questions (right? yeah? you with me? you know?): build in real questions (is everyone clear on the product we just described?) and get feedback
* Silence is powerful (you are in control of the silence, and people need time to digest: communication is more than presentation)
* Stay audience-centered rather than being wrapped up in your own goals and nerves: check in with them
* Breathe into your belly! (Especially if your mind goes blank.)

Stick the Landing

When you look to draw your presentation to a close, remember that your audience will recall best what you told them at the beginning (primacy effect) and what you remind them of at the end (recency effect). To reinforce the impact even more, leverage the verbal and nonverbal tools that we share above. To signal that you are reaching a different section of your presentation, for example, you might want to slow . . . your . . . pace. You might want to move to a different spot—if you were standing behind a lectern, maybe move closer to your audience. Then, as Barbara has said many times, you want to "stick the landing." Ending with the standard, "Thank you, any questions?" gets you the bronze medal. To go for the gold, choreograph the final few sentences of your presentation. To achieve the goal that you set, end by reminding the audience of your three main points, and even after answering questions, restate those three main points again so they are the last thing the audience remembers. For this Persuasive Communication section, those three main points are:

* You cannot not communicate, as 90 percent of what you communicate is in how you look and how you sound, not the content of the presentation
* Effective communication is Goal-oriented and Audience-centered
* WIIFM helps you to stay focused on what matters to your audience

Conclusion

The last session of my courses and workshops has developed a reputation for being a somewhat emotional experience. Crying is not uncommon. Alumni from previous years often join us for a repeat performance. In these final sessions, I always share three things: Steve Jobs's graduation speech, a statement about success, and an expression of what the experience has meant to me.

STEVE JOBS

You can't connect the dots looking forward; you can only connect them looking backwards.

—Steve Jobs[1]

Even if you have already watched it, take fifteen minutes to watch this video of Steve Jobs's Stanford graduation speech. Somehow watching it in the context of learning the Entrepreneurial Process has a more profound impact, and it is often the trigger for those tears I mention above. I have to admit getting choked up myself when I've watched it since my father died of pancreatic cancer in 2017: youtube.com/watch?v=UF8uR6Z6KLc[2]

Doing what you love resonates with a consistent message of *See, Solve, Scale.* Seeing Steve Jobs say so, when we all know now that he did not overcome his cancer, makes his message about life being short all the more poignant.

I also love his insight about how "connecting the dots" looking forward is so challenging and how we can only do so looking backward. For me, the insight connects my study of history with my passion for teaching entrepreneurship: history allows us to look backward and connect dots. Entrepreneurship pushes us to look forward and create new ones.

SUCCESS

Here is Bessie Anderson Stanley's definition of success (often erroneously attributed to Ralph Waldo Emerson):

Success
by Bessie Anderson Stanley

To laugh often and much;
To win the respect of intelligent people
and the affection of children;
To earn the appreciation of honest critics
and endure the betrayal of false friends;
To appreciate beauty,
to find the best in others;
To leave the world a bit better,
whether by a healthy child,
a garden patch or a redeemed social condition;
To know even one life has breathed easier
because you have lived.
This is to have succeeded.

As inspirational as these words may be, they should not be anyone's definition of success, other than Stanley's. Remember passion and remember purpose.

Defining success is personal. Instead of appropriating Steve Jobs's or Bessie Anderson Stanley's definition of success, use their inspiration to help you find your own.

———

Excuse the corniness if I use the POCD structure to summarize what this interaction with you has meant for me.

PEOPLE

One of the challenges in sharing *See, Solve, Scale* here is not knowing who you are. This is not an academic exercise for me. Because teaching entrepreneurship is a participation sport, I hope my writing and your reading are only the first part of a relationship that can continue beyond this book.

OPPORTUNITY

I am forever grateful to Barrett Hazeltine for tapping me on the shoulder back in 2005 as he ignited what has become my life's professional purpose. The opportunity to teach something I love has been the most gratifying thing I have ever done in my career—in Simon Sinek's language, it has been my *why*. It has been the Value Proposition I have had the privilege to develop to address the unmet needs that at first I did not even know existed. To teach in this different medium now on a much larger scale is again something for which I am grateful. Thank you for participating in this opportunity with me.

CONTEXT

In one way, the context for this kind of teaching is clear: teaching via the written word. For you, context varies depending on all the different contexts in which you might be reading this. In writing it, I tried to heed the lessons from Knight Ridder and avoid the equivalent mistake of "putting the newspaper online." That is, although so much of the content and rhythm of this book reflects the same Entrepreneurial Process, this shift in context has required sensitivity to the different ways that you needed to absorb this content.

Here, too, I have tried to follow the steps of my own process, by doing anthropological and empathetic Bottom-Up Research; by teaching an MVP equivalent of this book via in-person courses and workshops; and then by taking seriously the urging of students to think big and write this book version. I do not know yet where this process will go from here, but I do anticipate over time amplifying this teaching even further to have even bigger long-term impact at scale. I hope that you will feel comfortable sharing your thoughts and suggestions about that with me. Even as I wrote the section on open source, I began thinking about how *New York Times* columnist and writer Thomas Friedman's insight about leveraging contributions from the public developer community would apply to me. Perhaps you can help me understand and envision how "the crowd" of readers can help me to make better and much more rapid progress than I would alone.

DEAL

Thanksgiving Assignment

Every November, I send out a Thanksgiving Assignment, which at Harvard Business School I learned from the same Professor Jeff Timmons whose "think big" content I quote above. When I sent this assignment out to my first class back in 2006, I had no idea that its ripples would create so much impact. Now that I send it out every year to a list of more than three thousand alumni and growing, many of them anticipate receiving it, and some get anxious if I don't send it out on the day they expect it. In hearing back about the impact this assignment has had, one theme is that it is spreading. In the language of *See, Solve, Scale*, it is starting to have long-term impact at scale. Some alumni now have a tradition to talk about this assignment at their Thanksgiving tables, or over their holiday season. In the same spirit, I am excited to offer it to you here, and I encourage you to share this.

Hi everyone,

As I have been doing for many years, I am sending this to all of my current students at Brown as well as to my alumni from various programs and workshops in the United States and around the world. I hope this finds you all doing well.

Alumni will no doubt remember this assignment, and as I have said in the past, even for my international students who do not celebrate American Thanksgiving, you still qualify. I was so pleased to receive a couple of emails already this week from a few alumni who had already anticipated this year's assignment and were excited to share their experience.

Way back in 1994, my Harvard Business School entrepreneurship professor, Jeff Timmons, gave us an assignment that I found meaningful and which I now want to pass along to all of you. Think of all of the people who have helped you get to where you are today. All of the coaches, advisers, supporters, teachers, employers, mentors, relatives, and friends. All the people who helped you by writing recommendations for your college applications. All of the references who spoke on your behalf for summer jobs. Even the categories, let alone all of the individual supporters, are endless for all of us.

Select one or two, and write them a handwritten note to let them know how you are doing and to thank them for helping you get here. I still remember back in 1994 sending notes to Brown professors Peter Heywood and Barrett Hazeltine, both of whom had written me recommendations for my business school applications.

We are all on both sides of this equation from time to time, and we all know how much we enjoy hearing from those whose lives we have influenced—especially hearing those simple and magical words, "Thank you."

I hope your doing so adds a little extra meaning to your Thanksgiving and to the Thanksgiving of those who will be hearing from you! Based on the phenomenal experiences many of you have shared with me that resulted from this simple gesture, I am confident that you will find this rewarding.

For those of you who will be celebrating American Thanksgiving, I hope you enjoy your break.

As always, I look forward to hearing from you and to being helpful to you however I can.

Best,
Danny

If, as I have emphasized throughout this book and especially in chapter 7, so much of the success of an entrepreneurial venture comes from the strength and diversity of your team, you might think of this letter as an opportunity to strengthen the ties that have weakened over time.

A FINAL STUDENT PERSPECTIVE

One of my alumni, Jonah Fisher, has set the record for participating in and hosting more of my entrepreneurship courses and workshops than any former student. I thought it would be appropriate, therefore, if Jonah shared a final student perspective with you about *See, Solve, Scale* from the various perspectives he has experienced it.

> Growing up among the skyscrapers of New York and arriving as a student at Brown, the concept of "business" had acquired an aura of detached mechanization, as if it was a world governed by its own unique financial weather patterns. In the first minute of my first day in Danny's classroom, as he opened the semester with the word "people" written in large letters on the board, this image immediately burst. Danny opened a door for me and so many others to see that if we can prioritize relationships in our personal lives and in the work we do, we can unlock something powerful. Without being didactic or dogmatic, Danny helped us understand that once the "people" side of the equation is in place, the opportunities, contexts, and deals organically follow.

Over the past fifteen years, Jonah and many other former students have shared with me the impact my teaching has had on them. They have told me how much the Entrepreneurial Process has influenced their professional and even life trajectories in a much wider range of contexts than I had ever imagined an entrepreneurship course could.

Many nudged me to write a book to share the process I had taught them along with thousands of other aspiring entrepreneurs. They pointed out that I had followed only the first two steps. I had found and validated an unmet need for aspiring entrepreneurs to learn entrepreneurship. And I had developed a Value Proposition of teaching a structured Entrepreneurial Process in the classroom at Brown and in intensive workshops around the world. What those former students argued to get me off the dime and write this book was that I was not following through on my own process. I was not creating a Sustainability Model. I wasn't amplifying that Value Proposition to have long-term impact at scale. I wasn't thinking big. Their clever strategy of using my own teaching persuaded me.

Most teachers will say that there is no better way to learn something than to teach it. Imagine how much students like Jonah and the others you have met in this book have taught me! And now how exciting it has been to evolve the process I have been teaching by writing this book.

As I said in chapter 1, practice and teaching have reinforced each other through a formal alumni network of my former students and workshop participants. That continuous feedback loop has enabled me to hone and improve the process based on their entrepreneurial experiences. I am excited to contribute this book venture to this loop.

STAY IN TOUCH

The Deal is to stay in touch with me and with your fellow readers. Many of my alumni have collaborated with each other on new ventures and have even visited each other when traveling to other countries. I am in touch with thousands of alumni in all sorts of ways. I have written hundreds of letters to help alumni get into graduate schools and other places. I have advised many others in their own entrepreneurial ventures.

About every week, I hear from alumni, sometimes several in one day. Yesterday, for example, I received this note from Melissa Diamond, who participated in a 2015 Seeds of Peace workshop I led in Jordan. Melissa is the founder of A Global Voice for Autism, which equips refugee and conflict-affected communities to support children on the autism spectrum and children with developmental disabilities in their classrooms, homes and communities. She has grown the organization from a concept into a successful nonprofit that has equipped over 16,000 individuals in thirteen conflict-affected and refugee communities. In yesterday's WhatsApp message, her enthusiasm demonstrated how powerful and meaningful this alumni network has become and how much impact it is having, often in ways I don't even know about.

> Last year, you introduced me to your former Brown student, Amelie, whose startup Formally is making it easier for refugees to fill out asylum forms online. She invited me to speak at the form.ally conference. I connected with one of the other speakers after the conference who is an immigration lawyer. During our conversation, I shared a story about a Syrian family that assisted our Global Voice team in Jordan and then subsequently returned to a very dangerous situation in Syria. The lawyer heard the story and reached out to her contacts, and we found a way to bring the family to the U.S.! . . . all thanks to the chance meeting you and I had in Jordan in 2015 and then your

introduction to Amelie. My next steps are finding a sponsor organization for the family, fundraising to support them during their first year and preparing for their arrival. There's lots to do, but I've never been more excited! Thank you!

Earlier that morning I had received a short WhatsApp video message from a former Tel Aviv University MBA student, Moe Mernick, in which he spoke about how seemingly insignificant gestures we make every day can have enormous unexpected impact. When I read Melissa's message, I knew what he meant.

In order to reinforce the connections through this growing alumni network, every Memorial Day weekend, I invite all of my alumni to join what used to be a gathering at my house, and is now hosted at the Nelson Center at Brown.

I invite you to do something similar through a new online network open to only those like you who have read this book. Remember, this process is a participation sport, not a spectator one, and it requires collaboration through diverse teams. As a next step in your entrepreneurial journey, I invite you to access additional current content and resources and to join this online group at dannywarshay.com.

I look forward to hearing from you to let me know how you are progressing—Seeing, Solving, and Scaling to turn problems into breakthrough successes—and how else I can help you do so.

ACKNOWLEDGMENTS

Like any entrepreneurial endeavor, writing this book has been a team effort. To form that team, I have tried to draw on both strong and weak network ties and to benefit from diverse perspectives. As I say above, I had not considered writing a book until my students nudged me to do so, and I hope I have made them proud. I am excited to see how the process of writing this book will inform my classroom teaching, and to see what impact this book has on a big scale and for the long term.

Rather than the typical list of random names, I will reference the context in which I know so many generous contributors. To honor the different ways in which I have collaborated with several, you may notice that some contributors appear in more than one context.

Entrepreneurial Process alumni: Ally Donahue, Rahul Dey, Jonah Fisher, Daniel Breyer, Liv Simmons, Emma Butler, Kristen Mashikian, Tyler Gage, Dylan Jardon, Laura Thompson, Julie Sygiel, Hina Cao, Grant Gurtin, Alicia Lew, Jude Jacob Kayton, Micah Hendler, Raissa Hacohen, Hina Cao, Scott Grace, Gwen Mugodi, Kaiti Yoo, Haley Hoffman-Smith, Ben Chesler, Dan Aziz, Curtis Stiles, Annelise Gates, Luke Sherwin, Neil Parikh, Nicole Shimer, Justin Hefter, Melissa Diamond, Mollie West Duffy

Teaching experts: Barrett Hazeltine (Brown), Barry Nalebuff (Yale School of Management), Teresa Amabile (Harvard Business School), Tiffany Watson (Spelman College), Marionette Holmes (Spelman College), Barbara Tannenbaum (Brown), Emily Ferrier (Brown), Ashley Champagne (Brown), Jennifer Nazareno (Brown), Banu Ozkazanc-Pan (Brown), Arnell Milhouse (CareerDevs), Jude Jacob Kayton (Tel Aviv University), Jonah Fisher (Tel Aviv University), Dan Nissimyan (Tel Aviv University), Troy

Henikoff (Kellogg School of Management), Drew Boyd (University of Cincinnati), Noam Wasserman (Yeshiva University)

Family: Dr. Deb Herman, Marin Warshay, Gabby Warshay, Matthew Warshay

Professional collaborators: Bob Johnston (Strategy Innovation Group), Marta Reis (Strategy Innovation Group), Doug Bate (Strategy Innovation Group), Manny Stern, Bill Stone (OutsideGC), Walter Callender (Practico Innovation), Manuel Cargnelutti (Instrumentation Technologies), Tom Runco, Emily Clay (illume hire), May El Batran (Member of Egyptian Parliament), Kris Brown (Goodwin Procter), Guy Kawasaki

Book writing experts: Tim Bartlett and Alice Pfeifer (my editors from St. Martin's Press), John Maas (my wonderful agent at Park & Fine), Howie Jacobson, Amnon Levav, John Landry, Dr. Deb Herman, JR Lowry, Matt Kursh, Terri Alpert, Anastasia Ostrowski (RSA Fellow), Tyler Gage, Mollie West Duffy

Content experts: Jayna Zweiman (Pussyhat Project), Patrick Moynihan (Haitian Project), Angela Mascena (Haitian Project), Colby Bowker (Haitian Project), Shannah Green (yoga teacher), Ben Chesler (Imperfect Foods), Emma Butler (Intimately), Bob Reiss (R&R)

Special thank you: A few supporters deserve special mention as they contributed far beyond what I had ever expected, and the quality of this book reflects as much their hard work as it does my own. No one's patience and wise contributions exceeded that of my wife, Deb Herman, and no one supported me like she did in this endeavor, as she has throughout most of my life. J. R. Lowry, whose writing talent I have known since reading his columns in the Harvard Business School *Harbus*, demonstrated his strategic and copy-editing skills and generous commitment through so many days and hours I cannot even fathom. The multi-talented Howie Jacobson has been my writing guide and conscience since I dared to create a first *See, Solve, Scale* Google Doc in 2018. In addition to all of his sage guidance through this writing process that leverages his own wealth of writing experience, what I value most is his honesty and creativity. Bill Stone has supported me as my attorney in all of my entrepreneurial pursuits for many years and notably throughout this publishing process. He also read several early versions of this book on which he gave invaluable guidance. And I will be forever grateful to my oldest friend, Matt Kursh, who I have known since he pelted me with chalk in fifth-grade Hebrew School. As the saying goes, Matt and I can finish each other's sentences. The sentences in this book are so much better because of Matt's brilliant insight, entrepreneurship expertise, and writing talent. It's all in the way you tell it.

NOTES

Introduction

1. Ashley Bittner and Brigette Lau, "Women-Led Startups Received Just 2.3% of VC Funding in 2020," *Harvard Business Review*, February 25, 2021, hbr.org/2021/02/women-led-startups-received-just-2-3-of-vc-funding-in-2020.

2. Ronald White, "Black, Latinx and Female Entrepreneurs Are Still Ignored by Most Venture Capitalists," *Los Angeles Times*, June 5, 2021, latimes.com/business/story/2021-06-05/black-latinx-and-female-entrepreneurs-are-still-ignored-by-most-venture-capitalists.

3. Gené Teare, "Highlighting Notable Funding to Black Founders in 2020," Crunchbase News, February 12, 2021, news.crunchbase.com/news/highlighting-notable-funding-to-black-founders-in-2020/.

4. Banu Ozkazanc-Pan and Susan Clark Muntean, *Entrepreneurial Ecosystems: A Gender Perspective* (Cambridge: Cambridge University Press, 2021), cambridge.org/core/books/entrepreneurial-ecosystems/F303A1FDC37C9609E1273613B3E0FF43.

5. Daniel Kahneman, *Thinking, Fast and Slow*, 1st edition (New York: Farrar, Straus and Giroux, 2013).

6. Gabrielle S. Adams et al., "People Systematically Overlook Subtractive Changes," *Nature* 592, no. 7853 (April 2021): 258–61, doi.org/10.1038/s41586-021-03380-y.

Chapter 2: The Benefits of Scarce Resources

1. Howard H. Stevenson, and Jose-Carlos Jarillo Mossi, "R&R," Harvard Business Publishing Education November 15, 1987, hbsp.harvard.edu/product/386019-PDF-ENG.

2. Bob later wrote a book, *Bootstrapping 101*, in which he describes in more tactical detail how to launch a startup when you do not have a lot of your own resources. In one example, he zeroed in on the retailer Restoration Hardware. Because so many of my students and other first-time entrepreneurs long for lots of capital and other early resources, I love sharing this counterintuitive insight from Restoration's founder, who said that "if sufficient capital had been available to him in the company's early stages, he might not have been as successful as he is." In other words, the limits that the company experienced early created a discipline that never left the company's culture.

Bob Reiss, *Bootstrapping 101: Tips to Build Your Business with Limited Cash and Free Outside Help* (Boca Raton, FL: R&R, 2009).

3. Reiss.

4. Shunryu Suzuki et al., *Zen Mind, Beginner's Mind: Informal Talks on Zen Meditation and Practice*, ed. Trudy Dixon (Boston: Shambhala, 2011).

5. "CNBC.Com 2019 Disruptor 50," May 15, 2019, cnbc.com/2019/05/14/casper-2019 -disruptor-50.html.

6. Saj-Nicole Joni, "Stop Relying On Experts For Innovation: A Conversation With Karim Lakhani," Forbes.com, accessed March 25, 2020, www.forbes.com/sites/forbesleader- shipforum/2013/10/23/break-out-of-relying-on-experts-for-innovation-a-conversa- tion-with-karim-lakhani/.

7. "Pussyhat Project™ Website," PUSSYHAT PROJECT™, pussyhatproject.com.

8. Scott Sonenshein, *Stretch: Unlock the Power of Less-and Achieve More Than You Ever Imagined* (New York: Harper Business, 2017).

9. Claude Lévi-Strauss, *The Savage Mind*, The Nature of Human Society Series (Chi- cago: University of Chicago Press, 1966), 11.

10. Ted Baker, "Resources in Play: Bricolage in the Toy Store(y)," *Journal of Business Ven- turing* 22, no. 5 (September 2007): 694–711, doi.org/10.1016/j.jbusvent.2006.10.008, 698.

11. Ted Baker and Reed E. Nelson, "Creating Something from Nothing: Resource Con- struction through Entrepreneurial Bricolage," *Administrative Science Quarterly* 50, no. 3 (September 2005): 333, doi.org/10.2189/asqu.2005.50.3.329.

12. Baker and Nelson, 356.

13. Baker and Nelson, 329.

14. Baker and Nelson, 349.

15. Scott Burnham, *This Could: How Two Words Create Opportunity, Increase Creativity, and Reduce Waste* (VRMNTR, 2021).

16. Baker and Nelson, "Creating Something from Nothing," 334.

17. Clark Gilbert, "Mercury Rising: Knight Ridder's Digital Venture," Harvard Business Publishing Education, October 16, 2003, 28.

18. Gilbert, 1.

19. Howard H. Stevenson, "A Perspective on Entrepreneurship," Harvard Business Pub- lishing Education, April 13, 2006, 3.

Part 2: The See, Solve, Scale Entrepreneurial Process

1. "NRDC: Wasted—How America Is Losing Up to 40 Percent of Its Food from Farm to Fork to Landfill," nrdc.org/sites/default/files/wasted-2017-report.pdf.

2. As of early 2021, according to Bloomberg, Imperfect had raised over $95 million from investors, its valuation had ballooned to $700 million, it had a subscriber base of 350,000 customers, and it had ended 2020 with a revenue run rate of over $500 million.

3. "Imperfect Foods, Perfect Opportunity: How Ben Chesler '15 Saves Ugly Foods, Reduces Waste, & Raised over $50M for His Startup," *Nelson Center for Entrepre- neurship* (blog), entrepreneurship.brown.edu/event/interview-ben-chesler-15-co -founder-imperfect-foods/.

Chapter 3: Step 1: See: Find and Validate Unmet Needs

1.   Walter Isaacson, *Steve Jobs* (New York: Simon & Schuster, 2011).
2.   Daniel Simons, *Selective Attention Test*, youtube.com/watch?v=vJG698U2Mvo.
3.   Trafton Drew, Melissa L. H. Vo, and Jeremy M. Wolfe, "'The Invisible Gorilla Strikes Again: Sustained Inattentional Blindness in Expert Observers,'" *Psychological Science* 24, no. 9 (September 2013): 1848–53, doi.org/10.1177/0956797613479386.
4.   "Why Even Radiologists Can Miss a Gorilla Hiding in Plain Sight," NPR.org, accessed December 19, 2018, npr.org/sections/health-shots/2013/02/11/171409656/why -even-radiologists-can-miss-a-gorilla-hiding-in-plain-sight.
5.   Steven Johnson, "Where Good Ideas Come from | TED Talk," accessed December 20, 2018, ted.com/talks/steven_johnson_where_good_ideas_come_from?language=en.
6.   Derek Thompson, "Google X and the Science of Radical Creativity," *The Atlantic*, October 10, 2017, theatlantic.com/magazine/archive/2017/11/x-google-moonshot -factory/540648/.
7.   "The Top 20 Reasons Startups Fail," CB Insights Research, February 2, 2018, cbin sights.com/research/startup-failure-reasons-top/.
8.   Isaacson, *Steve Jobs*.
9.   Zoë Slote Morris, Steven Wooding, and Jonathan Grant, "The Answer Is 17 Years, What Is the Question: Understanding Time Lags in Translational Research," *Journal of the Royal Society of Medicine* 104, no. 12 (December 2011): 510–20, https://doi. org/10.1258/jrsm.2011.110180.

Chapter 4: Step 2: Solve: Develop a Value Proposition—Mindset Guidelines

1.   Doug Hall, *Jump Start Your Business Brain: Scientific Ideas and Advice That Will Immediately Double Your Business Success Rate* (Covington, KY: Clerisy Press, 2010).
2.   Rocio Wu, "10 Rules Entrepreneurs Need to Know Before Adopting AI," HBS Working Knowledge, February 11, 2020, http://hbswk.hbs.edu/item/10-rules-entrepreneurs-need-to-know-before-adopting-ai.
3.   Simon Sinek, *Start with Why: How Great Leaders Inspire Everyone to Take Action* (New York: Portfolio, 2011).
4.   Burnham, *This Could*.
5.   Ellen J. Langer and Alison I. Piper, "The Prevention of Mindlessness," *Journal of Personality and Social Psychology* 53, no. 2 (August 1987): 280–87, doi.org/10.1037 /0022–3514.53.2.280.
6.   During World War II, Ruth Noller served in the Navy. She was stationed at Harvard and was one of the first programmers of a computer that IBM had lent to the Navy. One day, after the computer crashed, Ruth identified the unexpected cause: a moth. That is the origin of the term computer "bug."
7.   "Knowledge, Imagination and Evaluation," Strategy Innovation Group, LLC, accessed February 19, 2019, strategyinnovationgroup.com/blog/2018/11/14/creativity -formula-ruth-noller.
8.   Lowell W. Busenitz and Jay B. Barney, "Differences between Entrepreneurs and Managers in Large Organizations: Biases and Heuristics in Strategic Decision-

Making," *Journal of Business Venturing* 12, no. 1 (January 1997): 9–30, doi.org/10 .1016/S0883–9026(96)00003–1.

9. Gerald E. Hills and Robert P. Singh, "Opportunity Recognition," in *Handbook of Entrepreneurial Dynamics: The Process of Business Creation*, ed. William B. Gartner et al. (Thousand Oaks, CA: SAGE, 2004), 259–72.

10. Roya Molaei et al., "The Impact of Entrepreneurial Ideas and Cognitive Style on Students Entrepreneurial Intention," *Journal of Entrepreneurship in Emerging Economies* 6, no. 2 (May 27, 2014): 140–62, doi.org/10.1108/JEEE-09–2013–0021.

11. Robert E. Johnston and J. Douglas Bate, *The Power of Strategy Innovation: A New Way of Linking Creativity and Strategic Planning to Discover Great Business Opportunities*, First edition (New York: AMACOM, 2013), 139.

12. Howard H. Stevenson and David E. Gumpert, "The Heart of Entrepreneurship," *Harvard Business Review*, March 1, 1985, https://hbr.org/1985/03/the-heart-of-entrepreneurship.

13. Johnston and Bate, 18–19.

14. Johnston and Bate, 289.

15. Clayton M. Christensen, *The Innovator's Dilemma: When New Technologies Cause Great Firms to Fail*, The Management of Innovation and Change Series (Boston: Harvard Business School Press, 1997).

16. Robin Wall Kimmerer, *Braiding Sweetgrass: Indigenous Wisdom, Scientific Knowledge and the Teachings of Plants* (Minneapolis, MN: Milkweed Editions, 2015).

17. Deborah Adele, *The Yamas & Niyamas: Exploring Yoga's Ethical Practice* (Duluth, MN: On-Word Bound Books, 2009), 92.

18. Kimmerer, *Braiding Sweetgrass*.

19. Melissa S. Cardon et al., "Measuring Entrepreneurial Passion: Conceptual Foundations and Scale Validation," *Journal of Business Venturing* 28, no. 3 (May 1, 2013): 373–96, doi.org/10.1016/j.jbusvent.2012.03.003.

20. Jon M. Jachimowicz et al., "The Gravitational Pull of Expressing Passion: When and How Expressing Passion Elicits Status Conferral and Support from Others," *Organizational Behavior and Human Decision Processes* 153 (July 1, 2019): 41–62, doi.org /10.1016/j.obhdp.2019.06.002.

21. Jachimowicz defines passion as "a strong feeling toward a personally important value/preference that motivates intentions and behaviors to express that value/preference." To measure it, he uses something called the "passion attainment scale."

22. Randy Komisar, *The Monk and the Riddle: The Art of Creating a Life While Making a Living* (Boston: Harvard Business Review Press, 2001).

23. Eva de Mol, "What Makes a Successful Startup Team," *Harvard Business Review*, March 21, 2019, hbr.org/2019/03/what-makes-a-successful-startup-team.

24. "Why Purpose?," Wayfinder, accessed May 5, 2019, projectwayfinder.com/why-purpose.

25. Melissa S. Cardon et al., "The Nature and Experience of Entrepreneurial Passion," *The Academy of Management Review* 34, no. 3 (2009): 511–32.

26. Jachimowicz et al., "The Gravitational Pull of Expressing Passion."

27. "Why Purpose?"

28. Eric S. Kim et al., "Purpose in Life and Reduced Risk of Myocardial Infarction among Older U.S. Adults with Coronary Heart Disease: A Two-Year Follow-Up,"

Journal of Behavioral Medicine 36, no. 2 (April 2013): 124–33, doi.org/10.1007/s10865 -012-9406–4.

29. Holger Patzelt and Dean A. Shepherd, "Negative Emotions of an Entrepreneurial Career: Self-Employment and Regulatory Coping Behaviors," *Journal of Business Venturing* 26, no. 2 (March 2011): 226–38, doi.org/10.1016/j.jbusvent.2009.08.002.

30. Komisar, *The Monk and the Riddle.*

31. Gloria Anzaldua, *Light in the Dark/Luz En Lo Oscuro: Rewriting Identity, Spirituality, Reality*, ed. AnaLouise Keating (Durham, NC: Duke University Press, 2015).

32. Steve Jobs, *Steve Jobs' 2005 Stanford Commencement Address*, accessed February 26, 2019, youtube.com/watch?v=UF8uR6Z6KLc.

33. Jeffrey Bussgang, *Entering StartUpLand: An Essential Guide to Finding the Right Job* (Boston: Harvard Business Review Press, 2017).

Chapter 5: Step 2: Solve: Develop a Value Proposition—Techniques

1. Sidney G. Winter and Gabriel Szulanski, "Replication as Strategy," *Organization Science; Linthicum* 12, no. 6 (December 2001): 730–43.

2. David J. Epstein, *Range: Why Generalists Triumph in a Specialized World* (New York: Riverhead Books, 2019).

3. Madeleine L'Engle, *A Wrinkle in Time* (New York: Farrar, Straus and Giroux, 1962).

4. Karl Duncker and Lynne S. Lees, "On Problem-Solving," *Psychological Monographs* 58, no. 5 (1945): i–113, doi.org/10.1037/h0093599.

5. "Systematic Inventive Thinking Website," *Systematic Inventive Thinking* (blog), accessed December 11, 2018, sitsite.com/method/.

6. There must be something in the water, because just like Ruth Noller thought through her own approach to creativity while serving in the United States Navy, Genrich Altshuller thought through much of this creative approach while serving in the Soviet Navy. He analyzed and categorized more than 200,000 patents, identifying a series of common templates and categories, which he called ARIZ, a Russian acronym for Algorithm for Inventive Problem Solving. Jacob Goldenberg et al., "Finding Your Innovation Sweet Spot," March 2003, 11.

7. Jacob Goldenberg and David Mazursky, "The Voice of the Product: Templates of New Product Emergence," *Creativity & Innovation Management* 8, no. 3 (September 1999): 157, doi.org/10.1111/1467–8691.00132.

8. Goldenberg et al., "Finding Your Innovation Sweet Spot."

9. Adams et al., "People Systematically Overlook Subtractive Changes."

10. Matthew Sparkes, "People Are Bad at Spotting Simple Solutions to Problems," New Scientist, accessed April 26, 2021, newscientist.com/article/2273931-people-are-bad -at-spotting-simple-solutions-to-problems/.

11. Adams et al., "People Systematically Overlook Subtractive Changes."

12. Goldenberg et al., "Finding Your Innovation Sweet Spot."

13. Drew Boyd and Jacob Goldenberg, *Inside the Box: A Proven System of Creativity for Breakthrough Results* (New York: Simon & Schuster, 2014).

14. Goldenberg et al., "Finding Your Innovation Sweet Spot."

15. Goldenberg et al.

16. Raymond H. Mak et al., "Use of Crowd Innovation to Develop an Artificial Intelligence–Based Solution for Radiation Therapy Targeting," *JAMA Oncology*, April 18, 2019, doi.org/10.1001/jamaoncol.2019.0159.

17. Martha Lagace, "Open Innovation Contestants Build AI-Based Cancer Tool," HBS Working Knowledge, April 18, 2019, hbswk.hbs.edu/item/open-innovation-contestants-build-ai-based-cancer-tool.

18. Lagace.

19. A. L. Delbecg and A. H. VandeVen, "A Group Process Model for Problem Identification and Program Planning." *Journal of Applied Behavioral Science* 7 (1971): 466–91.

20. John A. Sample, "Nominal Group Technique: An Alternative to Brainstorming," *Journal of Extension*, Ideas at Work, Volume 22, no. 2 (March 1984), https://archives.joe.org/joe/1984march/iw2.php.

21. Thomas Eisenmann, Eric Ries, and Sarah Dillard, "Hypothesis-Driven Entrepreneurship: The Lean Startup," Harvard Business Publishing Education, no. N9–812–095 (March 9, 2012): 8–9.

22. William A. Sahlman, "Parenting Magazine," Harvard Business Publishing Education, November 15, 1987, hbsp.harvard.edu/product/291015-PDF-ENG.

Chapter 6: Step 3: Scale: Create a Sustainability Model

1. J. A. Timmons and S. Spinelli, *New Venture Creation: Entrepreneurship for the 21st Century* (Boston: McGraw-Hill/Irwin, 2004), 85.

2. Vicky Phan, "Jayna Zweiman '01 Discusses Pussyhat Project, Welcome Blanket, and Social Entrepreneurship at Family Weekend," Nelson Center for Entrepreneurship (blog), November 20, 2019, https://entrepreneurship.brown.edu/2019/11/jayna-zweiman-family-weekend/.

3. L'Engle, *A Wrinkle in Time*.

4. Michael Collins and Charles A. Lindbergh, *Carrying the Fire: An Astronaut's Journeys* (New York: Farrar, Straus and Giroux, 2009).

5. Jeffrey Burton Russell, *A History of Heaven* (Princeton, NJ: Princeton University Press, 1998).

6. "About Hal Hershfield," accessed April 28, 2021, halhershfield.com/about.

7. Michael Blanding, "How Uber, Airbnb, and Etsy Attracted Their First 1,000 Customers," HBS Working Knowledge, July 13, 2016, hbswk.hbs.edu/item/how-uber-airbnb-and-etsy-attracted-their-first-1-000-customers.

8. "Turning One Thousand Customers into One Million," HBS Working Knowledge, November 16, 2016, hbswk.hbs.edu/item/turning-one-thousand-customers-into-one-million.

9. Julian Bleecker, "Design Fiction: A Short Essay on Design, Science, Fact and Fiction," March 2009, 49.

10. "About the Long Now," accessed February 2, 2021, longnow.org/about/.

11. Frank White and Charles E. Smith, "Bringing the Overview Effect Down to Earth," *Library of Professional Coaching*, April 15, 2013, https://libraryofprofessionalcoach-

ing.com/concepts/managing-stress-and-challenges/brining-the-overview-effect-down-to-earth/.

12. Tyler Gage, *Fully Alive: Using the Lessons of the Amazon to Live Your Mission in Business and Life* (New York: Atria Books, 2017).

13. Richard G. Hamermesh, Michael J. Roberts, and Taz Pirmohamed, "ProfitLogic," Harvard Business Publishing Education, May 5, 2003, hbsp.harvard.edu/product /802110-PDF-ENG?Ntt=profitlogic&itemFindingMethod=Search.

14. Gilbert, "Mercury Rising: Knight Ridder's Digital Venture," Harvard Business Publishing Education, 4.

15. Gilbert, 3.

16. Paul Saffo, "Failure Is the Best Medicine : Paul Saffo," *Newsweek*, March 25, 2002, https://www.saffo.com/essays/failure-is-the-best-medicine/.

17. Teresa Amabile and Steven Kramer, *The Progress Principle: Using Small Wins to Ignite Joy, Engagement, and Creativity at Work* (Boston: Harvard Business Review Press, 2011).

18. Thompson, "Google X and the Science of Radical Creativity."

19. Amabile and Kramer, *The Progress Principle*.

20. "X, the Moonshot Factory," accessed December 24, 2018, https://x.company.

21. Astro Teller, "The Secret to Moonshots? Killing Our Projects," *Wired*, February 16, 2016, wired.com/2016/02/the-secret-to-moonshots-killing-our-projects/.

22. "X, the Moonshot Factory."

23. Thompson, "Google X and the Science of Radical Creativity."

24. Kathryn Schulz, *On Being Wrong*, accessed February 5, 2019, ted.com/talks/kathryn _schulz_on_being_wrong.

25. Schulz.

26. Kathryn Schulz, *Being Wrong: Adventures in the Margin of Error* (New York: Ecco, 2011).

27. Jon J. Muth, *Zen Shorts* (New York: Scholastic Press, 2005), 32–33.

28. Karen Huang et al., "Mitigating Malicious Envy: Why Successful Individuals Should Reveal Their Failures," 2018, 65.

29. Huang et al., 65–66.

30. Dina Gerdeman, "Why Managers Should Reveal Their Failures," HBS Working Knowledge, December 5, 2018, hbswk.hbs.edu/item/why-managers-should-publicize -their-failures.

31. Daniella Kupor, Taly Reich, and Kristin Laurin, "The (Bounded) Benefits of Correction: The Unanticipated Interpersonal Advantages of Making and Correcting Mistakes," *Organizational Behavior and Human Decision Processes* 149 (November 1, 2018): 165–78, doi.org/10.1016/j.obhdp.2018.08.002.

32. Jim Whitehurst, "Be a Leader Who Can Admit Mistakes," *Harvard Business Review*, June 2, 2015, hbr.org/2015/06/be-a-leader-who-can-admit-mistakes.

33. "Anti-Portfolio · Bessemer Venture Partners—BVP," accessed February 7, 2019, www.bvp.com/anti-portfolio/.

34. For additional research about how making mistakes affects how others perceive us, I recommend learning more about the classic pratfall effect. A classic social psychology experiment is explained here: Elliot Aronson, Ben Willerman, and Joanne Floyd,

"The Effect of a Pratfall on Increasing Interpersonal Attractiveness," *Psychonomic Science* 4, no. 6 (June 1, 1966): 227–28, doi.org/10.3758/BF03342263.

35. Tim Herrera, "Do You Keep a Failure Résumé? Here's Why You Should Start," *New York Times*, February 7, 2019, nytimes.com/2019/02/03/smarter-living/failure -resume.html.

36. *Authority* Magazine, "Aishetu Fatima Dozie of Bossy Cosmetics: 5 Things I Wish Someone Told Me Before I Became CEO," Medium, September 22, 2020, medium .com/authority-magazine/aishetu-fatima-dozie-of-bossy-cosmetics-5-things-i-wish -someone-told-me-before-i-became-ceo-eacdffe4b2af.

37. Kennedy Odede, Jessica Posner, and Nicholas Kristof, *Find Me Unafraid: Love, Loss, and Hope in an African Slum* (New York: Ecco, 2016).

38. Thomas L. Friedman, *Thank You for Being Late: An Optimist's Guide to Thriving in the Age of Accelerations* (New York: Farrar, Straus and Giroux, 2016), 55.

39. Friedman, 58.

40. Friedman, 67.

41. Friedman, Thomas, *Thank You for Being Late* (New York: Farrar, Straus and Giroux, 2015), 68.

42. Mitch Wagner, "Red Hat CEO Jim Whitehurst: How Open Source Stopped Being 'Scary,'" *Light Reading*, February 13, 2019, www.lightreading.com/open-source/red- hat-ceo-jim-whitehurst-how-open-source-stopped-being-scary/a/d-id/749433.

43. "Red Hat CEO Jim Whitehurst."

44. PricewaterhouseCoopers, "Consumers Would Pay up to 16% More for Better Cus- tomer Experience, Say Companies Have Lost the Human Touch, According to PwC Survey," PwC, accessed January 22, 2021, pwc.com/us/en/press-releases/2018 /experience-is-everything-heres-how-to-get-it-right.html.

45. Troy Henikoff, *MATH 101: Why Is Troy Obsessed with CAC?*, 2019, vimeo.com /329687431.

46. Henikoff.

47. Richard G. Hamermesh and Indra A Reinbergs, "Shurgard Self-Storage: Expansion to Europe," Harvard Business Publishing Education, May 10, 2005, 29.

48. V. Kasturi Rangan, "Aravind Eye Hospital, Madurai, India: In Service for Sight," Harvard Business Publishing Education, May 15, 2009, hbsp.harvard.edu/product /593098-PDF-ENG.

49. Courtney Martin, "The Reductive Seduction Of Other People's Problems," Me- dium, June 27, 2019, brightthemag.com/the-reductive-seduction-of-other-people-s -problems-3c07b307732d.

50. "CNBC Transcript: Bank of America Chairman and CEO Brian Moynihan Speaks with CNBC's Becky Quick," CNBC, August 21, 2019, www.cnbc.com/2019/08/21/cn- bc-transcript-bank-of-america-chairman-and-ceo-brian-moynihan-speaks-with- cnbcs-becky-quick-today.html.

51. Dan Pallotta, *Uncharitable: How Restraints on Nonprofits Undermine Their Potential* (Medford, MA: University Press of New England, 2010).

52. Dan Pallotta, "Taking a Risk Is Not Immoral," *Harvard Business Review*, August 4, 2011, https://hbr.org/2011/08/taking-a-risk-is-not-immoral.

53. Dan Pallotta, "Transcript of 'The Way We Think about Charity Is Dead Wrong,'"

accessed January 26, 2020, www.ted.com/talks/dan_pallotta_the_way_we_think_about_charity_is_dead_wrong/transcript.

54. Dan Pallotta, "Why Nonprofits Should Invest More in Advertising," *Harvard Business Review*, May 26, 2009, https://hbr.org/2009/05/why-nonprofits-should-spend-mo.

Chapter 7: Step 3: Scale: Create a Sustainability Model—Growing Your Team

1. Noam Wasserman, *The Founder's Dilemmas: Anticipating and Avoiding the Pitfalls That Can Sink a Startup* (Princeton, NJ: Princeton University Press, 2013), 73.

2. David Beisel, "How to Divide Founder Equity: 4 Criteria to Discuss," *NextView Ventures* (blog), July 8, 2019, nextviewventures.com/blog/how-to-divide-founder-equity/.

3. Brian Uzzi, Teaming Up to Drive Scientific Discovery: Brian Uzzi, Ph.D. at TEDx-NorthwesternU, accessed March 26, 2020, www.youtube.com/watch?v=tyjohv6OdoU.

4. Noam Wasserman, "Understanding Founder's Dilemmas | Prof. Noam Wasserman," Business of Software USA, December 4, 2012, businessofsoftware.org/2012/12/noam-wasserman-understanding-founders-dilemmas/.

5. William A. Sahlman, "Some Thoughts on Business Plans," Harvard Business Publishing Education, 1996, 5.

6. Darmesh Shah, *INBOUND19: Facing Fears: Growing Better by Growing Bolder | Dharmesh Shah Keynote*, accessed March 16, 2020, www.youtube.com/watch?v=E82atOgbfj4&app=desktop.

7. David Tilman, "Causes, Consequences and Ethics of Biodiversity," *Nature* 405, no. 6783 (May 2000): 208, doi.org/10.1038/35012217.

8. Quamrul Ashraf and Oded Galor, "Cultural Diversity, Geographical Isolation, and the Origin of the Wealth of Nations," Working Paper (National Bureau of Economic Research, December 2011), doi.org/10.3386/w17640.

9. Richard Florida, "How Diversity Leads to Economic Growth," CityLab, accessed April 14, 2019, theatlanticcities.com/jobs-and-economy/2011/12/diversity-leads-to-economic-growth/687/.

10. Dorothy Leonard-Barton and Walter C. Swap, *When Sparks Fly: Harnessing the Power of Group Creativity* (Boston, Mass: Harvard Business School Press, 2005).

11. Laurie Joan Aron, "Bright Ideas: The Creative Power of Groups," HBS Working Knowledge, October 12, 1999, hbswk.hbs.edu/item/bright-ideas-the-creative-power-of-groups.

12. Dorothy Leonard and Susaan Straus, "Putting Your Company's Whole Brain to Work," *Harvard Business Review*, July 1, 1997, hbr.org/1997/07/putting-your-companys-whole-brain-to-work.

13. Linda A. Hill et al., "Collective Genius," *Harvard Business Review*, June 1, 2014, hbr.org/2014/06/collective-genius.

14. Melissa Azofeifa and Anna Correa, "'Bohemian Rhapsody': Story of the Killer 'Queen,'" *The Statesman* (blog), accessed February 19, 2019, sbstatesman.com/2018/12/02/bohemian-rhapsody-story-of-the-killer-queen/.

15. David J. Epstein, *Range: Why Generalists Triumph in a Specialized World* (New York: Riverhead Books, 2019).

16. Stephen Dunmore, "The Most Unexpected Lesson I Learned at Harvard Business

School | LinkedIn," accessed February 3, 2019, linkedin.com/pulse/most-unexpected -lesson-i-learned-harvard-business-school-dunmore/.

17. Susan Cain, *Quiet: The Power of Introverts in a World That Can't Stop Talking* (New York: Broadway Books, 2013).

18. Cain.

19. Cain, 80–81.

20. Jonah Lehrer, "Steve Jobs: 'Technology Alone Is Not Enough,'" *The New Yorker*, accessed July 1, 2020, newyorker.com/news/news-desk/steve-jobs-technology-alone-is -not-enough.

21. Steven Johnson, *Where Good Ideas Come from: The Natural History of Innovation* (New York: Riverhead Books, 2010).

22. Isaacson.

23. Susan Cain, "The Rise of the New Groupthink," *The New York Times*, January 13, 2012, nytimes.com/2012/01/15/opinion/sunday/the-rise-of-the-new-groupthink.html.

24. Cain, *Quiet*.

25. Tom DeMarco and Tim Lister, "Programmer Performance and the Effects of the Workplace," 1985, 5.

26. Cain, "Opinion | The Rise of the New Groupthink."

27. *The Terminator*, accessed February 26, 2019, imdb.com/title/tt0088247/.

28. Zack Lapinski, "How to Stop Worrying and Love the Robot Apocalypse (Ep. 461)," *Freakonomics* (blog), accessed June 24, 2021, freakonomics.com/podcast/cobots/.

29. Andrew McAfee, "Did Garry Kasparov Stumble into a New Business Process Model?," *Harvard Business Review*, February 18, 2010, hbr.org/2010/02/like-a-lot-of-people.

30. John E. Kelly III, "Computing, Cognition and the Future of Knowing. How Humans and Machines Are Forging a New Age of Understanding," *IBM Global Services*, 2015, 5.

31. Friedman, *Thank You for Being Late*, 107.

32. Michela Tindera, "Robot Wars: $60B Intuitive Surgical Dominated Its Market for 20 Years. Now Rivals Like Alphabet Are Moving In," Forbes, accessed May 21, 2019, forbes.com/sites/michelatindera/2019/02/14/intuitive-surgical-stock-robot-surgery -da-vinci-alphabet-jnj-ceo-gary-guthart/.

33. "New Study: 64% of People Trust a Robot More than Their Manager," accessed October 28, 2020, oracle.com/corporate/pressrelease/robots-at-work-101519.html.

34. "Algorithmic Justice League-Unmasking AI Harms and Biases," accessed June 10, 2021, ajl.org/.

35. Wasserman, *The Founder's Dilemmas*, 99–101.

36. Wasserman, 91.

37. Dina Gerdeman, "Who Has Potential? For Many White Men, It's Often Other White Men," HBS Working Knowledge, May 10, 2021, hbswk.hbs.edu/item/who-has -potential-for-white-men-its-usually-other-white-men.

38. The gendered and racialized ways in which entrepreneurial ecosystems are organized is the topic of my colleague's book: B. Ozkazanc-Pan and S. Clark Muntean, *Entrepreneurial Ecosystems: A Gender Perspective* (New York: Cambridge University Press, 2021).

39. J. Yo-Jud Cheng and Boris Groysberg, "Innovation Should Be a Top Priority for Boards. So Why Isn't It?," *Harvard Business Review*, September 21, 2018, hbr.org/2018 /09/innovation-should-be-a-top-priority-for-boards-so-why-isnt-it.

40. Michael Blanding, "Everyone Knows Innovation Is Essential to Business Success— Except Board Directors," HBS Working Knowledge, January 3, 2019, hbswk.hbs .edu/item/everyone-knows-innovation-is-essential-to-business-success-and-mdash -except-board-directors.

41. Wasserman, *The Founder's Dilemmas*, 103.

42. Wasserman, "Understanding Founder's Dilemmas | Prof. Noam Wasserman."

43. Mark S. Granovetter, "The Strength of Weak Ties," *American Journal of Sociology* 78, no. 6 (1973): 1360–80.

44. Malcolm Gladwell, "Six Degrees of Lois Weisberg," *The New Yorker* 74, no. 41 (January 11, 1999): 52.

45. Gladwell.

46. Frances X. Frei and Anne Morriss, "Begin with Trust," *Harvard Business Review*, May 1, 2020, hbr.org/2020/05/begin-with-trust.

47. David Rock, Heidi Grant, and Jacqui Grey, "Diverse Teams Feel Less Comfortable— and That's Why They Perform Better," *Harvard Business Review*, September 22, 2016, https://hbr.org/2016/09/diverse-teams-feel-less-comfortable-and-thats-why-they-per- form-better.

48. "Zipcar: Refining the Business Model, Video (DVD)," Harvard Business Publishing Education, accessed January 31, 2020, hbsp.harvard.edu/product/806717-VID -ENG.

49. Noam Wasserman, "Ockham Technologies: Living on the Razor's Edge," Harvard Business Publishing Education, July 29, 2013, hbsp.harvard.edu/product/804129 -PDF-ENG.

50. Tim Ferriss, "The Tim Ferriss Show Transcripts: Gary Keller—How to Focus on the One Important Thing (#401)," The Blog of Author Tim Ferriss, December 18, 2019, tim.blog/2019/12/18/gary-keller-transcript/.

51. Beisel, "How to Divide Founder Equity: 4 Criteria to Discuss."

Chapter 8: Step 3: Scale: Create a Sustainability Model—Raising Financial Resources

1. Carolynn Levy, "Startup Documents," Safe Financing Documents, September 2018, ycombinator.com/documents/#stq=&stp=0.

2. William A. Sahlman, "E Ink: Financing Growth," Harvard Business Publishing Education, December 9, 1999, 20.

3. Gilbert, "Mercury Rising: Knight Ridder's Digital Venture," Harvard Business Publishing Education, 5.

4. Mike Troiano, "Why You're Not Even Getting in the Door," *G20 Ventures* (blog), November 19, 2018, medium.com/g20-ventures/why-youre-not-even-getting-in-the -door-daa10ccb4911.

5. Rob Go, "Doing Due Diligence on Potential Investors," *NextView Ventures* (blog), January 30, 2020, nextviewventures.com/blog/doing-due-diligence-on-potential-investors/.

6. Paul Gompers, "Honest Tea," Harvard Business Publishing Education, October 17, 2001, hbsp.harvard.edu/product/201076-PDF-ENG.

7. Linda Cyr, "Noodles & Co.," Harvard Business Publishing Education, March 9, 2004, hbsp.harvard.edu/product/803174-PDF-ENG.

8. Cyr, 14–15.
9. Ivan Stevanovic, "40+ Crucial Crowdfunding Stats In 2021 | SmallBizGenius," January 6, 2021, www.smallbizgenius.net/by-the-numbers/crowdfunding-stats/.
10. "Advantages and Disadvantages of Crowdfunding | Nibusinessinfo.Co.Uk," accessed January 29, 2021, nibusinessinfo.co.uk/content/advantages-and-disadvantages-crowdfunding.

Chapter 9: Three Related Pitch Documents

1. William A. Sahlman, "Some Thoughts on Business Plans."
2. Guy Kawasaki, "Guy Kawasaki—The Art of the Executive Summary," *Guy Kawasaki* (blog), April 2, 2006, guykawasaki.com/the_art_of_the_-3/.
3. "Imperfect Foods Impact Report 2020," accessed May 16, 2021, imperfect.cdn.prismic.io/imperfect/669a6dac-c9d4–4692–93ad-16843fd5bd1f_210309-IF-ImpactReport-Final.pdf.
4. "NRDC: Wasted—How America Is Losing Up to 40 Percent of Its Food from Farm to Fork to Landfill."
5. Guy Kawasaki, "Guy Kawasaki—The Only 10 Slides You Need in Your Pitch," *Guy Kawasaki* (blog), March 5, 2015, guykawasaki.com/the-only-10-slides-you-need-in-your-pitch/.
6. Seth Godin, "Really Bad Powerpoint," *Seth's Blog* (blog), January 29, 2007, seths.blog/2007/01/really_bad_powe/.

Chapter 10: Pitching Mistakes to Avoid

1. "Turning One Thousand Customers into One Million."

Chapter 11: Persuasive Communication

1. Albert Mehrabian and Susan R. Ferris, "Inference of Attitudes from Nonverbal Communication in Two Channels," *Journal of Consulting Psychology* 31, no. 3 (June 1967): 248–52, doi.org/10.1037/h0024648.
2. While Mehrabian's study was limited to the impact of utterances, not full presentations, and his data were 55, 38, and 7 percent other studies have documented that the visual impact on audiences is even greater (see Nalini Ambady's work on first impressions). Barbara uses 60, 30, 10 because it captures the relative weights of verbal, nonverbal, and message elements of a presentation in a memorable way. The research results may vary in the specific weights, but the concept is valid.

Conclusion

1. Jobs.
2. Jobs.

BIBLIOGRAPHY

"About the Long Now." longnow.org/about/.

Adams, Gabrielle S., Benjamin A. Converse, Andrew H. Hales, and Leidy E. Klotz. "People Systematically Overlook Subtractive Changes." *Nature* 592, no. 7853 (April 2021): 258–61. doi.org/10.1038/s41586-021-03380-y.

Adele, Deborah. *The Yamas & Niyamas: Exploring Yoga's Ethical Practice*. Duluth, MN: On-Word Bound Books, 2009.

"Advantages and Disadvantages of Crowdfunding | Nibusinessinfo.Co.Uk." www .nibusinessinfo.co.uk/content/advantages-and-disadvantages-crowdfunding.

"Algorithmic Justice League-Unmasking AI Harms and Biases." www.ajl.org/.

Amabile, Teresa, and Steven Kramer. *The Progress Principle: Using Small Wins to Ignite Joy, Engagement, and Creativity at Work*. Boston: Harvard Business Review Press, 2011.

"Anti Portfolio · Bessemer Venture Partners — BVP." Accessed February 7, 2019. https:// www.bvp.com/anti-portfolio/.

Anzaldúa, Gloria. *Light in the Dark/Luz En Lo Oscuro: Rewriting Identity, Spirituality, Reality*. Edited by AnaLouise Keating. Durham, NC: Duke University Press, 2015.

Aron, Laurie Joan. "Bright Ideas: The Creative Power of Groups." HBS Working Knowledge, October 12, 1999. http://hbswk.hbs.edu/item/bright-ideas-the-creative-power -of-groups.

Aronson, Elliot, Ben Willerman, and Joanne Floyd. "The Effect of a Pratfall on Increasing Interpersonal Attractiveness." *Psychonomic Science* 4, no. 6 (June 1, 1966): 227–28. https://doi.org/10.3758/BF03342263.

Ashraf, Quamrul, and Oded Galor. "Cultural Diversity, Geographical Isolation, and the Origin of the Wealth of Nations." Working Paper. National Bureau of Economic Research, December 2011. https://doi.org/10.3386/w17640.

Authority magazine. "Aishetu Fatima Dozie of Bossy Cosmetics: 5 Things I Wish Someone Told Me Before I Became CEO." Medium, September 22, 2020. https://medium

.com/authority-magazine/aishetu-fatima-dozie-of-bossy-cosmetics-5-things-i-wish
-someone-told-me-before-i-became-ceo-eacdffe4b2af.

Baker, Ted. "Resources in Play: Bricolage in the Toy Store(y)." *Journal of Business Venturing* 22, no. 5 (September 2007): 694–711. https://doi.org/10.1016/j.jbusvent.2006.10.008.

Baker, Ted, and Reed E. Nelson. "Creating Something from Nothing: Resource Construction through Entrepreneurial Bricolage." *Administrative Science Quarterly* 50, no. 3 (September 2005): 329–66. https://doi.org/10.2189/asqu.2005.50.3.329.

Beisel, David. "How to Divide Founder Equity: 4 Criteria to Discuss." *NextView Ventures* (blog), July 8, 2019. https://nextviewventures.com/blog/how-to-divide-founder-equity/.

Bittner, Ashley, and Brigette Lau. "Women-Led Startups Received Just 2.3% of VC Funding in 2020." *Harvard Business Review*, February 25, 2021. https://hbr.org/2021/02/women-led-startups-received-just-2-3-of-vc-funding-in-2020.

Blanding, Michael. "Everyone Knows Innovation Is Essential to Business Success—Except Board Directors." HBS Working Knowledge, January 3, 2019. http://hbswk.hbs.edu/item/everyone-knows-innovation-is-essential-to-business-success-and-mdash-except-board-directors.

———. "How Uber, Airbnb, and Etsy Attracted Their First 1,000 Customers." HBS Working Knowledge, July 13, 2016. http://hbswk.hbs.edu/item/how-uber-airbnb-and-etsy-attracted-their-first-1-000-customers.

Bleecker, Julian. "Design Fiction: A Short Essay on Design, Science, Fact and Fiction," March 2009, 49.

Boyd, Drew, and Jacob Goldenberg. *Inside the Box: A Proven System of Creativity for Breakthrough Results*. New York: Simon & Schuster, 2014.

Burnham, Scott. *This Could: How Two Words Create Opportunity, Increase Creativity, and Reduce Waste*. VRMNTR, 2021.

Busenitz, Lowell W., and Jay B. Barney. "Differences between Entrepreneurs and Managers in Large Organizations: Biases and Heuristics in Strategic Decision-Making." *Journal of Business Venturing* 12, no. 1 (January 1997): 9–30. https://doi.org/10.1016/S0883-9026(96)00003-1.

Bussgang, Jeffrey. *Entering StartUpLand: An Essential Guide to Finding the Right Job*. Boston: Harvard Business Review Press, 2017.

Cain, Susan. "The Rise of the New Groupthink." *New York Times*, January 13, 2012. www.nytimes.com/2012/01/15/opinion/sunday/the-rise-of-the-new-groupthink.html.

———. *Quiet: The Power of Introverts in a World That Can't Stop Talking*. New York: Broadway Books, 2013.

Cardon, Melissa S., Denis A. Gregoire, Christopher E. Stevens, and Pankaj C. Patel. "Measuring Entrepreneurial Passion: Conceptual Foundations and Scale Validation." *Journal of Business Venturing* 28, no. 3 (May 1, 2013): 373–96. doi.org/10.1016/j.jbusvent.2012.03.003.

Cardon, Melissa S., Joakim Wincent, Jagdip Singh, and Mateja Drnovsek. "The Nature and Experience of Entrepreneurial Passion." *Academy of Management Review* 34, no. 3 (2009): 511–32.

CB Insights Research. "The Top 20 Reasons Startups Fail," February 2, 2018. www .cbinsights.com/research/startup-failure-reasons-top/.

Cheng, Yo-Jud, and Boris Groysberg. "Innovation Should Be a Top Priority for Boards. So Why Isn't It?" *Harvard Business Review*, September 21, 2018. hbr.org/2018/09 /innovation-should-be-a-top-priority-for-boards-so-why-isnt-it.

Christensen, Clayton M. *The Innovator's Dilemma: When New Technologies Cause Great Firms to Fail*. The Management of Innovation and Change Series. Boston: Harvard Business School Press, 1997.

CNBC. "CNBC Transcript: Bank of America Chairman and CEO Brian Moynihan Speaks with CNBC's Becky Quick," August 21, 2019. www.cnbc.com/2019/08/21/ cnbc-transcript-bank-of-america-chairman-and-ceo-brian-moynihan-speaks-with-cnbcs-becky-quick-today.html.

"CNBC.Com 2019 Disruptor 50," May 15, 2019. www.cnbc.com/2019/05/14/casper-2019 -disruptor-50.html.

Collins, Michael, and Charles A. Lindbergh. *Carrying the Fire: An Astronaut's Journeys*. New York: Farrar, Straus and Giroux, 2009.

Correa, Melissa Azofeifa, and Anna Correa. "'Bohemian Rhapsody': Story of the Killer 'Queen.'" *The Statesman*. www.sbstatesman.com/2018/12/02/bohemian-rhapsody -story-of-the-killer-queen/.

Cyr, Linda. "Noodles & Co.," Harvard Business Publishing Education, March 9, 2004. hbsp.harvard.edu/product/803174-PDF-ENG.

Delbecq, André L., and Andrew H. Van de Ven. "A Group Process Model for Problem Identification and Program Planning." *The Journal of Applied Behavioral Science* 7, no. 4 (July 1, 1971): 466–92. https://doi.org/10.1177/002188637100700404.

DeMarco, Tom, and Tim Lister. "Programmer Performance and the Effects of the Workplace," 1985, 5.

Drew, Trafton, Melissa L. H. Vo, and Jeremy M. Wolfe. "'The Invisible Gorilla Strikes Again: Sustained Inattentional Blindness in Expert Observers.'" *Psychological Science* 24, no. 9 (September 2013): 1848–53. https://doi.org/10.1177/0956797613479386.

Duncker, Karl, and Lynne S. Lees. "On Problem-Solving." *Psychological Monographs* 58, no. 5 (1945): i–113. https://doi.org/10.1037/h0093599.

Dunmore, Stephen. "The Most Unexpected Lesson I Learned at Harvard Business School | LinkedIn." www.linkedin.com/pulse/most-unexpected-lesson-i-learned-harvard -business-school-dunmore/.

Eisenmann, Thomas, Eric Ries, and Sarah Dillard. "Hypothesis-Driven Entrepreneurship: The Lean Startup." Harvard Business Publishing Education, no. N9–812–095 (March 9, 2012): 23.

Epstein, David J. *Range: Why Generalists Triumph in a Specialized World*. New York: Riverhead Books, 2019.

Ferriss, Tim. "The Tim Ferriss Show Transcripts: Gary Keller—How to Focus on the One Important Thing (#401)." https://tim.blog/2019/12/18/gary-keller-transcript/.

Florida, Richard. "How Diversity Leads to Economic Growth." CityLab. www.theatlanticcities .com/jobs-and-economy/2011/12/diversity-leads-to-economic-growth/687/.

"40+ Crucial Crowdfunding Stats in 2021 | SmallBizGenius," January 6, 2021. www .smallbizgenius.net/by-the-numbers/crowdfunding-stats/.

Frei, Frances X., and Anne Morriss. "Begin with Trust." *Harvard Business Review*, May 1, 2020. https://hbr.org/2020/05/begin-with-trust.

Friedman, Thomas L. *Thank You for Being Late: An Optimist's Guide to Thriving in the Age of Accelerations*. New York: Farrar, Straus and Giroux, 2016.

Gage, Tyler. *Fully Alive: Using the Lessons of the Amazon to Live Your Mission in Business and Life*. New York: Atria Books, 2017.

Gerdeman, Dina. "Who Has Potential? For Many White Men, It's Often Other White Men." HBS Working Knowledge, May 10, 2021. http://hbswk.hbs.edu/item/who-has-potential-for-white-men-its-usually-other-white-men.

——. "Why Managers Should Reveal Their Failures." HBS Working Knowledge, December 5, 2018. http://hbswk.hbs.edu/item/why-managers-should-publicize-their-failures.

Gilbert, Clark. "Mercury Rising: Knight Ridder's Digital Venture," Harvard Business Publishing Education, October 16, 2003, 28.

Gladwell, Malcolm. "Six Degrees of Lois Weisberg." *The New Yorker* 74, no. 41 (January 11, 1999): 52.

Go, Rob. "Doing Due Diligence on Potential Investors." *NextView Ventures*, January 30, 2020. https://nextviewventures.com/blog/doing-due-diligence-on-potential-investors/.

Godin, Seth. "Really Bad Powerpoint." *Seth's Blog* (blog), January 29, 2007. https://seths.blog/2007/01/really_bad_powe/.

Goldenberg, Jacob, Roni Horowitz, Amnon Levav, and David Mazursky. "Finding Your Innovation Sweet Spot," March 2003, 11.

Goldenberg, Jacob, and David Mazursky. "The Voice of the Product: Templates of New Product Emergence." *Creativity & Innovation Management* 8, no. 3 (September 1999): 157. doi.org/10.1111/1467–8691.00132.

Gompers, Paul. "Honest Tea," Harvard Business Publishing Education, October 17, 2001. https://hbsp.harvard.edu/product/201076-PDF-ENG.

Granovetter, Mark S. "The Strength of Weak Ties." *American Journal of Sociology* 78, no. 6 (1973): 1360–80.

Hall, Doug, and Tom Peters. *Jump Start Your Business Brain: Scientific Ideas and Advice That Will Immediately Double Your Business Success Rate*. Covington, KY: Clerisy Press, 2010.

Hamermesh, Richard G., and Indra A Reinbergs. "Shurgard Self-Storage: Expansion to Europe," Harvard Business Publishing Education, May 10, 2005, 29.

Hamermesh, Richard G., Michael J. Roberts, and Taz Pirmohamed. "ProfitLogic," Harvard Business Publishing Education, May 5, 2003. https://hbsp.harvard.edu/product/802110-PDF-ENG.

HBS Working Knowledge. "Turning One Thousand Customers into One Million," November 16, 2016. http://hbswk.hbs.edu/item/turning-one-thousand-customers-into-one-million.

Henikoff, Troy. *MATH 101: Why Is Troy Obsessed with CAC?*, 2019. https://vimeo.com/329687431.

Herrera, Tim. "Do You Keep a Failure Résumé? Here's Why You Should Start." *New York Times*, February 7, 2019, sec. Smarter Living. nytimes.com/2019/02/03/smarter-living/failure-resume.html.

Hershfield, Hal. "About Hal Hershfield." halhershfield.com/about.

Hill, Linda A., Greg Brandeau, Emily Truelove, and Kent Lineback. "Collective Genius." *Harvard Business Review*, June 1, 2014. https://hbr.org/2014/06/collective-genius.

Hills, Gerald E., and Robert P. Singh. "Opportunity Recognition." In *Handbook of Entrepreneurial Dynamics: The Process of Business Creation*, edited by William B. Gartner, William C. Gartner, Kelly G. Shaver, Nancy M. Carter, and Paul D. Reynolds, 259–72. SAGE, 2004.

Huang, Karen, Ryan W. Buell, Laura Huang, Alison Wood Brooks, and Brian Hall. "Mitigating Malicious Envy: Why Successful Individuals Should Reveal Their Failures," 2018, 82.

"Imperfect Foods Impact Report 2020." https://imperfect.cdn.prismic.io/imperfect /669a6dac-c9d4–4692–93ad-16843fd5bd1f_210309-IF-ImpactReport-Final.pdf.

Isaacson, Walter. *Steve Jobs*. New York: Simon & Schuster, 2011.

Jachimowicz, Jon M., Christopher To, Shira Agasi, Stéphane Côté, and Adam D. Galinsky. "The Gravitational Pull of Expressing Passion: When and How Expressing Passion Elicits Status Conferral and Support from Others." *Organizational Behavior and Human Decision Processes* 153 (July 1, 2019): 41–62. https://doi.org/10.1016/j.obhdp.2019.06.002.

Jobs, Steve. *Steve Jobs' 2005 Stanford Commencement Address*. www.youtube.com/watch ?v=UF8uR6Z6KLc.

Johnson, Steven. *Where Good Ideas Come from: The Natural History of Innovation*. New York: Riverhead Books, 2010.

———. "Where Good Ideas Come From | TED Talk." ted.com/talks/steven_johnson _where_good_ideas_come_from?language=en.

Johnston, Robert E., and J. Douglas Bate. *The Power of Strategy Innovation: A New Way of Linking Creativity and Strategic Planning to Discover Great Business Opportunities*. New York: AMACOM, 2013.

Joni, Saj-Nicole. "Stop Relying On Experts For Innovation: A Conversation With Karim Lakhani." Forbes.com. Accessed March 25, 2020. https://www.forbes.com/sites/ forbesleadershipforum/2013/10/23/break-out-of-relying-on-experts-for-innovation- a-conversation-with-karim-lakhani/.

Kahneman, Daniel. *Thinking, Fast and Slow*. New York: Farrar, Straus and Giroux, 2013.

Kawasaki, Guy. "Guy Kawasaki—The Art of the Executive Summary https://guykawasaki .com/the_art_of_the_-3/.

———. "Guy Kawasaki—The Only 10 Slides You Need in Your Pitch." March 5, 2015. https://guykawasaki.com/the-only-10-slides-you-need-in-your-pitch/.

Kelly III, John E. "Computing, Cognition and the Future of Knowing. How Humans and Machines Are Forging a New Age of Understanding." *IBM Global Services*, 2015.

Kim, Eric S., Jennifer K. Sun, Nansook Park, Laura D. Kubzansky, and Christopher Peterson. "Purpose in Life and Reduced Risk of Myocardial Infarction among Older U.S. Adults with Coronary Heart Disease: A Two-Year Follow-Up." *Journal of Behavioral Medicine* 36, no. 2 (April 2013): 124–33. https://doi.org/10.1007/s10865-012-9406-4.

Kimmerer, Robin Wall. *Braiding Sweetgrass: Indigenous Wisdom, Scientific Knowledge and the Teachings of Plants*. Minneapolis, MN: Milkweed Editions, 2015.

Komisar, Randy. *The Monk and the Riddle: The Art of Creating a Life While Making a Living*. Boston: Harvard Business Review Press, 2001.

Kupor, Daniella, Taly Reich, and Kristin Laurin. "The (Bounded) Benefits of Correction: The Unanticipated Interpersonal Advantages of Making and Correcting Mistakes." *Organizational Behavior and Human Decision Processes* 149 (November 1, 2018): 165–78. https://doi.org/10.1016/j.obhdp.2018.08.002.

Lagace, Martha. "Open Innovation Contestants Build AI-Based Cancer Tool." HBS Working Knowledge, April 18, 2019. http://hbswk.hbs.edu/item/open-innovation -contestants-build-ai-based-cancer-tool.

Langer, Ellen J., and Alison I. Piper. "The Prevention of Mindlessness." *Journal of Personality and Social Psychology* 53, no. 2 (August 1987): 280–87. https://doi.org/10.1037 /0022-3514.53.2.280.

Lapinski, Zack. "How to Stop Worrying and Love the Robot Apocalypse (Ep. 461)." https://freakonomics.com/podcast/cobots/.

Lehrer, Jonah. "Steve Jobs: 'Technology Alone Is Not Enough.'" *The New Yorker.* www .newyorker.com/news/news-desk/steve-jobs-technology-alone-is-not-enough.

L'Engle, Madeleine. *A Wrinkle in Time.* New York: Farrar, Straus and Giroux, 1962.

Leonard, Dorothy, and Susaan Straus. "Putting Your Company's Whole Brain to Work." *Harvard Business Review,* July 1, 1997. https://hbr.org/1997/07/putting-your -companys-whole-brain-to-work.

Leonard-Barton, Dorothy, and Walter C. Swap. *When Sparks Fly: Harnessing the Power of Group Creativity.* Boston: Harvard Business School Press, 2005.

Lévi-Strauss, Claude. *The Savage Mind.* The Nature of Human Society Series. Chicago: University of Chicago Press, 1966.

Levy, Carolynn. "Startup Documents." Safe Financing Documents, September 2018. ycombinator.com/documents/#stq=&stp=0.

Mak, Raymond H., Michael G. Endres, Jin H. Paik, Rinat A. Sergeev, Hugo Aerts, Christopher L. Williams, Karim R. Lakhani, and Eva C. Guinan. "Use of Crowd Innovation to Develop an Artificial Intelligence–Based Solution for Radiation Therapy Targeting." *JAMA Oncology,* April 18, 2019. doi.org/10.1001/jamaoncol.2019.0159.

Martin, Courtney. "The Reductive Seduction of Other People's Problems." Medium, June 27, 2019. https://brightthemag.com/the-reductive-seduction-of-other-people-s -problems-3c07b307732d.

McAfee, Andrew. "Did Garry Kasparov Stumble into a New Business Process Model?" *Harvard Business Review,* February 18, 2010. https://hbr.org/2010/02/like-a-lot-of -people.

Mehrabian, Albert, and Susan R. Ferris. "Inference of Attitudes from Nonverbal Communication in Two Channels." *Journal of Consulting Psychology* 31, no. 3 (June 1967): 248–52. https://doi.org/10.1037/h0024648.

Mol, Eva de. "What Makes a Successful Startup Team." *Harvard Business Review,* March 21, 2019. https://hbr.org/2019/03/what-makes-a-successful-startup-team.

Molaei, Roya, Mohammad Reza Zali, Mohhammad Hasan Mobaraki, and Jahngir Yadollahi Farsi. "The Impact of Entrepreneurial Ideas and Cognitive Style on Students Entrepreneurial Intention." *Journal of Entrepreneurship in Emerging Economies* 6, no. 2 (May 27, 2014): 140–62. https://doi.org/10.1108/JEEE-09-2013-0021.

Morris, Zoë Slote, Steven Wooding, and Jonathan Grant. "The Answer Is 17 Years, What Is the Question: Understanding Time Lags in Translational Research." *Journal of the*

Royal Society of Medicine 104, no. 12 (December 2011): 510–20. https://doi.org/10 .1258/jrsm.2011.110180.

Muth, Jon J. *Zen Shorts.* New York: Scholastic Press, 2005.

Nelson Center for Entrepreneurship. "Imperfect Foods, Perfect Opportunity: How Ben Chesler '15 Saves Ugly Foods, Reduces Waste, & Raised over $50M for His Startup." https://entrepreneurship.brown.edu/event/interview-ben-chesler-15-co-founder -imperfect-foods/.

"New Study: 64% of People Trust a Robot More than Their Manager." www.oracle.com /corporate/pressrelease/robots-at-work-101519.html.

NPR.org. "Why Even Radiologists Can Miss a Gorilla Hiding in Plain Sight." www.npr .org/sections/health-shots/2013/02/11/171409656/why-even-radiologists-can-miss-a -gorilla-hiding-in-plain-sight.

"NRDC: Wasted—How America Is Losing Up to 40 Percent of Its Food from Farm to Fork to Landfill." www.nrdc.org/sites/default/files/wasted-2017-report.pdf.

Odede, Kennedy, Jessica Posner, and Nicholas Kristof. *Find Me Unafraid: Love, Loss, and Hope in an African Slum.* New York: Ecco, 2016.

Ozkazanc-Pan, Banu, and Susan Clark Muntean. *Entrepreneurial Ecosystems: A Gender Perspective.* Cambridge: Cambridge University Press, 2021. cambridge.org/core /books/entrepreneurial-ecosystems/F303A1FDC37C9609E1273613B3E0FF43.

Pallotta, Dan. "Taking a Risk Is Not Immoral." *Harvard Business Review,* August 4, 2011. https://hbr.org/2011/08/taking-a-risk-is-not-immoral.

———. "Transcript of 'The Way We Think about Charity Is Dead Wrong.'" Accessed January 26, 2020. https://www.ted.com/talks/dan_pallotta_the_way_we_think_about_ charity_is_dead_wrong/transcript.

———. *Uncharitable: How Restraints on Nonprofits Undermine Their Potential.* Medford, MA: University Press of New England, 2010.

———. "Why Nonprofits Should Invest More in Advertising." *Harvard Business Review,* May 26, 2009. https://hbr.org/2009/05/why-nonprofits-should-spend-mo.

Patzelt, Holger, and Dean A. Shepherd. "Negative Emotions of an Entrepreneurial Career: Self-Employment and Regulatory Coping Behaviors." *Journal of Business Venturing* 26, no. 2 (March 2011): 226–38. https://doi.org/10.1016/j.jbusvent.2009.08.002.

Phan, Vicky. "Jayna Zweiman '01 Discusses Pussyhat Project, Welcome Blanket, and Social Entrepreneurship at Family Weekend." Nelson Center for Entrepreneurship (blog), November 20, 2019. https://entrepreneurship.brown.edu/2019/11/jayna-zwei- man-family-weekend/.

PricewaterhouseCoopers. "Consumers Would Pay up to 16% More for Better Customer Experience, Say Companies Have Lost the Human Touch, According to PwC Survey." PwC. www.pwc.com/us/en/press-releases/2018/experience-is-everything-heres -how-to-get-it-right.html.

PUSSYHAT PROJECT™. "Pussyhat Project™ Website." www.pussyhatproject.com.

Rangan, V. Kasturi. "Aravind Eye Hospital, Madurai, India: In Service for Sight," Harvard Business Publishing Education, May 15, 2009. https://hbsp.harvard.edu/product /593098-PDF-ENG.

Reiss, Bob. *Bootstrapping 101: Tips to Build Your Business with Limited Cash and Free Outside Help.* Boca Raton, FL: R&R, 2009.

Rock, David, Heidi Grant, and Jacqui Grey. "Diverse Teams Feel Less Comfortable — and That's Why They Perform Better." *Harvard Business Review,* September 22, 2016. https://hbr.org/2016/09/diverse-teams-feel-less-comfortable-and-thats-why-they-perform-better.

Russell, Jeffrey Burton. *A History of Heaven.* Princeton, NJ: Princeton University Press, 1998.

Saffo, Paul. "Failure Is the Best Medicine : Paul Saffo." *Newsweek,* March 25, 2002. www.saffo.com/essays/failure-is-the-best-medicine/.

Sahlman, William A. "E Ink: Financing Growth," Harvard Business Publishing Education, December 9, 1999, 20.

———. *"Parenting Magazine,"* Harvard Business Publishing Education, November 15, 1987. https://hbsp.harvard.edu/product/291015-PDF-ENG.

———. "Some Thoughts on Business Plans," Harvard Business Publishing Education, 1996, 30.

Sample, John A. "Nominal Group Technique: An Alternative to Brainstorming." *Journal of Extension,* Ideas at Work, Volume 22, no. Number 2 (March 1984). https://archives.joe.org/joe/1984march/iw2.php.

Schulz, Kathryn. *Being Wrong: Adventures in the Margin of Error.* New York: Ecco, 2011.

———. *On Being Wrong.* www.ted.com/talks/kathryn_schulz_on_being_wrong.

Shah, Darmesh. *INBOUND19: Facing Fears: Growing Better by Growing Bolder | Dharmesh Shah Keynote.* Accessed March 16, 2020. https://www.youtube.com/watch?v=E82atOgbfj4&app=desktop.

Simons, Daniel. *Selective Attention Test.* www.youtube.com/watch?v=vJG698U2Mvo.

Sinek, Simon. *Start with Why: How Great Leaders Inspire Everyone to Take Action.* New York: Portfolio, 2011.

Sonenshein, Scott. *Stretch: Unlock the Power of Less—and Achieve More Than You Ever Imagined.* New York: HarperBusiness, 2017.

Sparkes, Matthew. "People Are Bad at Spotting Simple Solutions to Problems." New Scientist. www.newscientist.com/article/2273931-people-are-bad-at-spotting-simple-solutions-to-problems/.

Stevenson, Howard H. "A Perspective on Entrepreneurship," Harvard Business Publishing Education," April 13, 2006, 13.

Stevenson, Howard H., and David E. Gumpert. "The Heart of Entrepreneurship." *Harvard Business Review,* March 1, 1985. https://hbr.org/1985/03/the-heart-of-entrepreneurship.

Stevenson, Howard H., and Jose-Carlos Jarillo Mossi. "R&R," Harvard Business Publishing Education, November 15, 1987. https://hbsp.harvard.edu/product/386019-PDF-ENG.

Strategy Innovation Group, LLC. "Knowledge, Imagination and Evaluation." www.strategyinnovationgroup.com/blog/2018/11/14/creativity-formula-ruth-noller.

Stevanovic, Ivan. "40+ Crucial Crowdfunding Stats In 2021 | SmallBizGenius," January 6, 2021. www.smallbizgenius.net/by-the-numbers/crowdfunding-stats/.

Suzuki, Shunryu, Huston Smith, Richard Baker, and David Chadwick. *Zen Mind, Beginner's Mind: Informal Talks on Zen Meditation and Practice.* Edited by Trudy Dixon. Boston: Shambhala, 2011.

Systematic Inventive Thinking. "Systematic Inventive Thinking Website." www.sitsite.com/method/.

Teare, Gené. "Highlighting Notable Funding to Black Founders in 2020." Crunchbase

News, February 12, 2021. https://news.crunchbase.com/news/highlighting-notable
-funding-to-black-founders-in-2020/.

Teller, Astro. "The Secret to Moonshots? Killing Our Projects." *Wired*, February 16, 2016.
www.wired.com/2016/02/the-secret-to-moonshots-killing-our-projects/.

Thompson, Derek. "Google X and the Science of Radical Creativity." *The Atlantic*, October 10, 2017. www.theatlantic.com/magazine/archive/2017/11/x-google-moonshot
-factory/540648/.

Tilman, David. "Causes, Consequences and Ethics of Biodiversity." *Nature* 405, no. 6783
(May 2000): 208. https://doi.org/10.1038/35012217.

Timmons, J. A., and S. Spinelli. *New Venture Creation: Entrepreneurship for the 21st Century.* Boston: McGraw-Hill/Irwin, 2004.

Tindera, Michela. "Robot Wars: $60B Intuitive Surgical Dominated Its Market for
20 Years. Now Rivals Like Alphabet Are Moving In." *Forbes.* www.forbes.com
/sites/michelatindera/2019/02/14/intuitive-surgical-stock-robot-surgery-da-vinci
-alphabet-jnj-ceo-gary-guthart/.

Troiano, Mike. "Why You're Not Even Getting in the Door." *G20 Ventures* (blog), November 19, 2018. https://medium.com/g20-ventures/why-youre-not-even-getting-in
-the-door-daa10ccb4911.

Uzzi, Brian. Teaming Up to Drive Scientific Discovery: Brian Uzzi, Ph.D. at TEDxNorth-
westernU. Accessed March 26, 2020. www.youtube.com/watch?v=tyjohv6OdoU.

Wagner, Mitch. "Red Hat CEO Jim Whitehurst: How Open Source Stopped Being 'Scary.'"
Light Reading, February 13, 2019. www.lightreading.com/open-source/red-hat-ceo-
jim-whitehurst-how-open-source-stopped-being-scary/a/d-id/749433.

Wasserman, Noam. *The Founder's Dilemmas: Anticipating and Avoiding the Pitfalls That
Can Sink a Startup.* Princeton, NJ: Princeton University Press, 2013.

———. "Ockham Technologies: Living on the Razor's Edge," Harvard Business Publishing Education, July 29, 2013. https:/hbsp.harvard.edu/product/804129-PDF
-ENG

———. "Understanding Founder's Dilemmas | Prof. Noam Wasserman." Business of
Software USA, December 4, 2012. https://businessofsoftware.org/2012/12/noam
-wasserman-understanding-founders-dilemmas/.

Wayfinder. "Why Purpose?" www.projectwayfinder.com/why-purpose.

White, Frank, and Charles E. Smith. "Bringing the Overview Effect Down to Earth." *Library of Professional Coaching*, April 15, 2013. https://libraryofprofessionalcoaching.
com/concepts/managing-stress-and-challenges/brining-the-overview-effect-down-
to-earth/.

White, Ronald. "Black, Latinx and Female Entrepreneurs Are Still Ignored by Most Venture Capitalists." *Los Angeles Times*, June 5, 2021. www.latimes.com/business/story
/2021–06–05/black-latinx-and-female-entrepreneurs-are-still-ignored-by-most
-venture-capitalists.

Whitehurst, Jim. "Be a Leader Who Can Admit Mistakes." *Harvard Business Review*, June
2, 2015. https://hbr.org/2015/06/be-a-leader-who-can-admit-mistakes.

Winter, Sidney G., and Gabriel Szulanski. "Replication as Strategy." *Organization Science;
Linthicum* 12, no. 6 (December 2001): 730–43.

Wu, Rocio. "10 Rules Entrepreneurs Need to Know Before Adopting AI." HBS Working

Knowledge, February 11, 2020. http://hbswk.hbs.edu/item/10-rules-entrepreneurs-need-to-know-before-adopting-ai.

"X, the Moonshot Factory." Accessed December 24, 2018. https://x.company.

"Zipcar: Refining the Business Model," Video (DVD) Harvard Business Publishing Education. https://hbsp.harvard.edu/product/806717-VID-ENG.

INDEX